CW01238431

LIBRARY OF HEBREW BIBLE/
OLD TESTAMENT STUDIES

707

Formerly Journal for the Study of the Old Testament Supplement Series

Editors
Laura Quick, Oxford University, UK
Jacqueline Vayntrub, Yale University, USA

Founding Editors
David J. A. Clines, Philip R. Davies and David M. Gunn

Editorial Board
Sonja Ammann, Alan Cooper, Steed Davidson, Susan Gillingham,
Rachelle Gilmour, John Goldingay, Rhiannon Graybill, Anne Katrine Gudme,
Norman K. Gottwald, James E. Harding, John Jarick, Tracy Lemos,
Carol Meyers, Eva Mroczek, Daniel L. Smith-Christopher,
Francesca Stavrakopoulou, James W. Watts

TRANSGRESSION AND TRANSFORMATION

Feminist, Postcolonial and Queer Biblical
Interpretation as Creative Interventions

Edited by

L. Juliana Claassens, Christl M. Maier
and Funlọla O. Ọlọjẹde

t&tclark

LONDON • NEW YORK • OXFORD • NEW DELHI • SYDNEY

T&T CLARK
Bloomsbury Publishing Plc
50 Bedford Square, London, WC1B 3DP, UK
1385 Broadway, New York, NY 10018, USA
29 Earlsfort Terrace, Dublin 2, Ireland

BLOOMSBURY, T&T CLARK and the T&T Clark logo
are trademarks of Bloomsbury Publishing Plc

First published in Great Britain 2021

Copyright © L. Juliana Claassens, Christl M. Maier, Funlọla O. Ọlọjẹde and contributors, 2021

L. Juliana Claassens, Christl M. Maier and Funlọla O. Ọlọjẹde have asserted their right under the
Copyright, Designs and Patents Act, 1988, to be identified as Editors of this work.

Cover design: Charlotte James

All rights reserved. No part of this publication may be reproduced or transmitted in any form or by
any means, electronic or mechanical, including photocopying, recording, or any information storage
or retrieval system, without prior permission in writing from the publishers.

Bloomsbury Publishing Plc does not have any control over, or responsibility for, any third-party
websites referred to or in this book. All internet addresses given in this book were correct at the
time of going to press. The author and publisher regret any inconvenience caused if addresses have
changed or sites have ceased to exist, but can accept no responsibility for any such changes.

A catalogue record for this book is available from the British Library.
Library of Congress Control Number: 2021939009.

ISBN: HB: 978-0-5676-9625-0
       ePDF: 978-0-5676-9626-7
       eBook: 978-0-5676-9628-1

Series: Library of Hebrew Bible/Old Testament Studies, volume 707
ISSN 2513–8758

Typeset by: Forthcoming Publications Ltd

To find out more about our authors and books visit www.bloomsbury.com
and sign up for our newsletters.

Contents

Notes on Contributors — vii
List of Abbreviations — xi

INTRODUCTION:
FROM TRANSGRESSION TO TRANSFORMATION — 1

Part I
Transgressive Measures

Chapter 1
NUMBERED WITH THE TRANSGRESSORS:
THE STORY OF THE DAUGHTERS OF ZELOPHEHAD AS RETOLD BY NOAH
  Funlọla O. Olọjẹde — 11

Chapter 2
SILENCE BREAKERS:
WOMAN ZION AND THE #METOO MOVEMENT—LAMENTATIONS 2:20–22'S
PATH TO TRANSFORMATION
  Gina Hens-Piazza — 20

Chapter 3
RECLAIMING JEZEBEL AND MRS JOB:
CHALLENGING SEXIST CULTURAL STEREOTYPES AND THE CURSE
OF INVISIBILITY
  Lerato Mokoena — 36

Chapter 4
INTERVENTIONS TO THE DRAMA OF A BROKEN FAMILY IN JEREMIAH 2:1–4:4
  Christl M. Maier — 52

Chapter 5
INTERRUPTIONS:
STRENGTHENING INSTITUTIONS AS TRANSFORMATIVE TRANSGRESSION
  Jacqueline E. Lapsley — 67

Chapter 6
TORAH AS INSTRUCTION TO ESTABLISH JUSTICE:
RETHINKING CHILDBIRTH AND CULTIC PURITY ACCORDING TO LEVITICUS 12
   Hendrik L. Bosman   80

PART II
TRANSGRESSIVE METHODOLOGIES

Chapter 7
EXCAVATING TRAUMA NARRATIVES:
HAUNTING MEMORIES IN THE STORY OF LOT'S DAUGHTERS
   L. Juliana Claassens   99

Chapter 8
NORMATIVE MASCULINITIES TURNED UPSIDE DOWN?
READING GENESIS 19:30–38 SIDE BY SIDE WITH SELECTED
AFRICAN PROVERBS
   Madipoane Masenya (Ngwan'a Mphahlele)   115

Chapter 9
JUSTICE FOR RAHAB AND THE GIBEONITES IN THE BOOK OF JOSHUA?
THE ELUSIVE COMMUNITIES OF JUSTICE IN IMPERIAL/COLONIAL CONTEXTS
   Dora Rudo Mbuwayesango   128

Chapter 10
COME ON, COME OUT, COME HERE, COME HERE… QUEER EXPRESSIONS
OF DESIRE IN GENESIS 28–31
   Charlene van der Walt   145

Chapter 11
POSTCOLONIAL BOTHO/UBUNTU:
TRANSFORMATIVE READINGS OF RUTH IN THE BOTSWANA URBAN SPACE
   Musa W. Dube   161

Chapter 12
TAMAR SUMMONS JESUS: A TRANS-TEXTUAL (2 SAMUEL 13:1–22;
MARK 5:22–43; MATTHEW 20:17–34) SEARCH FOR SECTORIAL SOLIDARITY
WITH RESPECT TO GENDER AND MASCULINITY
   Gerald O. West   184

Index of References   204
Index of Authors   208

CONTRIBUTORS

Professor Hendrik L. Bosman is Emeritus Professor of Old Testament at the Faculty of Theology, Stellenbosch University. In 2018, he formed part of a research group of twelve scholars at the Centre for Theological Inquiry (Princeton NJ, USA) concerned with issues related to "Religion and Migration." He is author of numerous articles and essays in the field of Old Testament ethics and theology with special attention to the exodus as a narrative concerned with origin and migration and constitutive of religious identity. He can be contacted at hlb1@sun.ac.za

Professor L. Juliana Claassens is Professor in Old Testament and Head of the Gender Unit at the Faculty of Theology, Stellenbosch University. She is the author of *Writing/Reading to Survive: Biblical and Contemporary Trauma Narratives in Conversation* (Sheffield Phoenix 2020); *Claiming Her Dignity: Female Resistance in the Old Testament* (Liturgical, 2016); *Mourner, Mother, Midwife: Reimagining God's Liberating Presence* (Westminster John Knox, 2012) and *The God who Provides: Biblical Images of Divine Nourishment* (Abingdon, 2004). She can be contacted at jclaassens@sun.ac.za

Professor Musa W. Dube is Professor in New Testament at the Candler School of Theology, Emory University, Atlanta, GA and the current continental Coordinator of the Circle of Concerned African Women Theologians (2019–2024). A Humboldtian awardee (2011), she was based at the University of Botswana until 2021. Her books include *Postcolonial Feminist Interpretation of the Bible* (Chalice, 2000), and *The HIV and AIDS Bible: Some Selected Essays* (Scranton, 2008). She is also a research fellow at the Department of Religion and Classical Studies, University of South Africa. She can be contacted at mudube00@gmail.com

Professor Gina Hens-Piazza, Professor of Biblical Studies, holds the Joseph S. Alemany Endowed Chair at the Jesuit School of Theology at Santa Clara University. She is the author of the recently published *Wisdom Commentary on Lamentations* (2017) and *The Supporting Cast of the*

Bible: Reading on Behalf of the Multitude (2020) as well as several other books. She can be contacted at ghenspiazza@scu.edu

Professor Jacqueline E. Lapsley serves as Dean and Vice President of Academic Affairs and is Professor of Old Testament at Princeton Theological Seminary. She has written or co-edited several books, including *Whispering the Word: Hearing Women's Stories in the Old Testament*; the 3rd edition of *A Women's Bible Commentary*; *After Exegesis: Feminist Biblical Theology*; and most recently, *Bible and Ethics in the Christian Life*. She can be contacted at jacqueline.lapsley@ptsem.edu

Professor Christl M. Maier is Professor of Old Testament at Philipps-Universität Marburg, Germany. Her works include *Daughter Zion, Mother Zion: Gender, Space, and the Sacred in Ancient Israel* (Minneapolis: Fortress, 2008), and most recently in collaboration with Carolyn J. Sharp, a commentary on Jeremiah 1–25 for the new Kohlhammer series *International Exegetical Commentary on the Old Testament* (IECOT), published in English and German. She also served as the co-editor of a number of collections of essays, among them *Prophecy and Power: Jeremiah in Feminist and Postcolonial Perspective*, ed. C. M. Maier and C. J. Sharp, LHBOTS 577 (New York: T&T Clark, 2013) and *The Writings and Later Wisdom Books*, ed. C. M. Maier and N. Calduch-Benages, The Bible and Women 1/3 (Atlanta: Society of Biblical Literature, 2014). She can be contacted at christl.maier@uni-marburg.de

Dr Lerato Makoena is Senior Lecturer in Old Testament at Northwest University. One of The Mail and Guardian's top 200 Young South Africans, Lerato received her PhD at University of Pretoria in 2020. Her research interests include Deuteronomistic History, Feminist Biblical Interpretation, Philosophy and Religion, Wisdom Literature (Ecclesiastes). She can be contacted at lerato.mokoena@nwu.ac.za

Professor Madipoane Masenya (Ngwan'a Mphahlele) is Professor of Old Testament Studies in the Department of Biblical and Ancient Studies at the University of South Africa, Pretoria. She has published numerous scientific articles and chapters in specialist books in the area of the Hebrew Bible and gender, especially in African contexts. She served as one of the associate editors of *The Africana Bible: Reading Israel's Scriptures from Africa and the African Diaspora* (Fortress, 2009) and is the author of *How Worthy is the Woman of Worth? Rereading Proverbs 31:10–31* (Peter Lang, 2004). She can be contacted at Masenmj@unisa.ac.za

Professor Dora Rudo Mbuwayesango is Dean of Students, George E. and Iris Battle Professor of Old Testament and Languages in Hood Theological Seminary, Salisbury, NC. She has published extensively in various academic journals and edited collections, most recently, "The Challenge of Feminist Bible Translation in African Contexts," in *Oxford Handbook of Feminist Approaches to the Hebrew Bible*, ed. Susanne Scholz, online publication November 2020; "Numbers," in *Postcolonial Commentary and the Old Testament*, ed. Hemchang Gossai (T&T Clark, 2019); "The Bible as a Tool of Colonization: The Zimbabwean Context" in *Colonialism and the Bible: Contemporary Reflections form the Global South*, ed. Tat-siong Benny Liew and Fernando F. Segovia (Lexington Books, 2018). In 2012, she co-edited with Andrew Mbuvi, *Postcolonial Perspectives in African Biblical Hermeneutics* (Society of Biblical Literature). She can be contacted at dmbuwayesango@hoodseminary.edu

Dr Funlọla O. Ọlọjẹde is a research associate and researcher in the Gender Unit of the Faculty of Theology, Stellenbosch University, South Africa. She is a co-editor of *Teaching for Change: Essays on Pedagogy, Gender, Health and Theology in Africa* (with Juliana Claassens, Charlene van der Walt & Funlọla O. Ọlọjẹde, SunMedia, 2019). Some of her publications are available at: https://www.researchgate.net/profile/Funlola_Olojede/contributions. She can be contacted at funlola@sun.ac.za

Professor Charlene van der Walt is the head of the Gender and Religion Department at the School of Religion, Philosophy, and Classics at the University of KwaZulu-Natal in South Africa. Charlene further functions as the deputy director of the Ujamaa Center for Biblical and Theological Community Development and Research at UKZN and is responsible for the work done in the Body Theology thematic area. She can be contacted at vanderwaltc@ukzn.ac.za

Professor Gerald O. West is Professor Emeritus at the School of Religion, Philosophy, and Classics at the University of KwaZulu-Natal, South Africa. He has worked extensively with the Ujamaa Centre for Community Development and Research for the past thirty years, a project in which socially engaged biblical scholars and ordinary African readers of the Bible from poor, working-class, and marginalised communities collaborate for social transformation. His most recent book is: *The Stolen Bible: From Tool of Imperialism to African Icon* (2016). He can be contacted at West@ukzn.ac.za

ABBREVIATIONS

AB	Anchor Bible
AOTC	Abingdon Old Testament Commentaries
ATANT	Abhandlungen zur Theologie des Alten und Neuen Testaments
BETL	Bibliotheca Ephemeridum Theologicarum Lovaniensium
Bib	*Biblica*
BibInt	*Biblical Interpretation*
BibOr	*Biblica et Orientalia*
BMW	Bible in the Modern World
BZAW	Beihefte zur Zeitschrift für die alttestamentliche Wissenschaft
CBQ	*Catholic Biblical Quarterly*
CBR	*Currents in Biblical Research*
FOTL	Forms of the Old Testament Literature
HBM	Hebrew Bible Monographs
HBS	Herders biblische Studien
HCOT	Historical Commentary on the Old Testament
HThKAT	Herders Theologischer Kommentar zum Alten Testament
ICC	International Critical Commentary
Int	*Interpretation*
ITC	International Theological Commentary
JAAR	*Journal of the American Academy of Religion*
JSOT	*Journal for the Study of the Old Testament*
JSOTSup	Journal for the Study of Old Testament: Supplement Series
JThSA	*Journal of Theology for Southern Africa*
KEH	Kurzgefasstes exegetisches Handbuch zum Alten Testament
KHC	Kurzer Hand-Commentar zum Alten Testament
LHBOTS	Library of Hebrew Bible/Old Testament Studies
NIB	*The New Interpreter's Bible*. Edited by Leander E. Keck. 12 vols. Nashville: Abingdon, 1994–2004
NIBC	New International Bible Commentary
NICOT	New International Commentary on the Old Testament
NIDB	*New Interpreter's Dictionary of the Bible*. Edited by Katharine Doob Sakenfeld. 5 vols. Nashville: Abingdon, 2006–2009
OTE	*Old Testament Essays*
OTL	Old Testament Library
POT	Prediking van het Oude Testament
SANt	Studia Aarhusiana Neotestamentica
SPSH	Scholars Press Studies in the Humanities

THOTC	Two Horizons Old Testament commentary
TynBul	*Tyndale Bulletin*
USQR	*Union Seminary Quarterly Review*
VT	*Vetus Testamentum*
VTSup	Supplements to Vetus Testamentum
WBC	Word Biblical Commentary
ZAW	*Zeitschrift für die alttestamentliche Wissenschaft*
ZBK	Zürcher Bibelkommentare

Introduction:
From Transgression to Transformation

L. Juliana Claassens, Christl M. Maier,
and Funlọla O. Ọlọjẹde

"Women always broke the curfews."[1]

So ruminates the narrator in Anna Burns' novel *Milkman*, which poignantly reflects a young woman's experience of being stalked against the backdrop of the so-called Troubles as she describes the Northern Ireland Conflict in the 1970s. The reason for the "traditional women" breaking the curfews was that their "patience would have been stretched far enough." As the narrator contends:

> It would have been over-tried, over-tested and the subsequent snapping of it would be directed towards any group of men, any religion, any side of the water, setting up rules and regulations, overreaching themselves with their rules and regulations, expecting everyone else too—meaning women—to go along with the preposterousness of the silliness they had concocted as rationale in their heads.[2]

When the traditional women have had enough, they would snap, "because life was going on—children to be fed, nappies to be changed, housework to be done, shopping to be got in," and the political problems were just a nuisance that should "be managed, skirted around or in some other way accommodated."[3] So these women would rise up and go ahead and break the curfew, "go[ing] out their doors in their hundreds and deliberately,

---

1. Anna Burns, *Milkman* (London: Faber & Faber, 2018), 159.
2. Ibid.
3. Ibid.

and permitless, after… hours… With them would be their children, their screaming babies, their housepets of assorted dogs, rabbits, hamsters and turtles."[4] The narrator describes this glorious chaos as follows:

> Also they'd be wheeling their prams and carrying their pennants, their banners, their placards and shouting, "CURFEW'S OVER! EVERYBODY IS TO COME OUT! CURFEW'S OVER!", thereby inviting all in the area who weren't already out, to come out, so that everybody could enter into state defiance and every time so far when the traditional women had done this, when they'd reclaimed sanity, the police and the military would find the latest curfew, right before their eyes, had stopped.[5]

The reason why these women's transgression could have this dramatic effect is that, as the narrator reflects, "[t]o shoot up a district of women, children, prams and goldfish otherwise, to run them through with swords much as one might like to, would not look good, would look grave, sexist, unbalanced, not only in the glare of the critical side of the home media, but also in the eyes of the international media."[6]

With the curfew over, the military and the state would go back to their war games, while "the traditional women—after further obligatory banner-waving, picketing, pressure protests and interviews—returning home in haste, emptying the streets in seconds, all to get in to get the evening tea on."[7]

This striking scene from *Milkman* captures some of the core themes that are at the heart of this collection of essays—transgression of rules and laws, and conventions that seem so self-evident to those in power, but really are not very practical, or life giving; and transformation, according to which individual and communal acts of transgression may result in some form of change that is beneficial to the community as a whole. In the example cited above, the curfew had been lifted. And, for a while at least, life could go on.

This example from *Milkman* moreover may help us consider some important features that are associated with the theme of transgression and transformation that informs this collection of essays. In the first instance, it is important to note that transgression cannot be enforced. It is once the individuals and the community have had enough that people may rise up and say, "Enough is enough." Transgression is thus very much linked to

4. Ibid., 160.
5. Ibid.
6. Ibid.
7. Ibid.

autonomy, attesting to a strong sense of self in which individuals and the community decide what is good for them and their families.

Second, transgression quite often does not occur by extraordinary means, but is to be found in small, rather ordinary actions that may have transgressive qualities. For instance, in the example cited above, the transgressive behavior of the traditional women is associated with their decision to go for a walk, taking their children and household pets with them! However, in some instances, as also in the example from *Milkman*, ordinary transgressive actions may have extraordinary transformative potential.

And third, as evident in the example from *Milkman*, rules and policies are not merely to be broken for the sake of breaking rules. It is indeed a case that one may be transgressive without being transformative. It is thus vitally important that transgressive practices have the intention, as well as the effect, of opening up life-giving spaces to others.

This connection between transgression and transformation, as compellingly represented in the contemporary novel of *Milkman*, extends also to the underlying premise of this book that considers the transgressive and transformative potential of exegetical and hermeneutical approaches such as feminist, postcolonial and queer biblical interpretation. In our exegetical endeavors that often are described as pushing exegetical and interpretative boundaries, many of us may have had the experience of people telling us: "You want to do what?" "It is impossible!" "It cannot be done." Nevertheless, it is precisely this transgression in terms of method and substance as evident in new hermeneutical and exegetical approaches that often has been responsible for breathing new life into tired and dusty corners of our discipline.

When it comes to engaging in exegetical and hermeneutical approaches that are deemed to be transgressive in nature, though, it is crucial to have a supportive community. Some of us may have had the experience of an encouraging professor or a colleague telling us: "You can argue what you want to, but you've got to be convincing!" We all need someone who understands what it is that we are seeking to do, and encourages us to develop the best possible arguments in order to be persuasive. Equally valuable is finding a kindred spirit in scholars who are trying to do the same thing, see the world in the same way, and move in the same general direction.

In some sense, this current collection of essays represents such a supportive community. This book was conceived in one of the Gender Unit conferences hosted by the Faculty of Theology at Stellenbosch University. Over the years, the Gender Unit has been seeking to offer a collaborative space in which scholars—experienced and emerging, local, national, and international—may come together and try out experimental exegetical and hermeneutical approaches that result in interpretations that take seriously the needs of the respective communities in which the interpreters find themselves.

The "Transgression and Transformation: The Role of Feminist, Postcolonial and Queer Biblical Interpretation in Fostering Communities of Justice" conference, which was held March 13–15, 2019 in collaboration with The Center for Theology, Women, and Gender of Princeton Theological Seminary, took its inspiration from what Carolyn Sharp considers a central task of feminist, postcolonial, and queer biblical interpreters:

> I define "lament" as socio-political protest that names woundedness and loss, making visible the vulnerability of cultural systems of meaning-making and declining to be complicit in the erasure of pain and brokenness from communal memory. I define "transgression" as the privileging of creative interventions, ancient and contemporary, that resist or reframe destructive social norms.[8]

These strategies are, according to Sharp, vital in "critique[ing] and resist[ing] any politics of Othering" in both text and society that includes such manifestations as misogyny, homophobia, violence and other forms of oppression.[9] The feminist critical enterprise is rooted furthermore in an intersectional understanding that focuses on the harm done to female bodies and psyche in the text and society, but also considers other forms of oppression and marginalization, and in particular, the wounds caused by racism, imperialism, heteronormativity and economic exploitation.

Ultimately, the goal of such reading practices is transformation. Sharp writes that the work of the feminist, postcolonial and queer biblical interpreter "must be sustained by the daily courage of communities of justice" that are focused on "working creatively to change oppressive paradigms."[10] According to Sharp, the goal is a "hermeneutically ethical world in which no interpreting subject is cast out."[11]

---

8. Carolyn J. Sharp, "Buying Land in the Text of Jeremiah: Feminist Commentary, the Kristevan Abject, and Jeremiah 32," in *Prophecy and Power: Jeremiah in Feminist and Postcolonial Perspective*, ed. Christl M. Maier and Carolyn J. Sharp, LHBOTS 577 (London: Bloomsbury T&T Clark, 2013), 155.

9. Ibid., 170.

10. Ibid., 171.

11. Ibid., 172.

Through innovate interpretative strategies, the participants in this conference, who were supplemented with a number of other like-minded contributors, can all be said to read against the grain of the text, and with the marginalized, the subordinated or subaltern others, both in the text and in the world. In the process, the contributors to this volume ask important questions regarding power and privilege, that is, whose voices are being heard and whose interests are being served? Knowing all too well the harm stereotypical constructions of the Other can do in terms of feeding, among others, racism, sexism, homophobia and imperialism in their respective interpretative communities, the contributors to this volume interrogate constructions of ethnicity, gender, sexual orientation, and class, both in the text as well as in their respective contexts.

In addition, the contributors to this volume, who come from very different social locations, have in common the commitment to create spaces for alternative life-giving interpretations that take seriously the experiences of those most vulnerable, amplifying those voices who are silenced, thereby challenging unjust structures and practices. Thus, by means of the thought-provoking interpretations collected in this volume, the contributors show their commitment to scholarship not just for the sake of scholarship, but for a scholarly ethos that in some shape or form contributes to the cultivation of more just, equitable societies.

Given their different social locations and constituencies, the contributors face a variety of challenges themselves. What counts as transgressive interpretation in one context may not be seen as innovative in another. A reading that is transformative in one location may not have any significant effect in another community. Therefore, contemporary readers are invited to assess the transgressive and transformative potential of any of the essays not only for themselves but also in relation to the author's context.

This volume is divided into two parts. In the first part, contributors consider what can be viewed as *Transgressive Measures* that pertain to some of the actions, both on the part of the characters, but more often on the part of the interpreters that counter, disrupt, or undo what is considered the norm, or "normal" in societies then and now. Read through a variety of different exegetical and hermeneutical lenses, these contributions include portrayals of female characters who rightly challenge the boundaries of what is considered normative in both ancient and contemporary societies. This section starts with an innovate first-person account by Noah, one of the Daughters of Zelophehad in Numbers 27, who, according to Funlọla Ọlọjẹde, is "numbered with the transgressors." This essay expertly shows how this woman and her sisters jointly act to transgress life-denying laws and customs when they bring a "class-action lawsuit" against the government of their day.

In her essay, which brings into conversation the representation of Woman Zion in the book of Lamentations and the #MeToo movement, Gina Hens-Piazza shows how Woman Zion's voice ruptures the silence which up to this point surrounds the biblical women's voices that might have cried "Me TOO." Despite the accusations indicting her, this city woman publicly names what happened to her and even confronts the abuser. In a few brief verses, she reclaims her autonomy, exercises agency and becomes a truth-teller. In the process, she rejects the blame and shame that have held her captive, boldly identifies where responsibility lies, and initiates the move toward resilience for herself and other women.

Focusing on probably two of the most vilified female transgressors in the Hebrew Bible, Lerato Mokoena seeks to challenge the sexist cultural stereotypes that have come to be associated with Jezebel, a seductress queen whose lust for power is depicted in 2 Kings 9–10, and Mrs. Job, who is portrayed as an unsympathetic and foolish character in the history of interpretation.

In an essay that seeks to deconstruct the gendered codes and the uneven discourse of voices in the drama of a broken family in Jer 2:1–4:4, Christl Maier argues that by challenging the divine monologue in terms of feminist, queer, and trauma perspectives, the fragility of the theological idea of human malice and divine justice that permeates the book of Jeremiah is revealed.

Transgressive action may also occur within the banal, mundane activities of quotidian institutional life. Employing the story of the woman of Shunem who pressed the king to return her land to her after her sojourn in Philistia (2 Kgs 8:1–6), Jacqueline Lapsley considers those instances in which merely following good laws already in the books, and pressing others to do so when they would rather not, become an act of creative transgression.

Continuing the conversation of following the law as an act of transgression, Hendrik Bosman considers the link between justice and the law in Leviticus 12 when it comes to safeguarding maternal health in the context of an exceedingly high mortality rate associated with childbearing in the ancient Near East, which continues also in many communities around the world today.

In these portrayals of the subversive or transgressive measures employed by subversive or transgressive female characters, one finds how biblical scholars, through a variety of exegetical and hermeneutical approaches, contribute to undoing or challenging cultural constructions and stereotypes, as well as unjust legal and cultural practices that prevent especially women, but also other vulnerable constituents, to reach their full potential.

In the second part of this book, *Transgressive Methodologies*, contributors seek to expand the conversation on the transgressive potential of exegetical and hermeneutical approaches such as trauma hermeneutics, gender critical, feminist, postcolonial, and queer biblical interpretation by pushing the methodological boundaries even further in the constant evolvement of innovative hermeneutical and exegetical strategies.

For instance, in the first of two treatments of the enigmatic story of Lot's daughters as told in Genesis 19, Juliana Claassens reads the deeply disturbing account of Lot's daughters sleeping with their father as a multilayered trauma narrative. In conjunction with such approaches as feminist and postcolonial interpretation, trauma hermeneutics is a helpful tool in interrogating, or one could say, excavating the multiple, intersecting levels of traumatic memories of Israel and her neighbors that continue to haunt them as they seek to make sense of their place in the world.

In the following essay, Claassens' fellow South African, Madipoane Masenya (Ngwan'a Mphahlele), reads the same text from a very different socio-cultural location as she brings Genesis 19 into conversation with selected African proverbs, specifically considering the question of what emerges when conventional notions of masculinities are transgressed.

Demonstrating the value of postcolonial interpretation for cultivating communities of justice, Dora Mbuwayesango proposes that a postcolonial analysis of narratives that depict the encounters of the Israelite colonial invaders and the indigenous Rahab and Gibeonites may help to honor the experiences of the victims of colonization and foster an authentic transformation of exploitative and oppressive social and economic paradigms.

Contemplating queer expressions of desire in Genesis 28–31, Charlene van der Walt seeks to counter the dominant thrust of the narrative trajectory presupposed by the heteropatriarchal ideology informing the construction and dominant interpretation of the Jacob narrative by reinterpreting Jacob's desire for Rachel to create space for tracing alternative strands of desire.

In their very interesting depiction of how Botswana women are reclaiming the exclusionary colonial and patriarchal urban space of Gaborone through the Naomi Shower movement, members of the Circle of Concerned African Women Theologians' chapter of the University of Botswana show how the divisive patriarchal ideology that often compels women to compete with one another is deconstructed. Musa Dube employs the wisdom of Botho//Ubuntu philosophy, which she utilizes in her depiction of how Gaborone women gather to read the book of Ruth to construct women-centered spaces and relationships in what is called the Naomi Shower.

And in the final essay, "Tamar Summons Jesus," Gerald West outlines an organic community-driven process in which the realities of violence against women summoned Contextual Bible Study work on (more) redemptive forms of African masculinity. Focusing on trans-textual interpretation that flows from 2 Sam 13:1–22 to Mark 5:22–43, and to Matt 20:17–34, West argues that these texts are to be understood as the remnants of redacted sources that reflect sectoral concerns about gender and masculinity, which may nurture interpretive and social transformation.

In the example cited from *Milkman* at the beginning of this introduction, it is clear that men from all religions, cultures and social locations will continue with their policies and procedures, rules and laws that are described by the narrator as a "toybox mentality."[12] Restrictive, suffocating, life-denying forms of controlling others in the name of good governance will thus continue. However, in terms of our exegetical work, those of us who are counting ourselves with the transgressors will continue to put into practice our exegetical and hermeneutical endeavors that can be considered transgressive in nature, precisely because we believe that a different way in the world is possible after all.

---

12. The narrator describes this "toybox mentality," as "the toy trains in the attic, the toy soldiers on the toy battlefield and, in the case of the state and the military, the particular toy of choice that they'd get out of the box every so often was curfews where the rules were, if you broke one without a permit after eighteen hundred hours and sometimes after just sixteen hundred hours, without fear or favour, without respect for station, on sight you would be shot" (Burns, *Milkman*, 159).

Part I

TRANSGRESSIVE MEASURES

Chapter 2

NUMBERED WITH THE TRANSGRESSORS:
THE STORY OF THE DAUGHTERS OF ZELOPHEHAD
AS RETOLD BY NOAH

Funlọla O. Ọlọjẹde
Stellenbosch University

1. A Voice Note from Noah

My name is Noah and I am the second of the five daughters of Zelophehad. Before I was born, my parents prayed earnestly for a son, but I turned out to be a girl anyway, so they gave me a boy's name.[1] So much has been said and written about my sisters and me, but we have never once spoken about ourselves. I thought it was time to tell you a little about my family even though I really don't owe you an explanation. You may choose to judge our action as right or wrong, but would you at least try to understand our situation before you do so?

I, Noah, was born in that great and terrible wilderness, where there were fiery serpents, and scorpions, and drought, and where there was no water.[2] So were my sisters Mahlah, Hoglah, Milcah and Tirzah. Our parents were gypsies in the desert of Sinai and part of the Israelite exodus from Egypt. But mother was a fragile person, and after the birth of five

---

1. "He named him Noah, saying, 'This one will bring us comfort from our labor and from the painful toil of our hands because of the ground that the LORD has cursed'... After Noah was 500 years old, *he* became the father of Shem, Ham, and Japheth" (Gen 5:30, 32, emphasis added). All Bible citations in this essay are taken from the New English Translation (NET) version, except otherwise stated.

2. Cf. "And who brought you through the great, fearful desert of venomous serpents and scorpions, an arid place with no water" (Deut 8:15).

babies her body could no longer withstand the rigor of desert life. Her soul also was much discouraged along the way because she could not bear a son in a culture which privileged sons above daughters. She died shortly after Tirzah was born. Our family was never the same again.

You have no idea what life in that wilderness was like. We wandered day and night in a land of deserts and of pits, a land of drought, and of the shadow of death, a land that no one passed through, and where no one dwelt.[3] I did not know any other life. Each day was the same. The weather was the same—either extremely hot or extremely cold. The food was the same, the landscape was the same, the pain was unbearably the same. We would go around in circles, ending up on the same spot we began.[4] The men would go to war sometimes, but for us girls, life had little meaning beyond the prospect of marriage and motherhood. Life was tough, but you had to keep going. The life we lived then, you cannot imagine; and the live you live now, we could not imagine. Imagine being quarantined for seven days every month simply because your female body was undergoing its natural cycle. Everyone knew what was happening in your body. There was no "sanitary pad drive," no bathroom, no privacy.

Instead, there were so many rules, so many sacrifices and rituals, so many taboos. Many people could not keep up with the myriad rules and regulations, most of which could result in death when violated. Father was one of the lawbreakers and, in time, he died for his sins.[5] My sisters and I were heartbroken. In the camp, we heard every day about the new world, the land that flowed with milk and honey. We were told that there was a promissory note by the LORD that he would take our people into that land—a land of wheat, and barley, and vines, and fig trees, and pomegranates; a land of olive oil, and honey, a land wherein we would

---

3. "…who brought us through the wilderness,
through a land of desert sands and rift valleys,
through a land of drought and deep darkness,
through a land in which no one travels,
and where no one lives?" (Jer 2:6).

4. "You have circled around this mountain long enough; now turn north" (Deut 2:3; cf. 1:6).

5. "Our father died in the wilderness, although he was not part of the company of those that gathered themselves together against the LORD in the company of Korah; but he died for his own sin, and he had no sons (Num 27:3). Cf. "But there was not a man among these who had been among those numbered by Moses and Aaron the priest when they numbered the Israelites in the wilderness of Sinai. For the LORD had said of them, 'They will surely die in the wilderness.' And there was not left a single man of them, except Caleb son of Jephunneh and Joshua son of Nun" (Num 26:64–65).

eat bread without scarceness and shall not lack any thing.[6] But we knew that with the death of our father Zelophehad, we would have no part in that hill country beyond the Jordan, except as drifters and squatters. The elders would not allocate any portion of the land to our father because he had no sons.[7] So life no longer had any meaning for us. Our hope was lost.

As Israelites in the aftermath of the exodus, we understood the meaning of homelessness, of landlessness, and of destitution. As orphan girls, my sisters and I understood grief, loneliness, and vulnerability. We were tired of roaming the desert but there was no other place to call home. We had no one else but ourselves, so we became very close. Soon, we learned to talk together, laugh together, cry together, and even tried to dream together; to dream of another land, and of a new day.

Then, we began to go to the Tent of the Meeting just to listen and catch a glimpse of the court proceedings as people brought different cases before the elders and before Moses. It was our own way of staying out of trouble. In the course of time, we perceived that if there would be any change in our lives, it would be through the law. The law was our only hope. But the law was against us. It discounted the girl child. How then could we transgress the boundaries of the law and live to tell the story? Moses was getting older and older and if we were to change our story, we would have to act fast before he died. Transforming policies and legislations appeared to be one of the few weapons that the powerless possessed. And so, for many months, we deliberated and prayed as we continued in the wilderness of Sinai. We then agreed to bring a class action suit before Moses. Our strength would be in our unity.

2. *Our Day in Court*

Let me talk a little about our day in court. The previous night, we could hardly sleep. We prayed, we plotted, we rehearsed our speech. Mahlah was to speak on our behalf—not only because she was the oldest but because she was bold, articulate, feisty and a truly great leader. She had been our second mother and our pillar of strength after the death of our parents.

---

6. "For the LORD your God is bringing you to a good land, a land of brooks, springs, and fountains flowing forth in valleys and hills, a land of wheat, barley, vines, fig trees, and pomegranates, of olive trees and honey, a land where you may eat food in plenty and find no lack of anything, a land whose stones are iron and from whose hills you can mine copper" (Deut 8:7–9).

7. "Now Zelophehad son of Hepher had no sons, but only daughters; and the names of the daughters of Zelophehad were Mahlah, Noah, Hoglah, Milcah, and Tirzah" (Num 26:33; cf. 27:3–4).

When our case was called, we were all so scared. My heart trembled, so did my hands. Tirzah clung to me, and I feigned a courage that I did not feel. We knew that Moses was a no-nonsense judge who followed the law to the letter. So we were quite uncertain of what would unfold. Would we get a fair hearing? Would he treat us as rebels and command the earth to swallow us as he did Korah, Dathan Abiram and On?[8] Would one of the congregation members attack us and stone us to death? Unquestionably, ours was an act of transgression. No woman had ever challenged Moses or the law. Miriam who was joined by Aaron to oppose their brother Moses was smitten with leprosy for seven days.[9]

Nonetheless, we approached Moses. We were in awe of him—this figure whose face would shine so much with the Shekinah glory of the LORD that he had to cover it with a veil.[10] I felt like running away, yet I wanted to etch that moment in my memory forever. We took the stand.[11] There was no lawyer or advocate. So Mahlah presented and argued our case. Our father died without having any son, but he died for his own sins; he was not a rebel. Our request was to inherit the portion of land that would have been allocated to him in the Promised Land. The irony was that we were demanding for the rights to a land our father never owned. We were relying only on the promise that the LORD made to our people even before we were born. It was an act of great faith on our part. Surprisingly, Moses was not rough with us. He had no daughters himself and he was willing to hear us out. But after hearing our demand, he was confused. He did not know what to do. The law made no provision for our case, so he decided to turn to the LORD for an answer.[12]

When we attended those court sessions in the past, we saw that, in some cases, Moses was unsure of what to do, for example, in the case of the men who missed the Passover because of the uncleanness of a dead person, or the case of the man who was caught gathering sticks on the Sabbath, or the case of the son of the Israelite woman who blasphemed the name of the LORD. In all these instances, the law was inadequate or unclear and Moses had to turn to the oracle for guidance.[13] We became a little apprehensive, then, not knowing what the response from the oracle would be. The outcome could be grim.

---

8. Num 16:30–33.
9. Num 12:1–15.
10. Exod 34:30–35.
11. Rolf P. Knierim and George W. Coats, *Numbers*, FOTL 4 (Grand Rapids, MI: Eerdmans, 2005), 274.
12. "So Moses brought their case before the LORD" (Num 27:5).
13. Num 9:1–14; 15:32–36; Lev 24:10–22.

In the end, we received a verdict and we all began to weep. The LORD had favored our cause. We were right. Moses was ordered to amend the law. He was to give us an inheritance among our father's brothers by transferring the inheritance of our father to us.[14] The victory that day was unprecedented—it was a victory for daughters, for mothers, and for all men who had no sons.[15] All the women came out singing and dancing outside the Tent of Meeting. It was a new day.

3. *Aftermath of the Case*

But our victory appeared short-lived. Sometime later, certain elders of our clan raised an objection to the ruling and went back to court.[16] They argued before Moses and Eleazar that if a daughter who inherited land from her father married into another tribe, the portion of land belonging to her father's tribe would be subverted. Their plea was that inherited land should remain within the clan so as not to alienate the land. A daughter who inherited her father's landed property should therefore not marry outside the clan unless she was ready to forfeit that inheritance.[17]

You see, before the initial ruling, no man looked in our direction because we were five orphan girls wandering through the wilderness of life without any inheritance or dowry. All of a sudden, my sisters and I were inundated with marriage proposals after the ruling. As you all probably know, some men also are gold diggers. Men from different Israelite tribes sought our hands in marriage because now they saw the economic potential in us. This was what prompted the elders to challenge the ruling in court. Moses therefore ruled in their favor. But we were not bothered by this outcome; some of our cousins were among our suitors, so we married

---

14. "The LORD said to Moses: 'The daughters of Zelophehad have a valid claim. You must indeed give them possession of an inheritance among their father's relatives, and you must transfer the inheritance of their father to them'" (Num 27:6–7).

15. "And you must tell the Israelites, 'If a man dies and has no son, then you must transfer his inheritance to his daughter; and if he has no daughter, then you are to give his inheritance to his brothers; and if he has no brothers, then you are to give his inheritance to his father's brothers; and if his father has no brothers, then you are to give his inheritance to his relative nearest to him from his family, and he will possess it. This will be for the Israelites a legal requirement, as the LORD commanded Moses'" (Num 27:8–11).

16. Num 36:1–13.

17. Knierim and Coats, *Numbers*, 330.

them.[18] Our male offspring could then bear the name of our late father and inherit his portion. But more importantly, they would have a better life than we did. It was a compromise we made in the circumstances and we decided not to pursue the case. We had already made our point.

On our side, we reasoned that since Moses granted the appeal of the elders, it meant that the law was not cast in stone. The book of Numbers, which contains our story, ended with the suggestion that there was no last word on the matter. In the future, there could be additional amendments to the inheritance law if the need arose because a paradigm has been set that showed that the law could be challenged and revised. And today, we are content to see that various nations have used our case as a reference point in their search for justice and equity.

Many generations have passed since the case of the *Zelophehad's Daughters versus the State*, but when my sisters and I hear what people continue to say about us, we are amazed and amused at the same time. Some say we are sons and not daughters,[19] while others compiled a list of all the tabloid gossip about us.[20] Some readers of our story accuse us of acting in the interest of men; that we were agents of patriarchy because we wanted to memorialize the name of our father. But we did not even know what patriarchy meant and we certainly did nothing for patriarchy but for love and for survival. And what is wrong with keeping our father's memory alive anyway? Father was our hero. After our mother died, he could have remarried but he chose to take care of us. He nursed us when we were sick. He carried us when we fell down and when we were too

---

18. "This is what the LORD has commanded for Zelophehad's daughters: 'Let them marry whomever they think best, only they must marry within the family of their father's tribe. In this way the inheritance of the Israelites will not be transferred from tribe to tribe. But every one of the Israelites must retain the ancestral heritage'… As the LORD had commanded Moses, so the daughters of Zelophehad did" (Num 36:6–7, 10). Cf. Num 27:1–11, which stipulates that the land must remain within the clan so as not to alienate the land. Hiebert explains that, "Land remained with male members of the family. Where the Bible records the transfer of land to women, besides the two cases of Pharaoh's daughter [1 Kgs 9:16] and Achsah…stipulations were legislated to cover this unique situation" (Paula S. Hiebert, "'Whence Shall Help Come to Me?' The Biblical Widow," in *Gender and Difference in Ancient Israel*, ed. Peggy L. Day [Minneapolis, MN: Fortress, 1989], 125–41 [137]).

19. Dora Rudo Mbuwayesango, "Can Daughters Be Sons? The Daughters of Zelophehad in Patriarchal and Imperial Context," in *Relating to the Text: Interdisciplinary and Form-Critical Insights on the Bible*, ed. Timothy J. Sandoval and Carleen Mandolfo, JSOTSup 384 (London: T&T Clark, 2003), 251–62.

20. L. Juliana M. Claassens, *Claiming Her Dignity: Female Resistance in the Old Testament* (Collegeville, MN: Liturgical, 2016), 84–91.

tired to walk. He comforted us when we grieved and longed for our mother. Our father was our world. And my sisters and I were his world. If you had a father like him, you also would try to immortalize his name. Zelophehad was not a man's man, he was a woman's man.

Some of those who judge us, who incidentally are daughters like us, call us imperialists.[21] They argue that by asking for the land we were depriving the women, children and men of Canaan their own inheritance. It is very painful to hear other women criticize us. It is easy to judge when you have never been in the shoes of those who have no shoes. They do not understand what drives us. We ourselves had been oppressed, slaves and vagabonds for many years. We never owned anything since we grew into a nation, and we reckoned that we should have a little share in the resources of the earth, that we also deserved a place under the sun. Or should we continue to live in tents forever? Surely, those who live in dream houses are at liberty to judge those who only dream of living in houses, aren't they?

We are told that, today, many women across the globe still do not own land. When you push people against the wall, something has to give—either they push back, or they push the boundaries in order to survive. When people have reached the limits of endurance, they act in desperate ways that transgress legal, moral and ethical boundaries. When a people has everything while the other has nothing at all, what we have is a recipe for disaster. We so-called Israelite invaders were not your regular run-of-the-mill imperialists but stateless "bandits" who were desperate to get a space under the heavens and have a share in the resources of the earth. The Canaanites had everything—houses full of good things, wells, vineyards, olive yards, fruit trees in abundance, cities fenced with high walls and gates and bars, and many unwalled cities as well.[22] But when a people has been in slavery for 430 years and wandered in the desert of life for another forty years without owning any immovable property, you would be desperate, my friend. When you have no life and your children have no hope, you would push boundaries.

---

21. Musa W. Dube, *Postcolonial Feminists Interpretation of the Bible* (St. Louis, MO: Chalice, 2000), 73–80; Mbuwayesango, "Can Daughters Be Sons?" 252, 261.

22. "...a land with large, fine cities you did not build, houses filled with choice things you did not accumulate, hewn out cisterns you did not dig, and vineyards and olive groves you did not plant..." (Deut 6:10–11). See also Deut 3:5, "All of these cities were fortified by high walls, gates, and locking bars; in addition there were a great many open villages"; Neh 9:25, "They captured fortified cities and fertile land. They took possession of houses full of all sorts of good things—wells previously dug, vineyards, olive trees, and fruit trees in abundance."

I, Noah, have been in that desert of life. When you live like we lived, what do you think will set in? It is the law of the jungle. You may choose not to acknowledge it, but we "Israelite invaders" are still among you today, and it may be a misnomer to see the Canaanites as the victims. Those who have nothing at all are the real victims in the game of life. They are no imperialists or conquerors; they have only been reduced to takers and grabbers, and die-hards by the very system that turned them away. When people refuse to share resources, when those who constitute themselves into moral police continue to act in arrogance and treat others with disdain, when other nation states are reduced to "shit-hole countries"[23] by those who shat/shit on them and there is no justice or equity in social, political or economic interactions, then, what you see is what you get, my friends.

My sisters and I abhor violence and we transgressed the Law of Moses at the risk of our own lives. We demanded that the law should make provision for us, but not just for us, or for a privileged few, but for all the landless, the vagabond, the underdog, those who have seen the dark side of life, and those whose lives have been fragmented by the vicissitudes of life, and whose names may not be remembered after they are gone. The law must accommodate children orphaned by dreaded diseases and those who have no formal education because they were born into the jungle of life. We wanted to set a precedent to let daughters everywhere know that they can present a united front and fight for their rights; that they can take the battle to the courts, the parliament and the *imbizos*[24] to demand for the amendment of every obnoxious law and every clause in the law that sidelines women and impinges on human rights; that they can advocate for the marginalized and the downtrodden, and support laws that would set the solitary in families.[25] We did not stand up for men—but for ourselves, for our family, for posterity.

By the way, my sisters Mahlah, Hoglah, Milcah and Tirzah said to let you know, to let you all know, that our voice is not merely the voice of women or the voice from a male script. Ours is the voice of the orphan and of the landless poor. It is the voice of the disenchanted and of the disenfranchised, the voice of the vagrant and of the migrant, the voice of the restless soul and of the tempest-tossed. Our voice is the voice of

---

23. In recent media reports, the former president of the United States, Donald Trump, allegedly referred to El Salvador, Haiti and certain African nations as "shithole countries."

24. An *imbizo* is a South African term for a gathering, usually called by a traditional leader.

25. Ps 68:6 (KJV).

all those who are united in pain and in hope. My sisters Mahlah, Hoglah, Milcah and Tirzah said to let you all know that, no matter what people say about us, we will always be proud that we were numbered with the *transgressors*.[26]

Bibliography

Claassens, L. Juliana M. *Claiming Her Dignity: Female Resistance in the Old Testament.* Collegeville, MN: Liturgical, 2016.

Dube, Musa W. *Postcolonial Feminist Interpretation of the Bible*. St. Louis, MO: Chalice, 2000.

Hiebert, Paula S. "'Whence Shall Help Come to Me?' The Biblical Widow." In *Gender and Difference in Ancient Israel*, edited by Peggy L. Day, 125–41. Minneapolis, MN: Fortress, 1989.

Knierim, Rolf P., and George W. Coats. *Numbers*. FOTL 4. Grand Rapids, MI: Eerdmans, 2005.

Mbuwayesango, Dora Rudo. "Can Daughters Be Sons? The Daughters of Zelophehad in Patriarchal and Imperial Context." In *Relating to the Text: Interdisciplinary and Form-Critical Insights on the Bible*, edited by Timothy J. Sandoval and Carleen Mandolfo, 251–62. JSOTSup 384. London: T & T Clark, 2003.

The NET Bible: The New English Translation. Dallas, TX: Biblical Studies Press, 2005.

---

26. Isa 53:12.

Chapter 2

Silence Breakers:
Woman Zion and the #MeToo Movement—
Lamentation 2:20–22's
Path to Transformation*

Gina Hens-Piazza

Jesuit School of Theology of Santa Clara University

Give sorrow words:
grief that does not speak knits up the o'er wrought heart
and bids it break.

Shakespeare, *Macbeth*

1. *Introduction*

The well-worn expression "Silence is golden" is only the first half of a proverb, the origin of which has been obscured by time but dates back to ancient Egypt. In 1831, the poet Thomas Carlyle translated it into English. The actual proverb reads "Silence is golden, speech is silver." Gold being worth more than silver indicates that speaking is good but silence is better. Hence, saying nothing is preferable to speaking.

* The #MeToo Movement began in October 2016 as a hashtag which spread virally on social media in an effort to educate the public on the frequency of sexual harassment and assault. The hashtag #MeToo was actually coined in 2006 by Tarana Burke, an American social activist and community organizer. Since 2017, victims have been encouraged to "tweet" about their experience in order to document the scope of the problem and the need for social change.

Yet, there is a silence in the biblical tradition that argues against the wisdom of this old adage. In Genesis 34, when Dinah passed through the fields, she was seized and raped by Shechem the Hivite (Gen 34:1–2). No account described her trauma and no direct discourse sounded her pain. When Bathsheba, who was spotted during her private bath, inquired about, sent for, brought to the king, slept with, and impregnated, no narrative space was allotted to her to claim with Dinah, "Me Too." When Moses ordered that all the Midianite female captives who had never known a man be handed over to Israel's soldiers (Num 31), no sound of their collective cry of "Me Too" was ever recorded. Following the legislation in Deut 21:14, any of the anonymous female war captives could be kept as concubines by the Israelite warriors. Yet, their collective lament, "Me Too," which might have begun a healing, never made its way into the tradition. Tamar, whose half-brother meticulously planned the sexual overture that turned into rape, never had a chance to go public and give voice to her trauma. The dancing maidens of Shiloh who were carried off by the Benjaminites as wives, and were isolated from one another also never had the collective support to declare, "Me Too." Lastly, in the unreadable story in Judges 19, the voice of Levite's concubine who was gang raped, left for dead, and who perhaps in her dying moments painfully whispered, "Me Too," remains forever silenced.

Breaking the silence around trauma is a necessary step on the road to healing and resilience. The muting of the #MeToo victims of the biblical stories has helped to shape the cultural message that women's experiences do not matter. And what is unimportant or is defined as unworthy of attention goes un-narrated or remains shrouded in silence. The capacity to emerge from trauma, to be transformed from victimhood to wholeness, requires breaking the silence.

Feminist scholars have long played their part in documenting the case of violence and trauma against women in the biblical traditions. Their work continues to make clear the abuse, blame, and trauma to which the numerous women in these biblical stories have been subjected, beginning with the blaming of the first woman in Gen 3:12. But feminist interpretations have also played an important role in subverting some of these traditions as well as highlighting often neglected counter stories in which women resist subjugation and act to secure their own liberation and that of others.

In these biblical texts resides the portrait of one woman who against all odds raised her voice against the violence, blame, and abuse unjustly foisted upon her. Breaking the silence, she not only spoke out against that which attempted to victimize her, her voice also resounds on behalf of others who have suffered unjust trauma—those silenced biblical figures as well as other silenced women across our world today. To understand this biblical woman's transition from abused victim to a figure of resilience and wholeness, three stages identified by trauma theorists will be enlisted to interpret her transformation.

2. *Trauma Theory and the Transition to Resilience*

When it comes to trauma, silence is definitely not golden. Therapists have long agreed on one underlying presumption. If one can talk about one's trauma—be it domestic violence, a sexual assault, being on site during 9/11, or returning home from fighting in Afghanistan—one can resolve it. The idea of bringing to memory the trauma and describing it in detail dates back to Freud's innovation called the "talking cure" in psychotherapy.[1] But talking about one's trauma as a means of resolving trauma is not so simple. The experience of traumatic events often eclipses words. Many people report that merely recalling in detail the traumatic event actually can re-traumatize an individual.

---

1. Sigmund Freud, *Inhibitions, Symptoms and Anxiety* (trans. Alix Strachey; London: Hogarth, 1949), 150. Since Freud, extensive literature from a variety of disciplines has focused on collective and individual trauma. Some of the more recent works often serving as resources for biblical scholars include Cathy Caruth, *Unclaimed Experience: Trauma, Narrative and History* (Baltimore, MD: The Johns Hopkins University Press, 1995); Cathy Caruth (ed.), *Trauma: Explorations in Memory* (Baltimore, MD: The Johns Hopkins University Press, 1995); Charles Whitfield, *Memory and Abuse: Remembering and Healing the Effects of Trauma* (Deerfield Beach: Health Communications, 1995); Judith Herman, *Trauma and Recovery: The Aftermath of Violence—From Domestic Abuse to Political Terror*, rev. ed. (New York: Basic, 1997); Ruth Leys, *Trauma: A Genealogy* (Chicago, IL: University of Chicago Press, 2000); Jeffrey Kauffman, *Loss of the Assumptive World: A Theory of Traumatic Loss* (New York: Brunner-Routledge, 2002); Sean Field, "Beyond 'Healing': Trauma, Oral History and Regeneration," *Oral History* 34 (2006): 31–42; Bessel A. van der Kolk, Alexander C. McFarlane, and Lars Weisaeth (eds.), *Traumatic Stress: The Effects of Overwhelming Experience on Mind, Body and Society* (New York: Guilford, 2007); Jeffrey C. Alexander, *Trauma: A Social Theory* (Cambridge: Polity, 2012); and Eve-Marie Becker, Jan Dochhorn, and Else K. Holt (eds.), *Trauma and Traumatization in Individual and Collective Dimensions: Insights from Biblical Studies and Beyond*, SANt 2 (Gottingen: Vandenhoeck & Ruprecht, 2014); Amir Kadhem, "Cultural Trauma as a Social Construct: 9/11 Fiction and the Epistemology of Communal Pain," *Intertexts* 18 (2014): 181–97.

Nonetheless, silence surrounding trauma is also deadly. Avram Finkelstein's *After Silence: A History of AIDS* gave birth to activists' rallying cry, "Silence equals death."[2] The author observes that in the face of trauma, silence imprisons a person with pain, with anxiety, and with awful memories. It locks up one's emotions that are tied to the horrible event with no place to exit or any avenue through which they can be expressed. Sometimes, it is tempting to think that one can regain control by not talking about what happened. But refraining from speaking about what was lost deludes one into thinking that the associated grief can be contained. Other times, shame, though often unfounded, prevents one from speaking about the emotional horror and physical pain one has endured. The very rawness of a memory often dissuades the victim from committing to words a recital of what took place. Hence, refusing to speak, though understandable, is motivated by a desperate attempt to manage the disabling effect of past trauma; yet it actually robs one of control. And in the end, remaining silent reinforces that deadly isolation of trauma.[3]

Speaking about trauma is difficult. It requires the mustering of a kind of vulnerability one would like to keep at bay. But breaking one's silence puts one on the path to resilience, and lifting one's voice to rupture the silence that surrounds trauma must meet certain requirements. First, one must be able to establish or reestablish *autonomy*. Second, in order to start making choices and asserting willpower, one will have to exercise agency. But choosing to speak (autonomy) and then actually doing so (agency) follow one more requirement. When one finally talks about one's trauma, one must become a *truth-teller*, no matter what.[4]

Speaking about one's trauma does not mean reciting every detail. Rather, it may involve merely naming the experience as a first step to putting one in control of the trauma instead of being controlled by it. Being able to cry out—"I am not doing well since the car accident I had that killed my child," or "I was abused by my uncle for five years," or "My father said it was for my own good but he beat me," or "I was raped"—reestablishes autonomy and agency, and helps one to begin telling the truth no matter what. When these dark places of silence are ruptured, what has been locked within starts to exit, healing can begin, life can be reclaimed, and the journey toward a transformed self begins.

---

2. Avram Finkelstein, *After Silence: A History of AIDS* (Berkeley, CA: University of California Press, 2017).

3. See Judith Herman's discussion of the elements that lead to silencing in *Trauma and Recovery*.

4. Ibid., 7–95.

3. *Woman Zion on the Path to Resilience*

Late in the Israelite traditions, a woman's voice ruptures the silence that up to that point surrounds the biblical women's voices that might have cried, "Me too!" Despite the accusations indicting her, Woman Zion publicly names what actually happened to her and even confronts her abuser. In a few brief verses, she reclaims her autonomy, exercises agency and becomes a truth-teller. In the process, she rejects the blame and shame that have held her captive, boldly identifies where responsibility lies, and initiates the move toward resilience for herself and other women. Though only a metaphor, she is a personified woman serving as a liberating symbol for those silenced women of the past and the present.

The book of Lamentations narrates the heartbreak and anguish of those who survived the destruction of Jerusalem and its subsequent siege in 587 BCE. With vivid description, these poems recount the pain and suffering of Zion's people in such a compelling way that it is virtually impossible, as a reader, not to be moved. The poems in Lamentations trace their form to ancient neighboring Mesopotamian city laments, in which an associated goddess is the dominant speaking subject who pleads on behalf of the survivors. Many have identified Woman Zion of Lamentations as the counterpart to the goddess of these Mesopotamian laments.[5] Like Woman Zion, the goddess is often portrayed as a mother figure. The Mesopotamian figure is also a weeping goddess who cries out to her deity (Enlil) and other deities on behalf of her people.[6] But despite the similarities in genre and in the portrayal of the key speaking figures in these laments, a significant aspect of the Israelite culture distinguishes Woman Zion from the Mesopotamian goddess. The poems of Lamentations appear to collapse the destroyed city and the lamenting goddess into one metaphoric figure—a weeping widow who is then made responsible for her own catastrophe. The development of her role across the five chapters also serves comprehensively to indict her, gradually deny her speech, and eventually obscure her presence. The cultural evolution of a pleading mother goddess in the ancient Mesopotamian laments into

---

5. F. W. Dobbs-Allsopp, *Weep, O Daughter of Zion: A Study of the City-Lament Genre in the Hebrew Bible*, BibOr 44 (Rome: Pontifical Biblical Institute, 1993), 77; Tikva Frymer-Kensky, *In the Wake of the Goddesses* (New York: Free, 1992), 170; W. C. Gwaltney, "The Biblical Book of Lamentations in the Context of Near Eastern Lament Literature," in *Scripture in Context II: More Essays on the Comparative Method*, ed. W. W. Hallo, J. C. Moyer, and L. G. Perdue (Winona Lake, IN: Eisenbrauns, 1983), 208–9.

6. Dobbs-Allsopp, *Weep, O Daughter of Zion*, 78–87.

a guilt-ridden widow depersonalized as "a filthy thing" (Lam 1:17d) in Israel's poems arouses legitimate suspicion. While what follows focuses on Lam 2:20–22, a summary of what precedes it sets the stage for the bold speech of this metaphoric woman who finally breaks the silence.

a. *The Backstory of Abuse*[7]

Lamentations 1 opens with striking equity. Two speakers, a male observer and Woman Zion, the personified city of Jerusalem, both recount their observations of the destruction of the city. Despite the differences in their perspectives, the quantity of space afforded each is remarkably balanced. Neither is privileged in terms of the opportunity to testify. Additionally, both speakers interrupt each other only once. The observer delivers a

---

7. Over the years, numerous works have studied the background and text of Lamentations using a variety of methods. See Norman K. Gottwald, *Studies in the Book of Lamentations* (Chicago, IL: A. Allenson, 1954.); Gwaltney, "The Biblical Book of Lamentations," 191–211; Francis Landy, "Lamentations," in *The Literary Guide to the Bible*, ed. Robert Alter and Frank Kermode (Cambridge, MA: Belknap, 1987), 305–19; Iain Provan, *Lamentations*, NCBC (Grand Rapids, MI: Eerdmans, 1991); Delbert Hillers, *Lamentations*, AB 7A (Garden City, NY: Doubleday, 1992); R. B. Salters, *A Critical and Exegetical Commentary on Lamentations*, ICC (New York: T&T Clark International, 1994); Claus Westermann, *Lamentations: Issues and Interpretation* (Minneapolis, MN: Fortress, 1994); Johan Renkema, *Lamentations*, trans. Brian Doyle, HCOT (Leuven: Peeters, 1998); Tod Linafelt, *Surviving Lamentations: Catastrophe, Lament, and Protest in the Afterlife of a Biblical Book* (Chicago, IL: University of Chicago Press, 2000); Adele Berlin, *Lamentations* (Louisville, KY: Westminster John Knox, 2002); F. W. Dobbs-Allsopp, *Lamentations*, Interpretation (Louisville, KY: John Knox, 2002); Kathleen O'Connor, *Lamentations and the Tears of the World* (Maryknoll, NY: Orbis, 2002), and "Lamentations," in *Women's Bible Commentary*, ed. Carol A. Newsom, Sharon H. Ringe, and Jacqueline E. Lapsley (Louisville, KY: Westminster John Knox, 2012), 178–82; Dianne Bergant, *Lamentations*, AOTC (Nashville, TN: Abingdon, 2003); Duane A. Garrett, and Paul R. House, *Song of Songs–Lamentations*, WBC 23B (Nashville, TN: Thomas Nelson, 2004); Elizabeth Boase, *The Fulfilment of Doom? The Dialogic Interaction between the Book of Lamentations and the Pre-Exilic/Early Exilic Prophetic Literature*, LHBOTS 437 (New York: T&T Clark International, 2006); Tremper Longman III, *Jeremiah, Lamentations*, NIBC (Peabody, MA: Hendrickson, 2008); Robin A. Parry, *Lamentations*, THOTC (Grand Rapids, MI: Eerdmans, 2010); Miriam J. Bier, *"Perhaps There Is Hope": Reading Lamentations as a Polyphony of Pain, Penitence, and Protest*, LHBOTS 603 (New York: Bloomsbury T&T Clark, 2015); Christopher Wright, *The Message of Lamentations* (Downers Grove, IL: InterVarsity, 2015); and Gina Hens-Piazza, *Lamentations*, Wisdom Commentary 30 (Collegeville, MN: Liturgical, 2017).

seemingly objective account that makes the destroyed city he describes a weeping mother whom he later blames for the catastrophe. Hence, he, the observer, speaks about the second speaker, Woman Zion. While it is not clear to whom he offers his report, he acknowledges bystanders and others who might be seeing what he sees. His description is dispassionate, though ultimately condemning. He notes that her friends have become her enemies, that her children have gone away, and that she is utterly alone. He also points out that her urban environment stands desolate. His account stems from his own observation. Yet at times, he reports rather intimate details of her experience. He notes that the enemies who have penetrated Woman Zion's narrow straits have stretched out their hands over her precious things. Her nakedness is made public, and she displays uncleanness in her skirts. In the course of his narration, the observer makes sense of these horrific and unfolding events twice by tying the catastrophe to the sinfulness of Woman Zion herself. Though never specifying the nature of this alleged sinfulness, the implication is clear. He accuses her of sexual impropriety. Finally, he defines the terror and desolation afflicting this female city figure as punishment for the "multitude of her transgressions" (1:5).

The former image of the Mesopotamian mother goddess, which he now describes as Woman Zion, is a female city figure which has been dismantled and decimated beyond repair. Her children, the inhabitants, lie in the streets dying. Her ramparts, walls, and gates lie in ruins. Without qualification, the observer offers an explanation for the destruction—her iniquity has instigated God's unbridled wrath.

b. *Assertion of Autonomy*

One of the core experiences of trauma is disempowerment. In addition to the damage done to a person's capacity to trust, to feel competent, or to make plans, a loss of the sense of autonomy is a core experience. Therefore, the first principle in the move toward resilience involves countering the dynamics of dominance. To become a survivor, one must be the author and arbiter of her own recovery. Martin Symonds advises that this subtle process involves overtures toward diminishing helplessness and building an awareness of what one wants.[8] Restoration of autonomy initiates a sense of flexibility, and self-possession that is sufficient to define one's own separateness and self-interest. For example, when abused women

---

8. Martin Symonds, "Victim Responses to Terror: Understanding and Treatment," in *Victims of Terrorism*, ed. F. Ochberg and D. Soskis (Boulder, CO: Westview, 1982), 98.

begin to conquer their fears and counter the dynamics of dominance that rob them of their autonomy and initiative, they begin to question their traditional acceptance of a subordinate role. They are even willing to examine whether their own socialization into some stereotypically feminine attitudes and behavior in the past has put them at risk. Hence, they begin to formulate ways to speak and act that represent *their* choices, that enlist *their* competences, and that are true to their experience. Yet the culture of subordination and blame poses a most challenging barrier. Such influences urge conformity, and discourage self-trust.

In Lam 2:20–22, Woman Zion will eventually raise her voice in an exercise of autonomy that counters the dynamics of dominance surrounding her. But just before she does so, she is not merely urged but commanded to conform to the cultural assessment of her—an abused woman who is responsible for her own victimization. With a barrage of imperatives, the observer instructs her to act like a stereotypical female and assume the stance of utter subordination before the deity:

> Cry out to the Lord
> O wall of daughter Zion!
> Let your tears stream down like a torrent
> day and night!
> Give yourself no rest
> your eyes, no respite!
> Arise, cry out in the night
> at the beginning of the watches!
> Pour out your heart like water
> before the presence of the Lord!
> Lift your hands to him
> for the lives of your children
> Who faint for hunger at the head of every street. (Lam 2:18–19, NRSV)

This observer directs Woman Zion to do the only thing he considers capable of stemming the mounting aftermath of her destruction. He directs her to turn her attention to the LORD and "cry aloud" (Lam 2:18a), "shed tears" (2:18b),[9] "give yourself no rest" (2:18c), "arise" (2:19a), "cry out in the night" (2:19a), "pour out your heart" (2:19b), and "lift up your hands" (2:19c). Thus, he orders her to make an emotional display before the LORD, to be ceaseless in this spectacle, to resist even resting,

---

9. Ulrich Berges, "The Violence of God in the Book of Lamentations," in *One Text, A Thousand Methods: Studies in Memory of Sjef van Tilborg*, ed. Patrick Chatelion Counet and Ulrich Berges (Boston, MA: Brill, 2005), 35.

and be demonstrative as in a prayerful appeal. Despite her brokenness, Woman Zion is urged to employ her whole being—with hands raised, tears streaming, voice crying out, and heart uplifted. She is to act like a guilty now penitent sinner with all her might in order to persuade the all-powerful deity to stop acting against her.

Though Woman Zion is afflicted with pain and guilt across these five poems, neither her cries nor the indictments against her have the last word. In a brief but nevertheless unprecedented speech, Woman Zion powerfully reclaims her autonomy. She lifts up her voice (Lam 2:20–22), which in this interpretation on behalf of traumatized women, becomes the focal point of the book. To do so, she must abandon self-blame. She must assume a resistant stance towards the bystanders, the observer, and the theological tradition that has indicted her.

Recognizing the dynamics of dominance that has almost cost her voice and conditioned her to believe that she was not capable of autonomy, Woman Zion acts contrary to culture, custom, and, some would say, common sense. Urged by the observer to turn to the LORD, Woman Zion speaks. But though instructed to be emotional, to pour out her tears, to plead, to cry, and to assume the posture of a desperate female supplicant, she does otherwise. In an exercise of autonomy, she abandons the identity of victim and the assessment of the self-blame before her abuser. Instead, she confronts her abuser and demands that responsibility for both the assault on her and others be redefined.

c. *Exercising Agency*

Resilience initiated by speech variously unfolds on a physical level, emotional level and/or spiritual level. And its development is as different as each person who achieves it. When a person returns from war minus a leg, resilience begins the day he or she stops lying in bed lamenting that the ability to walk has been lost. The huge physical effort it takes to learn to walk with prosthetics requires agency:

> Agency is the technical term for that feeling and action that lead to being in charge of your life: knowing where you stand, knowing that you have a say in what happens to you, knowing that you can say what happened to you, knowing that you have some ability to shape your circumstances.[10]

---

10. Bessel van der Kolk, *The Body Keeps the Score: Brain, Mind and Body in the Healing of Trauma* (New York: Penguin, 2014), 97.

This exercise of agency, the second step in achieving resilience, puts one on the road to transformation. In fact, Bessel van der Kolk, author of the *New York Times* best-selling book, *The Body Keeps the Score: Brain, Mind and Body in the Healing of Trauma*, explains that "resilience is the product of agency."[11] Doing something that changes the effect of the trauma constitutes agency. The exercise of agency begins to reestablish our sense of control that feels lost. We discover that we can change how we feel and can even learn new roles in difficult situations if they reoccur. We can act and speak in ways that renounce the burden of shame, guilt or even wrongly assigned responsibility, and place the burden on the circumstances or perpetrator where it belongs. As agency increases, it may take the form of confronting the traumatic situation or even confronting the abuser. And this is exactly what Woman Zion does. As she raises her voice, she begins by questioning the one responsible for such abuse:

> Look, O Lord, and consider!
> to whom have you done this?
> Should women eat their offspring
> the children they have borne?
> Should priest and prophet be killed
> in the sanctuary of the Lord?
> The young and the old are lying
> on the ground in the streets;
> My young women and my young men
> have died by the sword;
> In the day of your anger
> You have killed them
> slaughtering them without mercy!
> You invited my enemies from all around
> as if for a day of festival;
> And on the day of the anger of the Lord
> no one escaped or survived
> those whom I bore and reared
> my enemy has destroyed. (Lam 2:20–22, NRSV)

Woman Zion begins her confrontation by calling on the god of the theology that has condemned her to pay attention, and to ponder what this deity has done. In essence, she boldly invites this god to do some self-reflection. "Look, O LORD and consider! To whom have you done this?" (Lam 2:20). In contrast to this god's loss of control and excess

---

11. Ibid.

of violent display, Woman Zion practices a disciplined composure with measured and direct speech and employs an economy of words. No emotional outburst accompanies her speech. She has regained control. As a strong woman who has refused to be a victim, and who has abandoned self-blame before her abuser, she confronts this lord. With words aimed directly at her torturer, she paints a canvas portraying this deity's campaign of carnage with graphic images that eclipse the horror already narrated and includes horrific images yet to be blamed upon her. Not only have infants died at their mothers' breasts, but "women [also] eat their offspring, the children they have born" (Lam 2:20). The loss of maternal instinct that would allow a mother to eat her children has been portrayed elsewhere (2 Kgs 6:20–31). But cannibalizing one's children is not the consequence of a mere gustatory response to famine.[12] Rather, the image of mothers consuming their children in her speech exposes how extreme and oppressive social conditions had become as a result of the deity's acts of destruction. With this god, who has wielded such monstrous power amidst the powerless, lies the responsibility for such horrors. Moreover, the Lord's own behavior has been described persistently and thus experienced as "swallowing up" the people and their wellbeing (2:2, 5, 8, 16). Hence, mothers eating their own babies follows the circumstances narrated, as this god is "swallowing up" his own people. In addition, Woman Zion's speech uses the image of god "slaughtering" her inhabitants. The word "slaughtering" carries the connotation of killing for food. In Hebrew, the word "slaughter" (טבחת) is typically enlisted to describe the killing of animals for meat (Gen 43:16; Exod 21:37; 1 Sam 25:11). Therefore, when used metaphorically for the destruction of humanity, it not only bespeaks of an act of cruelty but also suggests the intention to consume or eat up.[13] As one scholar observes, "A fundamental difference between Zion and Yahweh has to be noted: they (the people) were forced to do what they did because he did not restrain his wrath but completed his anger."[14] Thus it follows, women consume their children because the LORD has consumed the people.

Next, she addresses the scope of this rampage. Despite her broken, violated core, Woman Zion's direct and straightforward speech suggests that she is exercising agency. She has found the courage to confront

12. See Gina Hens-Piazza, *Nameless, Blameless and without Shame: Two Cannibal Mothers before a King* (Collegeville, MN: Liturgical, 2003), 85–7, for a cultural exposition on cannibalism and how its manifestation coincides with the prevailing socio-political system.
13. Berges, "The Violence of God," 39.
14. Ibid., 38.

her aggressor with the brutal consequences of his deeds. Not only have children died terrible deaths, the city also is strewn with the bodies of young and old, lying lifeless in the streets. The hope of the future—young women and young men along with priest and prophet—have all been killed. Fearless and without qualification, she cites this god's violence three times. "You have killed," "You have slaughtered," and "without pity" (Lam 2:21c). Like a real human victim, the truth that this metaphoric woman speaks seems to fuel her confidence as she confronts her attacker. Finally, she holds the god responsible for what her enemies have been able to accomplish in shaming and overcoming her. She notes that this god summoned her enemies to contribute to her demise as if they were celebrating a festival. Invited by the deity, these hostile forces treated the execution of her citizens as a celebration (2:22). As a result, "no one escaped or survived" (2:22c). But her final pronouncement does not indict these other nations; it may well be heard as ultimately directed at the deity. Her concluding reference to "enemy" (2:23c) is congruent with the observer's earlier use of the term, where twice he saw God "like an enemy" (2:4, 5). Though Woman Zion's use of the term here comes on the heels of pointing to her enemies as this lord's instruments of destruction (2:22a), her closing words enlist "enemy" in the singular form. She narrates with striking clarity both the scope of destruction and the one she deems responsible for it. Consistent with all that she has said in this brief response, ultimately, the reigning image of god is cast as her foe:[15] "All whom I bore and reared, my enemy has destroyed" (2:23c).[16]

4. *Truth-telling No Matter What*

To disclose abuse, to name trauma, to tell the truth to family or friends who might question the narrative, or to confront an abuser comes with risks. But having established autonomy, and having begun exercising agency, such confrontations can be highly empowering, especially when an individual is ready to speak the truth as she knows it. That person does so without needing confirmation or without the fear of consequences. The

---

15. Archie Chi Chung Lee, "Mothers Bewailing: Reading Lamentations," in *Her Master's Tools? Feminist and Postcolonial Engagements of Historical-Critical Discourse*, ed. Caroline Vander Stichele and Todd C. Penner, GPBS 9 (Atlanta, GA: Society of Biblical Literature, 2005), 207; Berges, "The Violence of God," 39.

16. Reading "enemy" as singular with the MT, against the plural in the Peshitta and Targum, it is immaterial whether "enemy" refers to those hostile nations who are the instrument of divine wrath or to the LORD. Woman Zion aims her charge of injustice at God.

power of truth-telling in exposing abuse rests solely in the act of telling the truth. How others respond—the accuser, the bystander, the community, the authorities, the family—is immaterial to the one breaking the silence by telling the truth. She is ready to accept whatever the outcome may be. She no longer feels intimidated by or compelled to participate in a false narrative that encourages destructive relationships. No longer is she confined by secrecy, by being silenced, by being subordinate, or by being belittled as victim.

As a silence breaker, Woman Zion tells the truth in the face of resistance. At the end of ch. 2, Woman Zion has confronted the deity and those who indicted her. And the prophetic texts confirm her innocence. Again and again, prophetic pronouncements identify who is responsible for the day of destruction of the nation and the temple. They rivet their condemnations on the false prophets, the priests, the members of the royal counsel, the king and the landholders who are ultimately held responsible for the problems. They are the predominantly upper-class males and rulers who with their power have brought about this devastation that is duly authorized by their patriarchal god and its supporting theology.[17] Woman Zion, the metaphoric mother weeping for her children, does not bear responsibility for the destruction of Jerusalem, the Temple, and the annihilation of the people. Yet as is often the case, when the traumatized individual refuses to be victim any longer, and finally determines to speak the truth, there is pushback. Efforts to deny the truth are expended on the part of those who are hiding behind the lie, who deny their own experience, and who are afraid to confront the truth themselves.

As if to counter the strength that Woman Zion has mustered to face the God of the theological tradition who has afflicted her, and to match her strong affront of the male deity, Lamentations 3 opens immediately after her indicting speech with the introduction of a "strong man." His lament has been featured repeatedly as the centerpiece of the book because of the message of hope, fleeting though it is, which he offers. But it is a hope not founded on truth-telling. And it is a hope that dissipates by the end of the poem. This thin hope rests on an old theology that requires the denial of one's experience. It is an oration that lacks the strength of conviction of Woman Zion's final speech (2:20–22). The so-called strong man delivers a message weakened by his vacillations between confessing that he and the people have rebelled and then accusing God that they have not been forgiven. Moreover, his wavering between reporting his immense

---

17. Deryn Guest, "Hiding Behind the Naked Women in Lamentations: A Recriminative Response," *BibInt* 7 (1999): 413–48 (444).

suffering and then denying the truth of his experience enfeebles any claims of strength tied to his identity. That Woman Zion, who rises from her broken status as victim to become a strong and resilient truth-teller in the preceding chapter, now disappears in this poem, is not surprising. Her challenge to both the deity and to the hegemonic and socially stratified patriarchal culture that is backed by such a theology is unassailable.

5. *Conclusion*

Though Woman Zion is afflicted with pain and guilt across the five poems in Lamentations, neither her cries nor the indictments against her have the last word. Through her speech in Lam 2:20–22, she reasserts autonomy, exercises agency, and tells the truth about a broken theology that lays blame on a metaphoric woman rather than at the feet of those political and religious officials hiding behind her but who are responsible for this travesty. In her brief but unprecedented speech, Woman Zion lifts up her voice, names the abuse and confronts her abuser (Lam 2:20–22). From the standpoint of abused women, that speech becomes the focal point of the book. Abandoning self-blame, she assumes a stance of resistance towards the theological tradition that has indicted her. She demands that the divine take note of her suffering. Then she releases an angry tirade at the god of a bankrupt theological tradition through which she and others have been scapegoated. The warrior deity, who abuses, violently punishes, and makes innocent children victims, bears no resemblance to the ancient goddess weeping for her children. Such a tyrannical force conceived as a deity is at best the concoction and reflection of the competitive dynamism inherent in an oppressive hierarchical order. Named patriarchy, this subjugating order produces a theology reflective of itself. A patriarchal deity must wield unbridled power at the top to maintain its position, and in the process, it destroys community by stratifying social classes below.

Hence, when Woman Zion confronts the deity, she not only challenges this theology, but begins to pave the path to a transforming resilience. Audaciously, she names her trauma as abuse, and without apology, she defines this construction of the deity as "the enemy." She not only declares her own emancipation from the clutches of self-blame and victimhood by raising her voice, but also creates space for other victims of trauma to break their silence, to express their anger and their pain. She and these other bold silence breakers lift up their collective voice and tell the #MeToo truth. In so doing, they stand ready to move forward in an embrace of the full value of their lives and to begin to recognize the real Holy Presence in their midst.

Bibliography

Alexander, Jeffrey C. *Trauma: A Social Theory*. Cambridge: Polity, 2012.
Becker, Eve-Marie, Jan Dochhorn, and Else K. Holt (eds.). *Trauma and Traumatization in Individual and Collective Dimensions: Insights from Biblical Studies and Beyond*. SANt 2. Göttingen: Vandenhoeck & Ruprecht, 2014.
Bergant, Dianne. *Lamentations*. AOTC. Nashville, TN: Abingdon, 2003.
Berges, Ulrich. "The Violence of God in the Book of Lamentations." In *One Text, a Thousand Methods: Studies in Memory of Sjef Van Tilborg*, edited by Patrick Chatelion Counet and Ulrich Berges, 21–44. Boston, MA: Brill Academic, 2005.
Berlin, Adele. *Lamentations*. Louisville, KY: Westminster John Knox, 2002.
Bier, Miriam J. *"Perhaps There Is Hope": Reading Lamentations as a Polyphony of Pain, Penitence, and Protest*. LHBOTS 603. New York: Bloomsbury T&T Clark, 2015.
Boase, Elizabeth. *The Fulfilment of Doom? The Dialogic Interaction between the Book of Lamentations and the Pre-Exilic/Early Exilic Prophetic Literature*. LHBOTS 437. New York: T&T Clark International, 2006.
Boase, Elizabeth, and Christopher G. Frechette (eds.). *The Bible through the Lens of Trauma*. Atlanta, GA: Society of Biblical Literature, 2016.
Caruth, Cathy. *Unclaimed Experience: Trauma, Narrative and History*. Baltimore, MD: The Johns Hopkins University Press, 1995.
Caruth, Cathy (ed.). *Trauma: Explorations in Memory*. Baltimore, MD: The Johns Hopkins University Press, 1995.
Dobbs-Allsopp, F. W. *Lamentations*. Interpretation. Louisville, KY: John Knox, 2002.
Dobbs-Allsopp, F. W. *Weep, O Daughter of Zion: A Study of the City-Lament Genre in the Hebrew Bible*. BibOr 44. Roma: Pontifical Biblical Institute, 1993.
Finkelstein, Avram. *After Silence: A History of AIDS*. Berkeley, CA: University of California Press, 2017.
Freud, Sigmund. *Inhibitions, Symptoms and Anxiety*. Translated by Alix Strachey. London: Hogarth, 1949.
Frymer-Kensky, Tikva. *In the Wake of the Goddesses: Women, Culture, and the Biblical Transformation of Pagan Myth*. New York: Ballentine, 1993.
Garrett, Duane A., and Paul R. House. *Song of Songs/Lamentations*. WBC 23B. Nashville, TN: Thomas Nelson, 2004.
Gottwald, Norman K. *Studies in the Book of Lamentations*. Chicago, IL: A. R. Allenson, 1954.
Guest, Deryn. "Hiding Behind the Naked Women in Lamentations: A Recriminative Response." *BibInt* 7 (1999): 413–48.
Gwaltney, W. C. "The Biblical Book of Lamentations in the Context of Near Eastern Lament Literature." In *Scripture in Context II: More Essays on the Comparative Method*, edited by W. W. Hallo, J. C. Moyer, and L. G. Perdue, 191–211. Winona Lake, IN: Eisenbrauns, 1983.
Hens-Piazza, Gina. *Lamentations*. Wisdom Commentary 30. Collegeville, MN: Liturgical, 2017.
Hens-Piazza, Gina. *Nameless, Blameless and without Shame: Two Cannibal Mothers before a King*. Interfaces. Collegeville, MN: Liturgical, 2003.
Herman, Judith. *Trauma and Recovery: The Aftermath of Violence—From Domestic Abuse to Political Terror*. Rev. ed. New York: Basic, 1997.
Hillers, Delbert R. *Lamentations*. AB 7A. Garden City, NY: Doubleday, 1992.

Kauffman, Jeffrey. *Loss of the Assumptive World: A Theory of Traumatic Loss*. New York: Brunner-Routledge, 2002.

Landy, Francis. "Lamentations." In *The Literary Guide to the Bible*, edited by Robert Alter and Frank Kermode, 305–19. Cambridge, MA: Belknap, 1987.

Lee, Archie Chi Chung. "Mothers Bewailing: Reading Lamentations." In *Her Master's Tools? Feminist and Postcolonial Engagements of Historical-Critical Discourse*, edited by Caroline Vander Stichele and Todd C. Penner, 195–210. Atlanta, GA: Society of Biblical Literature, 2005.

Linafelt, Tod. *Surviving Lamentations: Catastrophe, Lament, and Protest in the Afterlife of a Biblical Book*. Chicago, IL: University of Chicago Press, 2000.

Longman III, Tremper. *Jeremiah, Lamentations*. NIBC. Peabody, MA: Hendrickson, 2008.

O'Connor, Kathleen. "Lamentations." In *Women's Bible Commentary*, edited by Carol A. Newsom, Sharon H. Ringe, and Jacqueline E. Lapsley, 178–82. Louisville, KY: Westminster John Knox, 2012.

O'Connor, Kathleen. *Lamentations and the Tears of the World*. Maryknoll, NY: Orbis, 2002.

Parry, Robin A. *Lamentations*. THOTC. Grand Rapids, MI: Eerdmans, 2010.

Provan, Iain. *Lamentations*. NCBC. Grand Rapids, MI: Eerdmans, 1991.

Renkema, Johan. *Lamentations*. Translated by Brian Doyle. HCOT. Leuven: Peeters, 1998.

Salters, R. B. *A Critical and Exegetical Commentary on Lamentations*. ICC. New York: T&T Clark International, 1994.

Symonds, Martin. "Victim Responses to Terror: Understanding and Treatment." In *Victims of Terrorism*, edited by F. Ochberg and D. Soskis, 94–103. Boulder, CO: Westview, 1982.

Van der Kolk, Bessel, Alexander C. McFarlane, and Lars Weisaeth (eds.). *The Body Keeps the Score: Brain, Mind and Body in the Healing of Trauma*. New York: Penguin, 2014.

Van der Kolk, Bessel, Alexander C. McFarlane, and Lars Weisaeth (eds.). *Traumatic Stress: The Effects of Overwhelming Experience on Mind, Body and Society*. New York: Guilford, 2007.

Westermann, Claus. *Lamentations: Issues and Interpretation*. Minneapolis, MN: Fortress, 1994.

Whitfield, Charles. *Memory and Abuse: Remembering and Healing the Effects of Trauma*. Deerfield Beach: Health Communications, 1995.

Wright, Christopher. *The Message of Lamentations*. Downers Grove, IL: InterVarsity, 2015.

Chapter 3

Reclaiming Jezebel and Mrs Job: Challenging Sexist Cultural Stereotypes and the Curse of Invisibility

Lerato Mokoena

Northwest University

1. Introduction

Caron E. Gentry and Laura Sjoberg begin their essay, "The Gendering of Women's Terrorism," with the following quote by Helena Kennedy that goes to the heart of this essay on sexist cultural stereotypes pertaining to the biblical figure of Jezebel and Mrs Job:

> [I]n almost every culture and every period of history, a she-devil emerges as an example of all that is rotten in the female sex. This Medusa draws together the many forms of female perversion: a woman whose sexuality is debauched and foul, pornographic and bisexual; a woman who knows none of the fine and noble instincts when it comes to men and children; a woman who lies and deceives, manipulates and corrupts. A woman who is clever and powerful. This is a woman who is far deadlier than the male, in fact not a woman at all.[1]

The designation "Jezebel" in popular culture often presages a woman whose sexuality is debauched and foul, one who manipulates and corrupts

---

1. Helena Kennedy, *Eve Was Framed*, cited in Caron E. Gentry and Laura Sjoberg, "The Gendering of Women's Terrorism," in *Women, Gender and Terrorism*, ed. Laura Sjoberg and Caron E. Gentry (Athens, GA: University of Georgia Press, 2011), 57–80 (57).

through trickery. What immediately comes to mind when one hears the name Jezebel are pornographic images, sultry outfits, uncontrollable desires, and deadly kisses—a woman who should be avoided at all costs. The name Jezebel has its own conceptual history, a phenomenon that took on a life of its own but which *ipso facto* sponsors the cultural outcomes of the perpetual distribution of stereotyping and the policing of women's sexuality.

In an essay titled "Jezebel at the Welfare Office," it is shown how in the United States a racialized stereotype exists that is veiled in bureaucratic language. This study maintains that negative ideas about poor women's sexuality and fertility during job interviews adversely affect their applications. In defense, the welfare officers called their day-to-day talk with recipients a "measure of discretion." However, the study proves that their language or manner of communication continues to perpetuate the stigmatization of African American women's sexuality. There is also a marked increase in these racialized stereotypes of black women as Jezebels in terms of their interactions with Child Protection Services, which view the parenting of these women with suspicion. The choices of these women are moralized and, in condescending terms, associated with their sexuality.[2]

These stereotypes that affect especially black women's lives go back to the original biblical texts in which we first encounter the stories of Jezebel and of Mrs. Job who are among the most vilified women in the Old Testament. Jezebel, a seductress queen with a lust for power in 1 Kings 16–2 Kings 9, who is accused of "seducing" her husband into idolatry, would meet her death at the hands of Jehu. Mrs. Job, who is often depicted as unsympathetic towards her husband, would become a symbol of all that women should not aspire to be.

As shown in the example of contemporary stereotypes associated with Jezebel, modern-day accounts have since magnified Jezebel's seductiveness and Mrs. Job's foolishness. These two women's stories have been connected to contemporary interpretations that on the one hand sexualize women, and on the other hand render them invisible. It is the aim of this essay to redeem these two female biblical characters, Jezebel and Mrs. Job, from these negative connections by rereading their stories in order to challenge the sexist cultural stereotypes that have come to be associated with them, and so, render them invisible no longer.

---

2. Tatiana N. Masters, Taryn P. Lindhorst, and Marcia K. Meyers, "Jezebel at the Welfare Office: How Racialized Stereotypes of Poor Women's Reproductive Decisions and Relationships Shape Policy Implementation," *Journal of Poverty* 18, no. 2 (2014): 109–29.

In this regard, feminist biblical interpretation is an important tool. From the numerous feminist works, it is evident that there has never been a single method through which we can approach feminist biblical exegesis. The assertion that biblical texts can be interpreted in only one manner and that their meaning is univocal overlooks the fact that real flesh-and-blood readers are behind these interpretations. Schüssler Fiorenza affirms this position as follow:

> [A] feminist critical interpretation for liberation insists on the hermeneutical priority of feminist struggles in the process of interpretation… [L]iberation theologies of all "colours" take the experience and voices of the oppressed and marginalized, of those wo/men traditionally excluded from articulating theology and shaping communal life, as the starting point of hermeneutical reflection.[3]

A recovery reading of biblical texts seeks to engage in oppositional and/or resistant readings, with the aim of reshaping the dominant readings of these texts. Biblical texts are not social photographs but a complex construct of ideology, theology, culture and tradition. All of these factors need to be addressed through rigorous hermeneutics and exegesis to bridge the huge gap that separates the ancient and contemporary societies. Also, gender constructions need to be unearthed as they are sometimes inaudibly nuanced, and they shape interpretation. In this essay, feminist biblical interpretation through the method of recovery reading is one tool that is particularly well suited to the present task. Musa Dube argues that in our trained feminist ways of reading texts, we often highlight the gender constructions of a story and consider the ways in which they serve as ideological tools that normalize the subordination of women and other groups.[4]

This essay therefore aims at absolving women from violent narratives which reduce them to she-devils, king slayers, bad fortune, harlots, evil Medusas, Jezebels and alleged doomsayers like Job's wife through a liberating reading and interpretation of texts. The character of Jezebel will be viewed through an ideological critical analysis of the Deuteronomist redactional activity associated with the text in which she features, whilst

---

3. Elisabeth Schüssler Fiorenza (ed.), *Sharing Her Word: Feminist Biblical Interpretation in Context* (Boston, MA: Beacon, 1998).

4. Musa W. Dube, "Jumping the Fire with Judith: Postcolonial Feminist Hermeneutics," in *Feminist Interpretation of the Bible and the Hermeneutics of Liberation*, ed. Silvia Schroer and Sophia Bietenhard, JSOTSup 374 (London: Sheffield Academic, 2003), 61–76.

Mrs. Job's favorable portrayal in the Septuagint (LXX) and the *Testament of Job* will be analyzed in order to contest her invisibility. In this essay, therefore, Jezebel's and Mrs. Job's narratives will be reread in order to expose the historical contexts, evaluate their reception history, and probe how the reception history influences modern-day interpretations and promotes androcentrism.

2. *"Please Redeem Me": Jezebel*

The authors of the Deuteronomistic History (DH) are well known for their bias and their obsession with maintaining religious purity. It is thus no surprise that the stories of Jezebel, the quintessential foreign woman, play such a central role in this part of the canon. Foreign women are viewed with suspicion because they often, although not all the time, maintain their cultural identity and, in some cases, promote a kind of hybridity of religious beliefs and values. Typically, foreign women are described in hypersexualized terms in both the DH and in colonial/postcolonial literature.[5]

For example, in the DH, a postcolonial analysis of the literary characterization of foreign women exposes both the "colonial" entanglements of the Deuteronomistic authors and their agenda of portraying foreign women as capitulators or as seductresses of the people of Israel.[6]

Dagmar Pruin begins her essay, "What Is in a Text? Searching for Jezebel," with the provocative claim that, "The historical reconstruction of an epoch already contains a whole array of problems."[7] These problems seem to increase if such a reconstruction focuses on a single figure even with a particularly prominent reception-history. Within the DH, the portrayal of Jezebel as a literary figure is a case in point. She is often placed alongside Elijah as opponents in faith (Yahwism and Baalism), that is, besides being the wife of King Ahab. Diachronically, the book of Kings is said to have undergone an extensive Deuteronomistic redaction, which may mean additions or omissions and cast doubt on the historicity of the events altogether.[8]

---

5. Bradley L. Crowell, "Good Girl, Bad Girl: Foreign Women of the Deuteronomistic History in Postcolonial Perspective," *BibInt* 21 (2013): 1–18.
6. Ibid., 2.
7. Dagmar Pruin, "What Is in a Text? Searching for Jezebel," in *Ahab Agonistes: The Rise and Fall of the Omri Dynasty*, ed. Lester L. Grabbe, LHBOTS 421 (New York: T&T Clark, 2007), 205–35 (208).
8. Ibid., 208–35.

The Phoenician princess is often charged with the crime of introducing Baal worship in Israel, while the prophet of YHWH, Elijah, heroically fights for his God.[9] Elsewhere, I have argued that the claim that Jezebel introduced Baalism (1 Kgs 18:18–19) can and should be contested. I argue that due to the Deuteronomistic redaction, Jehu's coup is portrayed as zealous obedience in the name of Yahwism to triumph over Baal worship.[10]

Jezebel is entangled in the narrative of Ahab and Naboth in which her fate is sealed through a series of judgment oracles. The judgments against Ahab are outlined in four oracles: (1) God commands Elijah in 1 Kgs 21:19 to accuse Ahab of taking possession of Naboth's vineyard and to announce the punishment that dogs will lick Ahab's blood. (2) Elijah delivers the second oracle to Ahab in 1 Kgs 21:20–24 charging him with apostasy and pronouncing the punishment, which is that disaster will befall the house of Ahab. This oracle mentions Jezebel at the end: "and also concerning Jezebel the Lord says: 'Dogs will devour Jezebel by the wall of Jezreel.'" (3) The third oracle is Elijah's announcement to one of the guild of prophets in 2 Kgs 9:1–3, which sets the wheels in motion to make Jehu a champion of Yahwism by anointing him king over Israel. (4) In the last oracle in 2 Kgs 9:6–10, a member of the guild of prophets anoints Jehu and delivers Elijah's oracle against the house of Ahab. Here again, Jezebel is included among the condemned.

The redactor's hand can be seen clearly in the first inclusion of Jezebel since Elijah's original oracle was directed only against Ahab for the murder of Naboth and the dispossession of his vineyard with no mention of the charges later brought up in 1 Kgs 21:24–25.

Steven McKenzie argues for a post-Dtr addition that imitates the original Dtr's characteristics to include Jezebel.[11] The Deuteronomistic historian typically favors the Southern kings. For example, it is said of Jehu that "there was none like him," which is what Gary Knoppers calls the "incomparability formula." On the other hand, the Northern kings receive bad publicity or little attention (e.g., Omri, and Ahab).[12] The Deuteronomist had the tendency of judging Northern kings negatively

---

9. Ibid., 209–14.

10. See Lerato Mokoena, "The Roots of Jehu's Bloody Coup: A Violent Story of Religious Zealots, Retributive Justice or International Politics?" (MTh thesis, University of Pretoria, 2017).

11. Steven L. McKenzie, *The Trouble with Kings: The Composition of the Book of Kings in the Deuteronomistic History* (Leiden: Brill, 1991), 61–80.

12. Gary N. Knoppers, "'There Was None Like Him': Incomparability in the Books of Kings," *CBQ* 54 (1992): 411–31 (412).

because they worshipped Yahweh outside of Jerusalem.[13] Nonetheless, if we shift the focus from the bias of the Dtr redactor to the theme of his message, which is apostasy, then we free Jezebel from the Trojan horse. We find forgotten connections and recover unsettling truths, as supporting roles become elevated to protagonists, whilst protagonists are reduced to supporting roles.

The shift in focus recovers the fact that Israel was not an exclusively Yahwistic nation from the beginning. Monotheism and the exclusive worship of Yahweh is a culmination of a historical process that happened over time. Robert Gnuse refers to the development of monotheism in ancient Israel as a breakthrough or culmination of the intellectual and religious development of the ages.[14] This leads me to affirm that in the midst of many pantheons, Israel created monotheism as a means of identity formation, a way to set themselves apart in a foreign land that was at risk of cultural and religious assimilation of their exilic captors.

Monotheism as an Israelite religion emerged from the Babylonian exile breakthrough, long after the time of Ahab and Jezebel. Gnuse argues that the description of Israel's idolatry is not of some backsliding experienced by some foolish Israelites. Rather, it testifies to the everyday religious life of Israel, which the prophets and reformers were trying to change.[15] I would follow Gnuse because it is actually in the Deuteronomistic History where the polytheistic roots of Israel are more evident.[16]

Some notable passages both in the Pentateuch and DH support this claim. In Exod 12:12 and Num 33:4, YHWH instructs Moses to "execute judgment upon the gods of Egypt," Josh 24:2 speaks of "gods served by the ancestors in the region beyond the river," and 2 Kgs 17:29–41 mentions "gods" worshipped in Samaria. Extra-biblical material in the records of Sargon II refers to the booty he took from Samaria, which includes "the gods they trusted" prior to the fall of Samaria.[17]

---

13. Thomas Römer, *The Invention of God* (London: Harvard University Press, 2015), xx.

14. Cf. Robert. K. Gnuse, *No Other Gods: The Emergence of Monotheism*, JSOTSup 241 (London: Sheffield Academic, 1997).

15. Ibid., 179–80.

16. Gnuse argues that the DH was actually a historical narrative reflecting on Israelite and Judean life through Yahwistic lenses with certain guidelines about strict allegiance to Yahweh, rejection of other deities, rejection of native Yahwistic cultic practices, centralized worship at the temple, and a great deal of egalitarianism and social justice in society. Ibid., 177.

17. Gnuse, *No Other Gods*, 181.

Many things remain uncertain in the Bible. For instance, we do not know if Jezebel was indeed a historical figure, although we are certain of her literary existence. The gift of a story is that we can move characters as we wish. There is, however, a downside to this literary gift, namely that in the realm of fiction, characters can be manipulated to serve certain interests. We should note that synchronically Jezebel already bears in her name, which means "Baal carriers," the course of events, while the name Elijah means "My God is YHWH," making it evident that both protagonists carry the faith of their gods in their names.[18]

Jezebel is only once explicitly linked to the introduction of Baal in the narrator's comment that she "urged" her husband Ahab "to do what was evil in the sight of the YHWH" (1 Kgs 21:25). However, other texts that mention Ahab's worship of other deities (1 Kgs 16:31–33; 2 Kgs 10:18) do not link it explicitly to his marriage. Since the discovery of the Tel Dan inscription, which contradicts the events, as recorded in 2 Kings 9–10, this portrait of Jezebel as a devotee of Baal should be called into question. One may ask further why the authors of 2 Kings 9–10 portrayed Jezebel in such a negative way.[19]

Jezebel, when reread in the true light of her place in history, represents a vilified figure,[20] a woman who was accused of a crime she did not commit. She might have been guilty of many other things but she did not introduce Baal worship to Israel. She is used as a prototype of women who seduce men—a treacherous queen. Patriarchy does not accommodate women on their own terms and Jezebel was an example used to send a misogynist message to the rest of us. Jezebel later was adapted into the symbol of a controlling woman, a woman whom God forgot to sprinkle with a bit of morality when she was created. Her words are like poison and her sexuality is a warrant of policing.

3. *Call Me Dinah or Simply Mrs. Job*

In much of the history of interpretation, Job's wife is presented as an unsympathetic woman, uncaring about her husband's grief, a blasphemous heretic.[21] She is relegated to the shadows after her six-word cameo

---

18. Pruin, "What Is in a Text?" 210.
19. Ibid., 221. Cf. also Mokoena, "The Roots of Jehu's Bloody Coup," 74–100, for more on the Tel Dan inscription and Jehu's coup.
20. See Pruin, "What Is in a Text?" 229.
21. Emily O. Gravett, "Biblical Responses: Past and Present Retellings of the Enigmatic Mrs. Job," *BibInt* 20 (2012): 97–127.

(Job 2:9), and later resurfaces with a name and more emotion in the *Testament of Job* (the LXX also shows her some favor).[22] She is the symbol of invisibility and silence, a synonym for her name should be "shadow."

Although she is nameless and her exceedingly short speech is rather vague, Mrs. Job has been the subject of intense interpretation. Various text-critical readings, socio-historical and post-colonial perspectives, and even feminist-forensic approaches have focused on the dissection of this enigmatic persona. Rachel Magdalene argues that the anti-female readings are as notorious as her words. For instance, Augustine considered her the second Eve, one of Satan's handmaidens.[23] Emily Gravett argues that Mrs. Job has been relegated to the shadows through literary devices.[24] Firstly, in the Masoretic Text (MT), she is given neither name nor origin. This omission meant that she would not be given any attention; from the outset, nothing more should be expected from her. The narrator only refers to her as "his wife." Gravett problematizes the prenominal suffix "his."[25] Mrs. Job is allotted that single identity, which is strange for a tradition that places heavy emphasis on people's names, which encompass their whole identity and existence. She was being erased. In this narrative, she is tantamount to non-existence. These literary choices create not only a haze around the figure of Mrs. Job, but also a subtle distance between Mrs. Job and her husband.

Characteristically, important figures in a book are introduced first. However, we meet Mrs. Job, who is not even shown to be connected to Job through marriage in a typical betrothal scene, only in the second chapter, after Job, "his" children, his servants, his chattel, messengers, God and even Satan have been introduced.[26] Women were typically identified by their fathers, husbands or where they came from (e.g., Noah's wife, Jephthah's daughter, the unnamed concubine of Judg 19, "the women of the land"). Even more tellingly, Job appears as though he is frustrated with Mrs. Job altogether. As Gravett shows, the infinitive construct of "to speak" can be rendered as the simple present tense (as in the NRSV), which could imply a general and ongoing state—perhaps Job feels that his wife constantly utters such foolishness.[27]

---

22. Ibid., 97.
23. Rachel F. Magdalene, "Job's Wife as Hero: A Feminist-Forensic Reading of The Book of Job," *BibInt* 14 (2006): 209–58.
24. Gravett, "Biblical Responses," 109.
25. Ibid., 103.
26. Ibid., 104.
27. Ibid., 107.

Some scholars, for example Victor Sasson, argue that it is superfluous to mention the invisibility of Mrs. Job because she is not a major character.[28] In terms of literary function, Sasson makes a valid point that the invisibility of Mrs. Job may be connected to the general systematic oppression and silencing of women. Biblical texts are living entities, with harmful constructions being reproduced through a variety of interpretations that may come at a great cost. According to Sasson, Mrs. Job's narrative is used to encourage further silencing of women especially through sermons in church spaces. Moreover, invisibility is a fundamental aspect of being a woman in a patriarchal world,[29] although we must admit that we have no knowledge of her trials, her toils and how she experienced the grief of also losing her children, as the "sufferer" Job lost "everything."

Choon-Leong Seow states that Mrs. Job is condemned by interpreters as an unthinking fool, an irritating nag, a heretic, a temptress, an unwitting tool of the devil, or even a personification of the devil himself because of her speech. These "misinterpretations" skew her place in the history of interpretation and reception. Seow further states that a recovery can lead to a balanced and richer reading of her character in the book of Job.[30]

Thus, with Phyllis Trible's method of depatriarchalizing texts, a literary mode of reading neglected traditions to reveal counter voices in a patriarchal document, another side of Mrs. Job can be unearthed. In this portrayal, her previously neglected grief for the loss of her children is highlighted.[31] Gerald West argues that Mrs. Job has endured battering with no one paying attention to her own grief. Even though she is portrayed as a woman ignorant of her husband's suffering, the contrary seems to be true.[32]

---

28. Victor Sasson, "The Literary and Theological Function of Job's Wife in the Book of Job," *Bib* 79 (1998): 86–90.

29. Ibid., 90.

30. Choon-Leong Seow, "Job's Wife, with Due Respect," in *Das Buch Hiob und seine Interpretationen: Beiträge zur Hiob-Symposium auf dem Monte Verità vom 14.–19. August 2005*, ed. Thomas Krüger, AThANT 88 (Zurich: Theologischer Verlag, 2007), 350–70.

31. Phyllis Trible, "Depatriarchalizing in Biblical Interpretation," *JAAR* 41 (1973): 30–48.

32. Gerald West, "Hearing Job's Wife: Towards a Feminist Reading of Job," *OTE* 4 (1991): 107–31.

In the Old Greek translation of the book of Job (LXX), Mrs. Job's speech in Job 2:9 is expanded and these five additional verses throw a more sympathetic light on her plight:

> Then after a long time had passed, his wife said to him, "Look, how long will you persist and say, 'Look, I will hang on a little longer while I wait for the hope of my deliverance?' For, look, your legacy has vanished from the earth—sons and daughters, my womb's birth pangs and labors, for whom I wearied myself with hardships in vain. And you, you sit in the refuse of worms as you spend the night in the open air. As for me, I am one that wanders about and a hired servant—from place to place and house to house, waiting for when the sun will set, so I can rest from the distresses and griefs that now beset me. Now say some word to the Lord, and die." (Job 2:9, NETS)

In this expanded passage, Mrs. Job remains nameless, but she speaks of herself as also being afflicted by enormous suffering. Like Job, she also mourns the loss of their children, which has rendered her labors in birthing and caring for them a futile effort. Due to his illness, she has to wander the streets and look for work in order to sustain life. Being a temporary hired servant, she is perhaps easily mistreated by her employers, at which she only hints by talking about distresses and griefs. Certainly, this later portrait of Mrs. Job as a lamenting mother and wife renders her more visible and gives her at least a voice.

These words of Mrs. Job are taken up and interpreted in more detail in another writing from the history of interpretation, which seeks to bring Mrs. Job out of the shadows, the *Testament of Job*, an anonymous, apocryphal work, likely written originally in Greek. Here, the enigmatic Mrs. Job is given the name, Dinah. The introduction also shows that the first Mrs. Job had "died" a bitter death together with the other ten children.[33]

It is noteworthy to mention that the MT reads, "He also had seven sons and three daughters" (Job 42:13). While the MT does not indicate what Mrs. Job was doing during Job's testing and increasing incapacitation, we only learn about her existence when she speaks abruptly. The *Testament of Job* imagines what life must have been like for her at this time and could only conclude that it was difficult. This provides a sound back-story for the wife that is absent in the MT.

---

33. Gravett, "Biblical Responses," 109.

In addition to the exhaustion she feels from her labor, the *Testament of Job* also allows Mrs. Job to express her own despair over the deaths of her ten children, another set of details the MT does not provide. By doing so, the *Testament of Job* calls attention to the grief that could have been shared by both parents which is previously neglected in the Hebrew Bible's account.[34] The retelling in the *Testament of Job* responds to the biblical text in a depatriarchalizing way, which unearths a series of questions that may be asked: "what kind of relationship does she have with her husband?" and "what kind of life has she been living throughout her husband's trials?" or "why would Mrs. Job say such seemingly surprising and terrible words to her husband amidst his suffering?"

4. *Overcoming the Problem of Misinterpretation?*

This essay has argued that through complex literary devices and redactions both Mrs. Job and Jezebel have been misconstrued and adapted for purposes of subjugation, vilification, controlling and policing women's images and bodies. A rereading through a postcolonial feminist biblical hermeneutical lens can redeem these women and contest the stereotypes associated with them.

Metapsychology teaches us that if something is repeated often with succession, it alters perception and the performance of society.[35] The performance of a society begs for a psychoanalysis in the spaces where violence (stereotyping, erasing and policing) through repetitive performance becomes invisible.[36] This type of psychoanalysis is described as an approach that "constructs an ensemble of conceptual models which are far less removed from empirical reality. Examples that are the fiction of a psychical apparatus divided into agencies, the theory of instincts, the hypothetical process of repression and so on."[37]

If the essence of psychoanalysis lies in the repression of an instinct by withholding it from becoming conscious as metapsychology teaches us, then how do we arrive at the knowledge of the unconscious? In his 1915 lecture, Sigmund Freud argues that the possibility of translating material which eludes empirical reality into the conscious is through every day

---

34. Ibid., 112.
35. Patricia Kitcher and Kathleen V. Wilkes, "What Is Freud's Metapsychology?" *Proceedings of the Aristotelian Society*, Sup. 62 (1988): 101–37.
36. Pumla D. Gqola, *Rape: A South African Nightmare* (Johannesburg: MFBooks, 2015), 78–9.
37. Kitcher and Wilkes, "What Is Freud's Metapsychology?" 101–37.

lived experiences.[38] The unconscious simply has to be performed through repetition. Sonja Brown Givens and Jennifer Monahan argue that priming a stereotype functions both in controlled and uncontrolled spaces, where it is activated unconsciously because of frequent activation in the past.[39] The repetitions of unconscious acts for a while remain disconnected with the grammar of suffering, which we deem unintelligible but which eventually becomes rampant acts of the conscious mind that require us to trace their source. We then create complex systems which enable us to trace, account for and justify the behavior.

The repetition of the misinterpretation and deliberate misconstructions of female biblical figures like Jezebel and Job's wife have resulted in a phenomenon that reduces women to the weaker sex, destructive medusas, devil's handmaids. The consumption of Jezebel and Mrs. Job's images lead to further cultural reproduction outside of the realms of religion. A cultural reproduction of these images that aims at editing female identity is so clearly nuanced that one hardly notices the significance.[40] Frances Klopper similarly argues that biblical texts have a profound impact on how women are perceived in society due to the overwhelming ethos of patriarchy in those stories.[41] Schüssler Fiorenza clearly notes that the aim of feminist biblical interpretation is to serve as an apparatus with which the Bible can be read and understood in a way that transforms women's self-understanding and cultural patterns of oppression. The goal is simply to understand texts better. As Frances Klopper states, "interpretation is all we have."[42]

Madipoane Masenya (Ngwana' Mphahlele) also highlights the tension between the belief that the word of God is authoritative and infallible as well as how ordinary women experience the Bible. She observes that women are often trying to find a way to maneuver between advocacy for their agency and adherence to the Bible.[43] There is a clear cognitive

38. As cited in ibid., 102.

39. Sonja M. Brown Givens and Jennifer L. Monahan, "Priming Mammies, Jezebels, and Other Controlling Images: An Examination of the Influence of Mediated Stereotypes on Perceptions of African American Women," *Media Psychology* 7 (2005): 87–100.

40. Tamura Lomax, *Jezebel Unhinged: Loosing the Black Female Body in Religion and Culture* (Durham, NC: Duke University Press, 2018).

41. Frances Klopper, "Interpretation Is All We Have: A Feminist Perspective on the Objective of Fallacy," *OTE* 22 (2009): 88–101.

42. Ibid., 88.

43. Madipoane Masenya (Ngwana' Mphahlele), "Biblical Authority and the Authority of Women's Experience: Whither Way?" *Scriptura* 70 (1999): 229–40.

dissonance when a woman becomes consciously aware of her position in society, which sometimes contradicts biblical authority. The question is, how do female readers of the Bible respond to a document that has been used to justify the politics of male domination?[44]

Simply removing androcentric elements from the text does not unsettle the status quo, and simply naming them would be a lazy deconstruction of a complex system which is heavily layered. An example of this is the culturally cued readings of the Bible in which interpretation ends with the conclusion that biblical authors were merely expressing the worldviews of their time.[45] A second example is the canon-within-a-canon reading of the Bible, which highlights positive images of women in order to argue that the Bible is inherently not a patriarchal document.[46] Such an argument is flawed given the very few positive images that occur in contrast to an overwhelming number of patriarchal expressions.[47] Another method would be to move beyond the text, and via a historical approach, unearth the ordinary lives of women. This approach, though, is often criticized for its alleged objectivity and claim of scientific veracity, particularly given the fact that there exists little or any epigraphic, archaeological and literal evidence.[48]

Cultural appropriations of Jezebel, besides being used as an oversexualized stereotype for black women, especially prominent in the entertainment industry worldwide, help shape the perceptions of the sexuality of black women and girls.[49] According to Tina Pippin, the juxtaposition of the images of the Mammy and the Jezebel served as an apologetic for the exploitation of the female slave. Jezebel was initially a condescending term used for African American women during the time of slavery whereas the image of the Mammy was asexual, warm, maternal, dark-skinned, big, older, hair covered with a kerchief, loyal, religious and pious.[50] Women labelled as Jezebels were considered to be young, sexualized, comely, provocative in dress, rebellious and whores.

---

44. Eryl W. Davies, *The Dissenting Reader: Feminist Approaches to the Hebrew Bible* (Aldershot: Ashgate, 2003), 26–8.

45. Cf. Ibid., 20–1.

46. Cf. Ibid., 26–8.

47. Klopper, "Interpretation Is All We Have," 89.

48. Esther Fuchs, "The History of Women in Ancient Israel: Theory, Method, and the Book of Ruth," in *Her Master's Tools? Feminist and Postcolonial Engagements of Historical-critical Discourse*, ed. Caroline Vander Stichele and Todd Penner (Atlanta, GA: Society of Biblical Literature, 2005), 211–31.

49. Sjoberg and Gentry, "Reduced to Bad Sex," 69.

50. Tina Pippin, "Jezebel Re-vamped," *Semeia* 69/70 (1995): 221–33.

These images were created by white masters to control and dominate the female slave.[51] The Mammy represented the desire for a positive image for African American women whereas the Jezebel was an excuse for white masters to justify their violence. Jezebel thus comes to represent a term used particularly by white women in the United States in order to deny the oppression and rape of slave women as they often chose whiteness over their womanhood. It was safer.[52]

5. *Conclusion*

This essay has engaged in a recovery reading of two vilified biblical figures, Jezebel and Mrs. Job, to affirm that history has no blank pages. Feminist interpretation should always be centered on the quest to absolve women as we continue to write ourselves into existence. It should no longer be acceptable, with all the exegetical and hermeneutical tools at our disposal, to ignore harmful biblical texts as time evolves and women continue to recreate themselves.

The dominant perspectives about the two women are effectively contested as we show that redactional activity is preceded by ideology. Through ideological criticism, we have shown that Jezebel could be effectively absolved of the accusation that she was the chief bearer of Baalism and that the violence meted against her through harmful interpretation is unwarranted. The patriarchal portrayal of a wicked woman who subverts her husband begins to fade. In particular, black women may now see a more positive picture of themselves, as the Mammy and Jezebel analogy is challenged through a revisionist process, and even a performance of the word in mainstream pop culture.

A survey of the LXX and of the *Testament of Job*'s portrayals of Mrs. Job, which give her a name and a voice, has brought her out of the shadows to which she has been relegated. A reading that focuses on Mrs. Job by detailing her life and grief in the narrative privileges marginalized voices. This reading also provides positive affirmation that the subalterns can speak for themselves. The traditional understanding of Mrs. Job's role in the biblical narrative in contrast to that portrayed in the LXX and the *Testament of Job* then forces us to undermine the patriarchal molds in which she has been cast and to view her as a feminist metaphor of the contestation of invisibility.

51. Ibid.
52. Ibid.

Women across the world are victims of patriarchy and sexism—as Tsitsi Dangarembga states, the business of womanhood is a heavy burden![53] However, pointing out the cultural effects of negative images specifically on black women does not aim to mask or create further distance or differences. An intersectional approach begs for a multicultural reading of biblical texts, which, as Renita Weems argues, makes us aware of our different intellectual heritage, political baggage and social assumptions; one that forces us to declare on whose behalf we interpret.[54] However, as Weems also reminds us, "the risk of failure is no excuse for not trying to reach out to one another."[55] It remains a constant struggle of wanting to understand and wanting to be understood, navigating through each other's cultural baggage.

Bibliography

Brown Givens, M. Sonja, and Jennifer L. Monahan. "Priming Mammies, Jezebels, and Other Controlling Images: An Examination of the Influence of Mediated Stereotypes on Perceptions of African American Women." *Media Psychology* 7 (2005): 87–100.
Crowell, Bradley L. "Good Girl, Bad Girl: Foreign Women of the Deuteronomistic History in Postcolonial Perspective." *BibInt* 21 (2013): 1–18.
Dangarembga, Tsitsi. *Nervous Conditions*. New York: Women's Press, 2009.
Davies, Eryl W. *The Dissenting Reader: Feminist Approaches to the Hebrew Bible*. Aldershot: Ashgate, 2003.
Dube, Musa, W. "Jumping the Fire with Judith: Postcolonial Feminist Hermeneutics." In *Feminist Interpretation of the Bible and the Hermeneutics of Liberation*, edited by Silvia Schroer and Sophia Bietenhard, 61–76. JSOTSup 374. London: Sheffield Academic, 2003.
Fuchs, Esther. "The History of Women in Ancient Israel: Theory, Method, and the Book of Ruth." In *Her Master's Tools? Feminist and Postcolonial Engagements of Historical-critical Discourse*, edited by Caroline Van der Stichele and Todd Penner, 211–31. Atlanta, GA: Society of Biblical Literature, 2005.
Gentry, Caron E., and Laura Sjoberg. "The Gendering of Women's Terrorism." In *Women, Gender and Terrorism*, edited by Laura Sjoberg and Caron E. Gentry, 57–80. Athens, GA: University of Georgia Press, 2011.
Gnuse, Robert. K. *No Other Gods: The Emergence of Monotheism*. JSOTSup 241. London: Sheffield Academic, 1997.
Gqola, Pumla D. *Rape: A South African Nightmare*. Johannesburg: MFBooks, 2015.

---

53. Tsitsi Dangarembga, *Nervous Conditions* (New York: Women's Press, 2009), 16.
54. Renita J. Weems. "Re-Reading for Liberation: African American Women and the Bible," in Schroer and Bietenhard (eds.), *Feminist Interpretation of the Bible and the Hermeneutics of Liberation*, 19–33 (21).
55. Ibid., 22.

Gravett, Emily O. "Biblical Responses: Past and Present Retellings of the Enigmatic Mrs. Job." *BibInt* 20 (2012): 97–127.
Kitcher, Patricia, and Kathleen V. Wilkes. "What Is Freud's Metapsychology?" *Proceedings of the Aristotelian Society*, Sup. 62 (1988): 101–37.
Klopper, Frances. "Interpretation Is All We Have: A Feminist Perspective on the Objective of Fallacy." *OTE* 22 (2009): 88–101.
Knoppers, Gary N. "'There Was None Like Him': Incomparability in the Books of Kings." *CBQ* 54 (1992): 411–31.
Lomax, Tamura. *Jezebel Unhinged: Loosing the Black Female Body in Religion and Culture*. Durham, NC: Duke University Press, 2018.
Magdalene, Rachel F. "Job's Wife as Hero: A Feminist-Forensic Reading of the Book of Job." *BibInt* 14 (2006): 209–58.
Masenya (Ngwana' Mphahlele), Madipoane. "Biblical Authority and the Authority of Women's Experience: Whither Way?" *Scriptura* 70 (1999): 229–40.
Masters, N. Tatiana, Taryn P. Lindhorst, and Marcia K. Meyers. "Jezebel at the Welfare Office: How Racialized Stereotypes of Poor Women's Reproductive Decisions and Relationships Shape Policy Implementation." *Journal of Poverty* 18, no. 2 (2014): 109–29.
McKenzie, Steven L. *The Trouble with Kings: The Composition of the Book of Kings in the Deuteronomistic History*. Leiden: Brill Academic, 1991.
Mokoena, Lerato. "The Roots of Jehu's Bloody Coup: A Violent Story of Religious Zealots, Retributive Justice or International Politics?" MTh Thesis, University of Pretoria, 2017.
NETS. *A New English Translation of the Septuagint and the Other Greek Translations Traditionally Included under that Title*. Edited by Albert Pietersma and Benjamin G. Wright. New York: Oxford University Press, 2007.
Pippin, Tina. "Jezebel Re-vamped." *Semeia* 69/70 (1995): 221–33.
Pruin, Dagmar. "What Is in a Text? Searching for Jezebel." In *Ahab Agonistes: The Rise and Fall of the Omri Dynasty*, edited by Lester L. Grabbe, 205–35. LHBOTS 421. New York: T&T Clark, 2007.
Römer, Thomas. *The Invention of God*. London: Harvard University Press, 2015.
Sasson, Victor. "The Literary and Theological Function of Job's Wife in the Book of Job." *Bib* 79 (1998): 86–90.
Schüssler Fiorenza, Elisabeth (ed.). *Sharing Her Word: Feminist Biblical Interpretation in Context*. Boston, MA: Beacon, 1998.
Seow, Choon-Leong. "Job's Wife, with Due Respect." In *Das Buch Hiob und seine Interpretationen: Beiträge zur Hiob-Symposium auf dem Monte Verità vom 14.–19. August 2005*, edited by T. Krüger, 351–75. ATANT 88. Zurich: Theologischer Verlag, 2007.
Trible, Phyllis. "Depatriarchalizing in Biblical Interpretation." *JAAR* 41 (1973): 30–48.
Weems, Renita J. "Re-Reading for Liberation: African American Women and the Bible." In *Feminist Interpretation of the Bible and the Hermeneutics of Liberation*, edited by Silvia Schroer and Sophia Bietenhard, 19–33. JSOTSup 374. London: Sheffield Academic, 2003.
West, Gerald. "Hearing Job's Wife: Towards a Feminist Reading of Job." *OTE* 4 (1991): 107–31.

Chapter 4

INTERVENTIONS TO THE DRAMA OF A BROKEN
FAMILY IN JEREMIAH 2:1–4:4

Christl M. Maier

Philipps-Universität Marburg/Stellenbosch University

1. *Introduction*

The book of Jeremiah revolves around ancient Judah's demise as an independent state and the destruction of its capital Jerusalem by the Babylonians in 587 BCE. It presents different genres and topics—oracles of doom addressed to Judah and Jerusalem as well as to foreign nations, and long-winding speeches of the prophet that blame the audience for its own demise. Next to narratives about Jeremiah's maltreatment by state representatives are oracles of salvation that announce restoration. This multi-voiced book responds to the traumatic event of Jerusalem's destruction. It puts the traumatic experience of the Judean survivors into language in order to overcome the overwhelming feeling of helplessness, to contain their memory, and to seek healing of their wounds. As Kathleen O'Connor has demonstrated, contemporary studies of trauma and disaster, used as heuristic devices, help to untangle the book's multi-layered and multi-voiced message.[1] Inspired by O'Connor's reading and by

---

1. Cf. Kathleen M. O'Connor, "The Book of Jeremiah: Reconstructing Community after Disaster," in *Character Ethics and the Old Testament: Moral Dimensions of Scripture*, ed. M. Daniel Carroll R. and Jacqueline E. Lapsley (Louisville, KY: Westminster John Knox, 2007), 81–92; eadem, *Jeremiah: Pain and Promise* (Minneapolis, MN: Fortress, 2012).

feminist critique of the gendered biblical metaphors, my interpretation of Jer 2:1–4:4 seeks to contribute a reading that privileges the marginal voices in the text. After introducing the text's contents and rhetoric, I will first discuss O'Connor's interpretation of this text before offering some creative interventions against the text's seemingly androcentric and misogynist message.

2. *Jeremiah 2:1–4:4: Contents and Rhetoric*

After the initial call narrative, Jer 2:1–4:4 builds a kind of overture to the book that briefly presents the eventful history of God and his people and introduces the main themes. The text describes a conflict in the relationship between God and his people and offers a seemingly straightforward solution to it. As many scholars have noted, several hands produced this text over a long time-span.[2] For instance, in vv. 1–2aα, Jerusalem is addressed, but this introduction to the speech is absent in the Old Greek and conflicts with the later description of the female collective. While I am aware of its growth, in this article, I aim at interpreting the text in its final form. This perspective compels me to balance the different and sometimes contradictory voices in the text.

Jeremiah 2:1–4:4 offers discomforting portraits of both its audience and the divine character whose words are presented by the prophetic voice. The text accuses its implied audience and tries to justify the necessity of divine punishment. Not only with regard to contents but also to form, Jeremiah 2–3 is disturbing due to abrupt changes of addressees and topics. Jeremiah 2:2aβb talks about female Israel's time in the wilderness as a time of love and loyalty towards God. In the next verse, however, Israel is a single male figure called "holy to the Lord" and "first fruit of the harvest" (2:3). Reviewing the history of Israel's ancestors from the exodus to the present time, the speaker then accuses the audience of having turned their back to YHWH and venerating other deities (2:4–13).

According to Jer 2:14–17, Israel, the male addressee who here represents the Northern Kingdom, was looted by its enemies, but Judah, personified as female, neither takes notice nor relents, and therefore will face a similar fate. Although the female collective is not named, the accusations reveal that it refers to Judah. This is evident in the rhetorical

---

2. For an overview on the redaction-critical interpretations of Mark Biddle, Dieter Böhler, and Maria Häusl, see my article "Reading Back and Forth: Gender Trouble in Jeremiah 2–3," in *Interested Readers: Essays on the Hebrew Bible in Honor of David J. A. Clines*, ed. James K. Aitken, Jeremy M. S. Clines, and Christl M. Maier (Atlanta, GA: Society of Biblical Literature, 2013), 139–41.

question in v. 18, "what do you (woman) gain by going to Egypt, to drink the waters of the Nile? Or what do you gain by going to Assyria, to drink the waters of the Euphrates?" which relates to Judah's alliances with the empires of that period. The prophetic voice interprets this policy of shifting coalitions as a false path that only leads to disaster because Judah has abandoned her own deity, the fountain of living waters (v. 13). Verses 23 and 24 compare female Judah to a young she-camel and a wild ass in heat, and thus accuse her of promiscuous sexual acts. With fictitious citations of the female figure, Jer 2:20–25 stages a dispute between Judah and YHWH. As she openly affirms her love of strangers (v. 25), she is accused of harlotry.

By alluding to the law that prohibits reunion by a divorced couple in Deut 24:1–4, Jer 3:1–5 argues that Judah has utterly spoiled herself by having sex with every passer-by and therefore YHWH cannot take her back.[3] The following prose passage in Jer 3:6–11, however, identifies the divorced woman as Israel, the Northern Kingdom, and accuses her sister Judah of not learning from Israel's punishment by God. Despite this harsh verdict, both wives are called to repent and return to their "husband" (3:12, 14, 19). In 3:19, Judah is suddenly addressed as "daughter" and promised a share of land as heritage among the sons, if she will be remorseful. The following penitential prayer (3:22b–25), however, represents the voice of the children, who articulate their guilt and shame. They receive the promise that they will be a blessing to the nations, like their father Abraham, if they return to YHWH, swear only to him, and remove the foreskin of their hearts (4:1–4). The solution to this marital conflict is therefore that YHWH divorces his unfaithful wives and approaches their children in order to restore the broken relation.

Rhetorically, Jer 2:1–3:5 consists of a divine monologue, an indictment speech, in which YHWH accuses his wife of "adultery" with political allies and other deities and cites her merely to demonstrate her stubbornness and denial of responsibility. God refers to the prohibition to remarry a once divorced wife and argues that due to her "whoring" reunion will be impossible. In 3:6, Jeremiah enters the stage and reports God's words to him (3:6–10, 11–20). Jeremiah tells the audience that God has asked him to witness the stubbornness of Israel and Judah, but

---

3. Whereas the Old Greek in Jer 3:1–5 only alludes to Deut 24:1–4, changes in the Masoretic Text create direct literary links to the prohibition to remarry; cf. my article, "Ist Versöhnung möglich? Jeremia 3,1–5 als Beispiel innerbiblischer Auslegung," in *"Gott bin ich, kein Mann". Beiträge zur Hermeneutik der biblischen Gottesrede: FS Helen Schüngel-Straumann*, ed. Ilona Riedel-Spangenberger and Erich Zenger (Paderborn: Schöningh, 2006), 295–305.

nevertheless sends him to invite Israel and all displaced children back. After Jeremiah's statements, a conversation ensues (3:21–4:4). When Jeremiah mentions that he hears the children crying (v. 21), YHWH repeats his call to return (v. 22a), to which the children respond with a penitential prayer (vv. 22b–25), which causes YHWH to pronounce a conditional oracle of salvation (4:1–4).

This distribution of voices clearly demonstrates that God is the main protagonist, while Jeremiah serves as his master's voice and witness. Judah is negatively portrayed and compared to her sister Israel, while her children suffer from the divorce, weep and repent. All responsibility for the disaster is laid on the shoulders of the two female figures, but God is exonerated. At first glance, any objection to the divine assessment seems futile. It is therefore not surprising that most commentators side with God and his prophet and condemn Judah, taking for granted her alleged misdeeds and character flaws.[4] Only a few interpreters are willing to deconstruct the text's gendered codes and uneven discourse of voices.

3. *Jeremiah 2:1–4:4 as Drama of a Broken Family*

Kathleen O'Connor interprets Jer 2:1–4:4 as "drama of the broken family" and argues that, "This extended metaphor of the family turns readers into voyeurs who watch a messed-up couple and their children interact and fail to connect with each other."[5] A close reading of the text reveals that the metaphor of the family's dissolution skillfully symbolizes the history of Israel and Judah as God's people, their successive military defeat, deportation, as well as the open question about the fate of the survivors and their relationship to the deity. As metaphors are culture-specific and time-bound, they generate associations and images in readers, and the views of readers, ancient and modern, certainly differ.

---

4. Cf., for example, William McKane, *A Critical and Exegetical Commentary on Jeremiah, vol. I: I–XXV*, ICC 24 (Edinburgh: T&T Clark, 1986), 34, 42, 45, 55, 63; Gunther Wanke, *Jeremia 1,1–25,14*, ZBK 20/1 (Zurich: Theologischer Verlag, 1995), 36–7, 41, 49; Georg Fischer, *Jeremia, Bd.1: Jeremia 1–25*, HThKAT (Freiburg: Herder, 2005), 162–3, 168–70, 178, 203. Only Carroll challenges the rhetoric of Judah's negative characterization and calls it an ideology; cf. Robert P. Carroll, *Jeremiah, vol. 1* (Sheffield: Sheffield Phoenix, 2006), 123–5, 128, 136, 142.

5. O'Connor, *Pain and Promise*, 35. Cf. also the detailed analysis of A. R. Pete Diamond and Kathleen M. O'Connor, "Unfaithful Passions: Coding Women Coding Men in Jeremiah 2–3 (4.2)," in *Troubling Jeremiah*, ed. A. R. Pete Diamond, Kathleen M. O'Connor, and Louis Stulman, JSOTSup 260 (Sheffield: Sheffield Academic, 1999), 121–45.

In ancient Israel's kin-based society, marriage was a hierarchical, heterosexual relationship in which the husband held all the power in social and juridical terms over his wife, children, and extended household, including other relatives and slaves; only he could initiate a divorce (cf. Deut 24:1). Whereas a man could marry several women (cf. Gen 29) and have sex with prostitutes (cf. Gen 38; Josh 2), any sexual contact of a betrothed or married woman with another man would infringe both her husband's property rights and his honor; therefore, it was strongly sanctioned (cf. Lev 20:10; Deut 22:22–29). To divorce an adulterous wife was perceived as the husband's right (Deut 24:1; Jer 3:8).[6] This concept of marriage sounds both outdated and horrific to modern readers, especially in Western societies, in which marriage partners are legally equal. The idea of male supremacy and privilege, however, has not fully disappeared in contemporary societies due to the unequal distribution of resources as well as patriarchal structures that remain extant. In the world of the text, the "wife" is punished for her adultery through divorce. Yet, one should not forget that this is a metaphor, which for ancient readers illustrates Israel's and Judah's failed relationship with their national deity YHWH, and serves as a reason for their political subjugation under foreign rule.

Diamond and O'Connor acknowledge that the text's rhetoric and use of the marriage metaphor were probably conventional to ancient readers. They identify its implied audience with the late exilic/early post-exilic Jewish community which lived in Jerusalem under Persian hegemony.[7] In appealing to them as the children of YHWH's unfaithful wife Judah, Jer 2:1–4:4 "constructs a rhetoric of sympathy for husband YHWH" and encourages the children to "side with their father" by representing the mother in an unsympathetic way.[8] Yet, Diamond and O'Connor rightly point to the metaphor's harmful effect on modern recipients. They find not only the sexualized image of the people but also the portrait of God immensely problematic because Jeremiah 2–4 contains "a male projection of betrayal and evil unto women" and the female character is "the principal tool used in a rhetoric of shaming to encode the infidelities of

---

6. Interestingly, there is no record in the Hebrew Bible that the husband would beat his wife since such physical assault was deemed an aberration; cf. Funlọla O. Ọlọjẹde, "Absence of Wife-battering in Old Testament Narratives: A Literary Omission or a Cultural Aberration?" in *Gender Agenda Matters: Papers of the "Feminist Section" of the International Meetings of the Society of Biblical Literature*, ed. I. Fischer (Newcastle upon Tyne: Cambridge Scholars, 2015), 87–98.
7. Diamond and Kathleen M. O'Connor, "Unfaithful Passions," 126.
8. Ibid., 142–3.

male Israel."[9] Therefore, the task of any modern interpreter of this family drama in Jeremiah is twofold. On the one hand, it is essential to *explain* why Judah's national disaster is told as estrangement and divorce, which has a huge impact on the children, that is, the following generations. On the other hand, one needs to *interpret* the metaphor for contemporary readers and thus in a postmodern cultural context.[10]

4. *Transgressing Cultural Assumptions and Gender Roles*

In outlining the task of the feminist and postcolonial interpreter, Carolyn Sharp identifies "transgression" as one important strategy for reading a biblical text like Jer 2:1–4:4. She defines "'transgression' as the privileging of creative interventions, ancient and contemporary, that resist or reframe destructive social norms."[11]

The unit of Jer 2:1–4:4 has been the subject of criticism by various feminist scholars due to its one-sided, hierarchical dichotomy of gender roles, its depiction of a powerful male protagonist and his obedient spokesman on the one hand, and of stigmatized female figures, which are accused, beaten and silenced, on the other. I concur that the androcentric and misogynist aspects of this broken family metaphor should be outlawed and rejected, as O'Connor, Gerlinde Baumann, Mary Shields and other feminist interpreters have argued.[12] Especially, the depiction of

---

9. Ibid., 143.
10. This double hermeneutical perspective pertains to all biblical metaphors and has been introduced by Gerlinde Baumann, *Love and Violence: Marriage as Metaphor for the Relationship between YHWH and Israel in the Prophetic Books*, trans. Linda M. Maloney (Collegeville, MN: Liturgical, 2003), 44–6; eadem, *Gottesbilder der Gewalt im Alten Testament verstehen* (Darmstadt: Wissenschaftliche Buchgesellschaft, 2006), 15–17, 79–83.
11. Carolyn J. Sharp, "Buying Land in the Text of Jeremiah: Feminist Commentary, the Kristevan Abject, and Jeremiah 32," in *Prophecy and Power: Jeremiah in Feminist and Postcolonial Perspective*, ed. Christl M. Maier and Carolyn J. Sharp, LHBOTS 577 (London: Bloomsbury T&T Clark, 2013), 155.
12. Cf. O'Connor, *Pain and Promise*, 147 n. 19; Baumann, *Love and Violence*, 238–40; Mary E. Shields, *Circumscribing the Prostitute: The Rhetorics of Intertextuality, Metaphor and Gender in Jeremiah 3.1–4.4*, JSOTSup 387 (London: T&T Clark, 2004); Maria Häusl, *Bilder der Not: Weiblichkeits- und Geschlechtermetaphorik im Buch Jeremia*, HBS 37 (Freiburg: Herder, 2003), 300–356; J. Cheryl Exum, "The Ethics of Biblical Violence against Women," in *The Bible in Ethics: The Second Sheffield Colloquium*, ed. John W. Rogerson, Margaret Davies, and M. Daniel Carroll R., JSOTSup 207 (Sheffield: Sheffield Academic, 1995), 265–69.

Judah as a young camel and a she-ass in heat (2:23–24) dehumanizes the female character and misrepresents female sexual desire.[13]

From a queer perspective, however, the sudden change in addressing Israel and Judah as male or female in Jer 2:1–4:4 indicates a breakdown of fixed gender roles. As Stuart Macwilliam convincingly argues, the text's disjointedness of gendered addressees cannot be solved by associating "female" Jerusalem/Judah with the marriage metaphor and "male" Israel with the politico-religious theme of apostasy.[14] While the marriage metaphor clearly exemplifies a heterosexual union, especially with regard to its sociological background in the ancient society, it includes a queer logic by requiring the male members of its implied audience "to think of themselves and their relationship to the divine in a way that wholly undermines their cultural expectations."[15] Moreover, Macwilliam perceives a queer relationship between YHWH and Jeremiah in Jer 15:16 and 20:7, which together with the prohibition to marry (Jer 16:2) destabilizes Jeremiah's role as a vigorous male prophet.[16] Similarly, Deryn Guest criticizes feminist interpretations of the marriage metaphor because they do not challenge the compulsory heteronormativity inherent in this metaphor.[17]

As a multi-layered and multi-voiced text, Jer 2:1–4:4 carries a certain potential of subverting the seemingly clear image of the powerful male deity, its male prophet, and its feminized human followers. At closer inspection, Jer 2:1–4:4 is highly ambiguous in both its character portraits and its scenery, and thus offers clues for deconstructing its apparently straightforward message of doom. Therefore, I will now use some of the story's inconsistencies as a starting point for intervention and re-framing the overall plot of a relationship gone awry. Ambiguities surround (a) the implied audience, (b) the debate about who is to blame for the disaster, and (c) the role of the prophet Jeremiah.

---

13. Cf. Baumann, *Love and Violence*, 117–18; Athalya Brenner and Fokkelien van Dijk-Hemmes, *On Gendering Texts: Female and Male Voices in the Hebrew Bible*, BibInt 1 (Leiden: Brill, 1993), 181–7; Shields, *Circumscribing the Prostitute*, 158–60; Maier, "Ist Versöhnung möglich?" 303–4.

14. Stuart Macwilliam, "Queering Jeremiah," *BibInt* 10 (2002): 384–404; idem, *Queer Theory and the Prophetic Marriage Metaphor in the Hebrew Bible* (Sheffield: Equinox, 2011), 89–92.

15. Macwilliam, *Queer Theory*, 95.

16. Stuart Macwilliam, "The Prophet and His Patsy: Gender Performativity in Jeremiah," in Maier and Sharp (eds.), *Prophecy and Power*, 173–5.

17. Deryn Guest, *Beyond Feminist Biblical Studies* (Sheffield: Sheffield Phoenix, 2012), 105–16.

(a) *Shifting Audience*

Analyzing the different addressees in Jer 2:1–4:4 reveals that the implied audience is shifting and unstable. While the late introduction in Jeremiah 2:1–2aα MT addresses Jerusalem, the rhetorical questions in Jeremiah 2:18 challenge Judah's politics in the last years of the monarchy. Used as a counterpart to Judah, the Northern Kingdom Israel is personified alternatively as a male slave (2:14–15) as well as YHWH's first wife (3:6–11), but in other instances, the name "Israel" refers to the entire people, both in historical retrospect (2:3, 26) and at present (2:4). There is *not only one* gendered image of the audience *but many* and this ambiguity blurs the seemingly clear-cut division between good and bad, male and female figures.

Moreover, if one assumes pre-exilic Judah as the first audience, it is mostly men forced to identify with the self-assured, lustful and stubborn woman.[18] The people's leading groups which are accused of neglecting God are priests, scribes, kings with their officials, and prophets (2:8, 26). Thus, linking the metaphor of the adulterous wife to its sociological background reveals its function to shame the pre-exilic Judeans, especially their leading men. Regarding this scenario, Guest points out that a male deity addressing a male audience through the use of a marriage metaphor carries homoerotic connotations, results in queerness, and thus may be read as deconstructing heteronormativity.[19] Certainly, the text's distinction between the wives and their children seems to circumvent this conclusion and helps to address the Judean survivors of war and deportation. These survivors, however, are called to reject their own history as a people, and thus part of their own identity.[20]

Why should modern readers endorse their voice of lament and repentance and side with their self-blame? Why not take Judah's words in Jer 2:23, "I am not defiled, I have not gone after the Baals," and in Jer 2:35, "I am innocent… I have not sinned," as an attempt at self-defense that challenges her negative portrayal by the divine voice? The postmodern interpreter may choose which voice she or he would like to emphasize. Instead of siding with the divine voice, one may foreground voices of other characters, especially because the dominant position of

---

18. Cf. also Shields, *Circumscribing the Prostitute*, 123; Exum, "Ethics of Biblical Violence," 250; Diamond and O'Connor, "Unfaithful Passions," 143; Macwilliam, *Queer Theory*, 93, 95.

19. Guest, *Beyond Feminist Biblical Studies*, 111.

20. Similarly, Sharp ("Buying Land," 164) notes that in the story of Jeremiah's sign-act to claim patrimonial land (Jer 32), Judah is characterized as a defiled and repulsive thing that is beyond recovery (32:23, 29–35).

the divine voice is challenged in the text and therefore should be deconstructed by the feminist interpreter.

(b) *Who Is to Blame for the Disaster?*

The text repeatedly blames the victims of the destruction of Jerusalem and Judah for their own demise, and in Jer 2:4–13 includes all generations from the time of the Exodus in a history of continuous iniquity and guilt. The main line of argument is that Judah was not aware of her bridal privilege, was unfaithful to her national deity, and affiliated with other empires and deities in order to survive. Despite its massive blaming, however, the text cannot fend off an alternative conclusion, namely, that YHWH was too weak to protect his people and failed to rescue Jerusalem, his chosen dwelling-place, from the hands of the Babylonians. In this regard, the question in Jer 2:31 may not be merely rhetorical:

> Have I been a wilderness to Israel, or a land of thick darkness?
> Why then do my people say, "We are free, we will come to you no more"?
> (Jer 2:31)

Taken as a genuine question, this verse challenges the divine reasoning that only Judah's self-assured obstinacy led to the break-up. Instead, it implies that YHWH contributed to the couple's estrangement.[21] Moreover, God is vulnerable in the relationship, and needs to stay in contact with his people. Why else would he call his "wives" to return? Why else would he even abrogate his own law that forbids the reunion of a divorced couple? After the decisive argumentation of 3:1–5 that a man cannot take back his divorced wife because of her multiple acts of "whoring," Jeremiah narrates twice that God has asked Israel to return to him (3:7, 12). According to Jer 3:19, God also reaches out to female Judah, saying:

> How would I set you among my children, and give you a pleasant land, the most beautiful heritage of all the nations. I said: You should call me, "My Father," and should not turn from following me. (3:19)

---

21. In Jer 44:15, the Judean survivors, who flee to Egypt in fear of the Babylonian retaliation after the assassination of Gedaliah, trace their calamity to their neglect of the Queen of Heaven, a goddess venerated in Judah's towns and Jerusalem. They offer an alternative reasoning to the one presented by YHWH in Jer 2–3. Cf. Christl M. Maier, "Listening to the Trauma of Refugees in Jeremiah 40–44," *lectio difficilior* 1/2017; http://www.lectio.unibe.ch/17_1/inhalt_d.htm.

Admittedly, this verse uses a father–daughter metaphor and therefore does not advocate a reunion of the couple. Yet, it is YHWH who makes the first move to resume the shattered relationship. There is no response from the wives, because what they represent is lost. The Northern Kingdom was extinguished from history and Judah lost its state with its capital being now subject to foreign rule. Thus, there is much to lament, and renewal can only be achieved by giving voice to the trauma. Only some of Judah's children who survived the disaster are able to respond to God's offer. O'Connor interprets the liturgical form of the response in 3:22–25 as a means for the survivors to overcome their passivity by gathering, using gestures and speech, and becoming active again.[22]

They march home in procession:

> Here we are; we come to you; for you are YHWH, our God. (3:22b)

They confess their idolatry:

> Truly, the hills were a delusion, a roaring the mountains. (3:23a)

They declare their praise:

> Truly, with YHWH our God is the deliverance of Israel. (3:23a)

They lament their losses in the disaster:

> Disgrace has devoured our ancestors' entire yield, from our youth,
> their flocks and their herds, their sons and their daughters. (3:24)

They prostrate themselves and confess their guilt:

> We have to lie down in our shame and dishonor will cover us;
> for we have sinned against YHWH, our God;
> we and our ancestors, from our youth even to this day;
> and we have not obeyed the voice of YHWH, our God. (3:25)

In its current context, however, God's invitation for a renewed relationship as well as the survivors' response "remains only a possibility, a hope, an introductory appeal of the book to its readers."[23] The book of

---

22. O'Connor, *Pain and Promise*, 41. The following rubrics are taken from O'Connor; the translation of the Hebrew is mine.
23. Ibid., 41.

Jeremiah abundantly expands the announcement of doom and the blaming of the victims; it details the threat of extinction while oracles about restoration are few, tentatively formulated, and always have a condition attached. This contingent restoration is introduced in Jer 4:1–2, which emphasizes a big "if":

> *If* you (masc.) return, O Israel, says YHWH, *if* you return to me, *if* you remove your abominations from my presence, and do not waver, and *if* you swear, "As YHWH lives!" in truth, in justice, and in uprightness, *then* nations shall be blessed by him (= Israel), and by him they shall boast.

In sum, there is no happy ending for the broken family. The wives' disappearance and the experience of death and deportation are indelibly ingrained in Israel's collective memory. Yet, my critical interventions in the reading of Jer 2:1–4:4 also show that all family members must be heard and that the privileging of the divine voice is fraught with uncertainties.

(c) *Ambiguities in Jeremiah's Role*

Finally, one wonders what the role of Jeremiah in all of this may be. Is he, indeed, the obedient spokesperson for God who consents to God's negative assessment of his people's history? At least, Jeremiah reports the children's lament:

> A voice on the bare heights is heard,
> a weeping, a supplication of Israel's children,
> because they have perverted their way,
> they have forgotten YHWH, their God. (3:21)

These words of the prophet seem to inspire another divine call to return and thus stimulate the next step in reconciliation.

In 2:1–4:4, Jeremiah does not respond to God, but in Jer 4:10, he accuses the deity of deception:

> Then I said, "Ah, my lord, YHWH, how utterly you have deceived this people and Jerusalem, saying, 'It shall be well with you,' even while the sword is at the throat!"

Although in most chapters of the book, Jeremiah compliantly announces God's words to the people, in this verse, he argues with the deity. In five poems of lament, spread over chs 11–20, Jeremiah also eloquently wrestles with God over the message of doom and the opposition that he faces as a prophet. However, in Jer 15:18, Jeremiah calls YHWH "a deceitful brook, water on which one cannot rely." In Jer 20:7, he further laments that YHWH has enticed and overpowered him, and made him a laughing-stock to his opponents. In Jer 20:14–18, Jeremiah even curses the day of his birth and wishes he never left his mother's womb. In his complaints, Jeremiah not only questions his own role, but also God's role in crushing his own people.

In the end, Jeremiah cannot prevent the calamity; he is unable to stop God's cruel plan. Although the narratives in the second part of the book describe him as mediator between the Judeans and God, he is forbidden to intercede and pray on behalf of the people—and this divine veto is mentioned three times (7:16; 11:14; 14:11). In my view, the repeated prohibition from interceding demonstrates that there may have been an alternative solution to the rupture in relationship, a way to avoid the harsh punishment.

5. Conclusion

Why are we still reading texts like Jer 2:1–4:4? How can our interpretation foster communities of justice? In my view, each interpretation of a biblical passage should not just paraphrase its message and consent, but wrestle with its meaning—past and present. In particular, texts like Jer 2:1–4:4 that deliver disturbing, multi-layered metaphors and theological statements need to be explained within their ancient socio-historical context and interpreted for postmodern readers whose views may differ from those of the implied audience, which the authors of the text had in mind.

On the one hand, Jer 2:1–4:4 comments on the history of Israel and Judah, both of which were crushed by foreign powers, while their inhabitants were killed, deported or left without resources in a devastated land. The text foregrounds the perspective of the national deity, YHWH, who justifies their downfall with their breach of relationship. He accuses them of having abandoned him and sought other deities as well as human allies in their quest for survival. Against this seemingly straightforward argumentation, the text, however, is ambiguous in its description of both the audience and the deity, and it includes the voices of the survivors. In this drama of a broken family, all members get wounded: While the "wife," the pre-exilic people of Judah including its former generations, is blamed and most negatively portrayed, the "husband," YHWH, who divorced his wife, can hardly justify his deeds and is bereft of his children, too. God is vulnerable in relationship, needs to stay in contact with his people, and thus repeatedly calls his children back. The "children," survivors of the catastrophe, have to carry the burden of loss and deportation, and they respond to their father's call, repent, and take the blame. Yet their liturgy of praying is only a first attempt to reconnect, and what God offers them in the future is only a conditioned oracle of salvation. Thus, healing will take some time, and it is not for free.

Why do the surviving Judeans take the blame? O'Connor argues that self-blaming is a coping mechanism in the midst of disaster.[24] Victims of trauma and disaster often blame themselves in order to take some responsibility for what happened and to regain agency. Instead of remaining helpless, overwhelmed and isolated in their pain, they want their God to be in control and powerful, even at the cost of portraying him as wrathful and punishing.[25] While I consent that this comparison explains how the massive blaming of Judah and the theory of divine retribution pervade the book of Jeremiah, I think that for postmodern readers this reasoning is inadequate. The sudden shifts of addressees and topics in Jer 2:1–4:4 signify that there is no simple solution and that the image of God as a furious and violent husband has to be challenged. This drama of the broken family also reveals a crisis of traditional theology, especially its idea of divine justice. In the face of the divorce, which signifies the survivors' trauma of being abandoned by their deity and crushed by the Babylonians, traditional images of God as leader in the wilderness, or protector of Jerusalem, or righteous judge have dissolved. Even the divine law no longer provides a solution because if God in his role as husband were to insist on his rights, he would be left alone without women and children. The solution to this family crisis is not to silence the "wives" and have the children repent. Rather, modern interpreters should deconstruct these seemingly fixed gender roles as well as their patriarchal and heterosexual norms.

If we recognize that the gender performance of God, Jeremiah, and the audience is unstable and shifting, the attribution of hierarchy and blame becomes inconclusive and the text's subversive potential comes to the fore. Within this constellation, God's attitude towards his people needs to change. God has to waive his male right to punish and divorce. A solution may be reached through the transformation of God as furious husband to benevolent parent who cares for his children no matter what they do. This transformation implies that God listens to the cries of those who suffer from trauma. The way to healing would be long and arduous—not only

---

24. O'Connor, "Reconstructing Community," 85–6; eadem, *Pain and Promise*, 43–4.
25. Ibid., 42–3.

in the past but also in the present. What we need for our contemporary faith communities are interpretations that transgress the trodden paths and transform traditional ideas of God as well as human hierarchies.

Bibliography

Baumann, Gerlinde. *Gottesbilder der Gewalt im Alten Testament verstehen.* Darmstadt: Wissenschaftliche Buchgesellschaft, 2006.
Baumann, Gerlinde. *Love and Violence: Marriage as Metaphor for the Relationship between YHWH and Israel in the Prophetic Books.* Translated by Linda M. Maloney. Collegeville, MN: Liturgical, 2003.
Brenner, Athalya, and Fokkelien van Dijk-Hemmes. *On Gendering Texts: Female and Male Voices in the Hebrew Bible.* BibInt 1. Leiden: Brill, 1993.
Carroll, Robert P. *Jeremiah, Volume 1.* Sheffield: Sheffield Phoenix, 2006.
Diamond, A. R. Pete, and Kathleen M. O'Connor. "Unfaithful Passions: Coding Women Coding Men in Jeremiah 2–3 (4.2)." In *Troubling Jeremiah*, edited by A. R. Pete Diamond, Kathleen M. O'Connor, and Louis Stulman, 121–45. JSOTSup 260. Sheffield: Sheffield Academic, 1999.
Exum, J. Cheryl. "The Ethics of Biblical Violence against Women." In *The Bible in Ethics: The Second Sheffield Colloquium*, edited by John W. Rogerson, Margaret Davies, and M. Daniel Carroll R., 248–71. JSOTSup 207. Sheffield: Sheffield Academic, 1995.
Fischer, Georg. *Jeremia, Band 1: Jeremia 1–25.* HThKAT. Freiburg: Herder, 2005.
Guest, Deryn. *Beyond Feminist Biblical Studies.* Sheffield: Sheffield Phoenix, 2012.
Häusl, Maria. *Bilder der Not: Weiblichkeits- und Geschlechtermetaphorik im Buch Jeremia.* HBS 37. Freiburg: Herder, 2003.
Maier, Christl M. "Ist Versöhnung möglich? Jeremia 3,1–5 als Beispiel innerbiblischer Auslegung." In *"Gott bin ich, kein Mann". Beiträge zur Hermeneutik der biblischen Gottesrede: FS Helen Schüngel-Straumann*, edited by Ilona Riedel-Spangenberger and Erich Zenger, 295–305. Paderborn: Schöningh, 2006.
Maier, Christl M. "Reading Back and Forth: Gender Trouble in Jeremiah 2–3." In *Interested Readers: Essays on the Hebrew Bible in Honor of David J. A. Clines*, edited by James K. Aitken, Jeremy M. S. Clines, and Christl M. Maier, 137–50. Atlanta, GA: Society of Biblical Literature, 2013.
Maier, Christl M. "Listening to the Trauma of Refugees in Jeremiah 40–44." *lectio difficilior* 1 (2017), http://www.lectio.unibe.ch/17_1/inhalt_d.htm.
Macwilliam, Stuart. "The Prophet and His Patsy: Gender Performativity in Jeremiah." In *Prophecy and Power: Jeremiah in Feminist and Postcolonial Perspective*, edited by Christl M. Maier and Carolyn J. Sharp, 173–88. LHBOTS 577. London: Bloomsbury T&T Clark, 2013.
Macwilliam, Stuart. *Queer Theory and the Prophetic Marriage Metaphor in the Hebrew Bible.* Sheffield: Equinox, 2011.
Macwilliam, Stuart. "Queering Jeremiah." *BibInt* 10 (2002): 384–404.
McKane, William. *A Critical and Exegetical Commentary on Jeremiah, Volume I: I–XXV.* ICC 24. Edinburgh: T&T Clark, 1986.
O'Connor, Kathleen M. "The Book of Jeremiah: Reconstructing Community after Disaster." In *Character Ethics and the Old Testament: Moral Dimensions of Scripture*, edited by M. Daniel Carroll R. and Jacqueline E. Lapsley, 81–92. Louisville, KY: Westminster John Knox, 2007.

O'Connor, Kathleen M. *Jeremiah. Pain and Promise*. Minneapolis, MN: Fortress, 2012.
Ọlọjẹde, Funlọla O. "Absence of Wife-battering in Old Testament Narratives: A Literary Omission or a Cultural Aberration?" In *Gender Agenda Matters. Papers of the "Feminist Section" of the International Meetings of the Society of Biblical Literature*, edited by Irmtraud Fischer, 87–98. Newcastle upon Tyne: Cambridge Scholars Publishing, 2015.
Sharp, Carolyn J. "Buying Land in the Text of Jeremiah: Feminist Commentary, the Kristevan Abject, and Jeremiah 32." In *Prophecy and Power: Jeremiah in Feminist and Postcolonial Perspective*, edited by Christl M. Maier and Carolyn J. Sharp, 150–72. LHBOTS 577. London: Bloomsbury T&T Clark, 2013.
Shields, Mary E. *Circumscribing the Prostitute: The Rhetorics of Intertextuality, Metaphor and Gender in Jeremiah 3.1–4.4*. JSOTSup 387. London: T&T Clark, 2004.
Wanke, Gunther. *Jeremia 1,1–25,14*. ZBK 20/1. Zurich: Theologischer Verlag, 1995.

Chapter 5

INTERRUPTIONS: STRENGTHENING INSTITUTIONS AS TRANSFORMATIVE TRANSGRESSION

Jacqueline E. Lapsley

Princeton Theological Seminary

1. *Introduction*

Transgression sounds radical and edgy, exercising whatever transformative power it possesses at the margins. But the transgression I want to explore in this essay takes place within the banal, mundane activities of quotidian institutional life. One destructive social norm that may manifest within even the best-intended institutions, ancient and contemporary, is the widespread disregard of good laws already on the books. Simply following those laws, and interrupting "business as usual" to follow those laws, becomes an act of creative transgression. The story of the woman of Shunem who, in 2 Kgs 8:1–6, interrupts the king—interrupts the "business as usual" of the king—in order to get her land, provides a useful biblical lens through which to reflect on the dynamics of institutional power when following the law is itself an act of transgression. The work of Reinhold Niebuhr will add a theological lens to these reflections.

In June of 2018, an article appeared in the *Chronicle of Higher Education* about the continuing prevalence of gender discrimination and sexual harassment perpetrated by Faculty members on college and university campuses. It was actually one in a series of articles on this topic throughout that summer. One of the steps that the author, Tricia Serio, argues will reduce the prevalence of gender discrimination on educational campuses is as follows:

> If the severity and/or frequency of the infractions rise to the level of termination and due process has been followed, colleges must be willing to follow their own guidelines… Employers, including universities, can and should play an important role in preventing [exploitation, harassment, and discriminatory treatment of students] by following policies and practices known to be effective.[1]

The clause of particular interest for the purposes of this paper is "*colleges must be willing to follow their own guidelines.*" Often schools have guidelines that are known to be effective, based on core principles such as those advocated by the U.S. government's Equal Opportunity Employment Commission. The principles include:

1. Committed and engaged leadership;
2. Consistent and demonstrated accountability;
3. Strong and comprehensive harassment policies;
4. Trusted and accessible complaint procedures; and
5. Regular, interactive training tailored to the audience and the organization.[2]

The difficulty pointed out in the present study is that, in practice, even where schools have the third item on the list—"strong and comprehensive harassment policies"—they often do not follow their own policies because they lack the second item, "consistent and demonstrated accountability."

The problem of gender discrimination in educational institutions is a good example of a larger issue within the academy; even where there is committed, engaged leadership, individuals can become so inured to allowing unethical behavior to continue that they do not *interrupt* the *institutional inertia* in order to implement their own policies. The result of these missing pieces is that the cultural norm in some institutions is to not follow their own policies. In such a context, pressing the leaders from within the institution itself to follow its own policies becomes an act of transgressing that cultural norm.

Of particular interest to me is the way in which even the best leaders, people with excellent intentions and principles, are caught up in systems

---

1. Tricia Serio, "How Colleges and Organizations Can Stop the Cycle of Faculty Sexual Abuse," *The Chronicle of Higher Education* (June 26, 2018), https://www.chronicle.com/article/How-CollegesOrganizations/243761.

2. U.S. Equal Employment Opportunity Commission, "Promising Practices for Preventing Harassment," https://www.eeoc.gov/eeoc/publications/promising-practices.cfm.

with their own fraught histories, and who then unwittingly make decisions that are unjust, even though the process itself is not inherently unjust. More careful attention to where good processes go wrong, and awareness of the ways in which the history of an institution can derail justice even when people are well-intentioned, can bring about transformation of institutional culture. But it may well require transgressive acts of interrupting business as usual, of holding institutions accountable to what is on their books—to their best values, practices, and policies.

Transgression is an effort, usually from the outside, to exert power to effect positive change. In this essay, I am focusing on how self-awareness by those *on the inside of an institution, how those with a certain degree of power*, can effect positive change. In our current cultural climate, to say that positive transgressive acts are available to those who already hold power is itself counter-cultural. In my context, there is currently widespread hostility to institutions, and widespread suspicion that institutions are rarely, if ever, capable of effecting positive change in the world. Institutions are seen as part of the problem, not part of the solution. I believe, by contrast, that institutions can be part, even a very large part, of the solution to injustice. But those who exercise power within institutions must be willing to transgress the norms of behavior when those norms sweep injustice under the rug. So, this essay addresses contexts in which persons already have a certain access to power, and how those persons might disrupt institutionalized patterns of injustice. It does not address the many contexts in which persons with little to no access to power attempt to disrupt unjust systems from outside; that is a critical area of activity, but it is not the focus of this essay.

Carolyn Sharp defines "transgression" as the "privileging of creative interventions, ancient and contemporary, that resist or reframe destructive social norms."[3] In what follows I want to reflect on transgression in this context through the lens of the story of the woman of Shunem in 2 Kings 8, who interrupts the king in order to press for a return of her land, and secondly, through a Reformed theological lens that considers the ways God's grace can flow through certain coercive actions within institutions.

For this last aspect of my reflection here, I will engage the work of Reinhold Niebuhr. Niebuhr laid out in both *The Nature and Destiny of Man* and in *Moral Man, Immoral Society*, the idea that even the

---

3. Carolyn J. Sharp, "Buying Land in the Text of Jeremiah: Feminist Commentary, the Kristevan Abject, and Jeremiah 32," in *Prophecy and Power: Jeremiah in Feminist and Postcolonial Perspective*, ed. Christl M. Maier and Carolyn J. Sharp (London: Bloomsbury T&T Clark, 2013), 159–72 (155). Cf. the Call for Papers for the Transgression and Transformation Conference for which this essay was written.

best-intentioned, "moral" human beings, often find themselves caught up in systems in which they make immoral decisions. For Niebuhr, strong institutions are not ones that wield a lot of power, necessarily, but are ones that are characterized by integrity, accountability, and committed, engaged leadership. Strong institutions are those through which God's grace, God's justice, flow out to bless all those they touch. But they require pressure to be exerted constantly from within in order for justice to be done. Coercion and grace are not opposed to one another but go hand in hand.

2. Transgressing Social Norms:
The Case of the Shunammite Woman (2 Kings 8)

But before we get to Niebuhr, I want to explore the problem through a biblical lens. The Hebrew Bible of course presents the law, the *torah*, as a gift from God for the benefit of the people. The law is meant to promote the people's flourishing. "Do these things so that it may go well with you..." is repeated throughout much of the legal material in the Pentateuch (Deut 6:8, 13, etc.). And there are numerous famous stories about individuals calling leaders to account by invoking the law, such as Nathan confronting the sexual predator and murderer, David (2 Sam 12), and Naboth confronting Ahab and Jezebel over their theft of his land (1 Kgs 21). There are also, of course, many famous transgressive women in the Hebrew Scriptures whom I might have focused on—Eve, Hagar, Rachel, Rebekah, the daughters of Zelophehad, Deborah, Abigail, Ruth, Esther, and so many others. But I here turn to a lesser-known story—the story recounted in 2 Kings 8 of the woman from Shunem who returns to Israel from a time in Philistia and goes to the king to reclaim her land. The story concerns a woman with a modicum of access and power, who invokes the law in order to exert pressure on those with the most power (in this case, the king) to see that justice is done. As Claudia Camp has observed, the Shunammite woman is one of the most remarkable in the Hebrew Bible.[4] She is powerful, intelligent, wealthy, pious, independent, observant, strategic, and persistent. She transgresses cultural norms, and in so doing accesses institutional power in order to bring about justice for herself. Precisely because the Shunammite woman is somewhat privileged—she has access to the king—her story is a useful lens for reflecting

---

4. Claudia Camp, "1 and 2 Kings," in *The Women's Bible Commentary*, ed. Carol A. Newsom and Sharon H. Ringe (Louisville, KY: Westminster John Knox, 1992), 106.

on how those with some privilege within institutions might transgress certain social norms in order to further justice in our own time.

First, a bit of background to the story told in 2 Kings 8. The Shunammite woman first meets Elisha the prophet in 2 Kings 4, where Elisha asks her how he can repay her for her unusually generous hospitality to him. She replies that she does not need anything ("I live among my own people," v. 13). But Elisha will not take no for an answer, so he asks his assistant, Gehazi, who answers *for the woman* that she must want a son. As feminist scholars have pointed out, Elisha and Gehazi provide us with early evidence for the phenomenon of mansplaining.[5] After these two men finish telling the woman what she must want, she says, "No, don't deceive me," which may mean that a child would be a gift beyond imagining, but also, "I'm not asking for this—don't set me up for crushing heartbreak." But lo and behold, she conceives and has a son, and heartbreak sure enough soon follows.

The woman's concern that she would be set up for tragedy turns out to be well-founded. She has the son, but then, horrifically, at a young age, the child dies. And so the woman experiences the crushing heartbreak she had emphatically said she did not want. Elisha is long gone by now, but this does not stop the woman from going after the "Mansplainer." She takes leave of her household responsibilities to travel to Mt. Carmel in search of Elisha. When she finds him, she confronts him with the death of her son. This idea of having a child, foisted on her by Elisha and Gehazi, has turned out badly. Elisha dispatches Gehazi to deal with the dead child, but the woman is adamant that Elisha himself must come, and she will accompany him to be sure that he does. Her dogged persistence in pursuing Elisha and holding him accountable is a powerful act of transgression; she interrupts the prophet's "business as usual." And it pays off. Elisha caves in, returns with her, and raises the boy from the dead.

Somewhat surprisingly, the woman of Shunem reappears in the narrative a few chapters later. In the intervening time, Elisha has performed a slew of miracles including feedings, healings, retrieving lost tools, miraculous military espionage, even rescuing a cooking experiment gone awry (2 Kgs 4:38–41). He has intervened in both military and political affairs such that he wields considerable power in the land by the beginning of ch. 8. At this

---

5. Yairah Amit, "A Prophet Tested Elisha, the Great Woman of Shunem and the Story's Double Message," *BibInt* 11 (2003): 287–8; Mary Shields, "Subverting a Man of God, Elevating a Woman," *JSOT* 58 (1993): 59–69; Danna N. Fewell, "The Gift: World Alteration and Obligation in 2 Kings 4:8–37," in *"A Wise and Discerning Mind": Essays in Honor of Burke O. Long*, ed. Saul M. Olyan and Robert C. Culley (Providence, RI: Brown Judaic Studies), 109–23.

point, it is revealed that Elisha had earlier told the woman of Shunem to leave Israel and sojourn in Philistia while Israel endured a famine (8:1). This time, she does not go to Elisha to advocate for herself and her family, but to the king. She literally "cries out" to the king for her house and her field, which have been taken from her (v. 3).

It seems that during the seven years she was away, her house and land were claimed either by encroaching neighbors, or by the crown itself.[6] In either case, by rights she should get her land back, though it requires pressing her case. Throughout Kings, the monarchy is presented as "extractive," to use Cameron Howard's word: "[the monarchy exists] only by means of—and for the sake of—extracting resources from [its] constituent social units."[7] That this is a woman with a certain access to power is attested by how easily she scores an audience with the king, which is likely due to her connection with Elisha. But when she arrives, the king is talking with Elisha's assistant, Gehazi, so she *interrupts* them by "crying out" for her house and her land (v. 5).[8] The two men are not just talking about any old thing, of course. No, the king is asking Gehazi to regale him with all the tremendous deeds of Elisha: "Tell me all the great things that Elisha has done" (v. 4). Business as usual often means powerful men sitting around talking about other powerful men.

This scene of the three of them, the two men and the woman of Shunem, in many ways parallels the earlier scene where Elisha and Gehazi decided, in front of the woman of Shunem, without asking her, that she really needed a son. In this scene, the two men discuss the amazing feats of Elisha, a subject on which the woman of Shunem might have some choice remarks, reflecting some ambivalent feelings. In parallel to the previous scene, the two men discuss in front of the woman of Shunem matters that are of import to her, and to which she might contribute with intelligence and knowledge. But she has to interrupt them in order to be heard.

---

6. Camp, "1 and 2 Kings," 108. Cameron Howard believes the king confiscated her land; see Cameron Howard, "1 and 2 Kings," in *Women's Bible Commentary*, ed. Jacqueline Lapsley, Carol Newsom and Sharon Ringe, 3d edn (Louisville, KY: Westminster John Knox, 2012), 176. Volkmar Fritz states: "In effect, to leave one's ground meant to give up one's property. In cases of abandonment, as also in cases of the death penalty, land would be confiscated as the king's property. The ownership of land was dependent on the actual use of property, the legal claim therefore tied to its possession rather than mere ownership." Volkmar Fritz, *1 and 2 Kings: A Continental Commentary*, trans. Anselm Hagedorn (Minneapolis, MN: Fortress, 2003), 273.

7. Howard, "1 and 2 Kings," 166.

8. How Gehazi gained a royal audience is puzzling, since by now he suffers from a leprosy-like skin disease that Elisha inflicted on him for his abuse of power and greed back in ch. 5.

Just at the moment when Gehazi is telling the king about Elisha's resuscitation of the child, here is the woman, and apparently also her son, as evidence of this miracle! But she did not come to be evidence for an account of Elisha's awesomeness. She has her own agenda, and she interrupts them. But there is an ambiguity. Verse 6 says, "When the king questioned the woman, she told him." She told him what? How fabulous Elisha was? Or why she has come? It is not clear, though most commentators think she echoes Gehazi in telling the king how fabulous Elisha is. The ambiguity of the text suggests another reading. It becomes clear that when she has her chance to speak she asks the king for her house and land back (v. 6). She has not come to join these powerful men in praising another powerful man. She has come to get justice. The king's response is to appoint an official to make sure that it happens, returning also the revenue of the field since the day she left.[9]

In sum, the woman of Shunem used the access she had to interrupt the "business as usual" of the monarchy in order to do what was just, to follow the law. And she does this without the help of the prophet. As Mark Roncace points out, "the woman efficiently gets things done on her own."[10] It is worth remembering that this is not the first time that this king[11] has heard a woman pressuring him for relief. Two chapters earlier in 2 Kings 6, another woman *cries out* to the king in the midst of the famine because she was just about to cannibalize her own child (2 Kgs 6:26). It is a parallel story, though even more grisly, to the story recounted in 1 Kings 3 where two women dispute whose child has been crushed in the night with the mother of the living child bringing the dispute to the king.

In 2 Kings 6, in the face of the grief-stricken mother of the about-to-be-cannibalized child, the king tears his clothes, but his main reaction is to attack Elisha. The king does not directly address the woman's concern. As Walter Brueggemann observes of the story of the cannibalizing mother, "She is an unexpected witness 'from below,' a marginalized woman who attests to the deep cost of famine and war brought about by patriarchal

---

9. Claudia Camp observes that the Shunammite's insistence on the return of her land leads the king to "implicitly recognize that, in Israel, the land is *not* the king's to control but rather God's." Camp, "1 and 2 Kings," 108. Contra Fritz, who sees the king as all powerful in this story, with the main point of the narrative being to show that though the woman had no rightful claim, the king is merciful (Fritz, *1 and 2 Kings*, 273).

10. Mark Roncace, "Elisha and the Woman of Shunem," *JSOT* 91 (2002): 121.

11. If it is the same king. It could be King Jehoram, but admittedly the story that begins in 2 Kgs 6:24, "Some time later King Ben-hadad of Aram…" may indicate that the chronology is disrupted between 2 Kgs 6 and 8.

power. Indeed, the makers of war rarely pay the costs of war regularly borne by the voiceless, surely the poor, always the mothers."[12] In Kings, women persistently interrupt the king by crying out, for it is they who suffer the most when institutions are broken.

In both the Shunammite's case, and that of the devastated, famine-struck mother, the king is focused on the deeds of a *man*, when it is actually a woman who interrupts, crying out for justice. The woman of Shunem's strong self-advocacy is transgressive in a society that is largely uninterested in her and others like her because the focus of those in power, the focus of the institution itself, is on men and male power. Unlike most of the stories involving Elisha, which recount supernatural miracles, note here that the Shunammite woman's powerful demand for economic justice involves no miracles—she simply transgresses the *extractive* norms, by interrupting patriarchal business as usual, in order to see justice is done.

3. *Moral Man, Immoral Society: The Niebuhrian Lens*

Having thought a bit on the Shunammite woman, I now want to reflect on transgression within institutions through a theological lens, and specifically a Reformed theological lens. In this section, I will consider Reinhold Niebuhr's argument that human beings are, as individuals, capable of ethical actions, but they are prone to be compromised when they find themselves within social and political systems.

In his work, especially in *Moral Man, Immoral Society*, but also in *The Nature and Destiny of Man*, Reinhold Niebuhr lays out a theological anthropology that drives a stake into the heart of liberal protestant theology of his day. Niebuhr understood that strong institutions are critically important to the health of society; when they are strong, they are bulwarks against the rampant spread of injustice. Niebuhr posits that "law contains within it the desire to do justice";[13] which does not mean that all laws are good, obviously. But that laws, when properly constituted, can be a vehicle for justice. "Justice is a relational term for Niebuhr; it is the relative embodiment of *agape* in the structures of society."[14] So, *agape* is not something that exists only within or between individuals, but it exists within institutions themselves, when they are marked by integrity and accountability.

---

12. Walter Brueggemann, *1 and 2 Kings* (Macon, GA: Smith & Helwys, 2000), 356.

13. Daniel F. Rice, "The Spirit of the Law in the Thought of Reinhold Niebuhr," *Journal of Law and Religion* 4, no. 2 (1986): 253–91 (257).

14. Ibid., 279.

But Niebuhr also saw how individuals of good will can become co-opted into unjust systems and perpetuate injustices within institutions. Niebuhr criticized the liberal view that saw reason as a bulwark against injustice; a view based on the idea that reason can master other human impulses. As Jeremy Luis Sabella says in speaking of Niebuhr's theological anthropology:

> ...Niebuhr argues that reason is enmeshed with non-rational social impulses, which are "more deeply rooted" in the will than is reason, and therefore [these non-rational impulses] can co-opt reason to serve their [own] purposes. While these impulses may be unselfish as well as selfish, the survival instinct predisposes the individual toward selfishness. Consequently, reason is "always, to some degree, the servant of self-interest." The efficacy of attempts to prompt social change hinges on the ability to acknowledge the ways that self-interest shapes reason, and to formulate strategies accordingly.[15]

In fact, it is not just that reason *might* further self-interest; rather, reason is *more likely* to intensify than to diminish self-interest. For Niebuhr, individuals can act *qua individuals* with apparent morality, but "as members of social groups—in class, racial, economic, or political matters—they [cannot] in any way escape doing and supporting injustice."[16]

---

15. Jeremy Luis Sabella, "Establishment Radical: Assessing the Legacy of Reinhold Niebuhr's Reflections on the End of an Era," *Political Theology* 18, no. 5 (2017): 377–98 (381).

16. Langdon B. Gilkey, "Introduction," in Reinhold Niebuhr, *Moral Man and Immoral Society: A Study in Ethics and Politics*, Library of Theological Ethics (Louisville, KY: Westminster John Knox, 1960 [orig. 1932]), xv. "Rationalism in morals may persuade men in one moment that their selfishness is a peril to society and in the next moment it may condone their egoism as a necessary and inevitable element in the total social harmony. The egoistic impulses are so powerful and insistent that they will be quick to take advantage of any such justifications" (Niebuhr, *Moral Man and Immoral Society*, 41). Niebuhr's perspective has, in the decades since he formulated his views, been subjected to a variety of critiques from various angles (e.g., liberationist, feminist/womanist). James H. Cone has famously criticized Niebuhr on the fact that asymmetrical power relations are built into his theology. A good summary of Cone's critique is available in Amy R. Barbour and Marvin E. Wickware, Jr., "Breaking the Chains of Chattel Teamwork: The Future of Black Liberation Theology," *USQR* 64 (2013): 44–51. Of course, Niebuhr's blindness to the failings of his own theology ironically argues for the persuasiveness of his theological claims, rather than negating them.

What are the implications of this human propensity toward selfishness? As Langdon Gilkey observes, for Niebuhr, "the only effective mechanism of achieving social justice is to set the interests of competing groups against one another in a way that ameliorates injustice for society as a whole. Such confrontations between social units invariably involve coercion, whether violent or non-violent."[17] Therefore, coercion of one kind or another is necessary for change, and that coercion sometimes takes the form of transgressive interventions when institutions have fallen into the ruts of doing things as they always have. Niebuhr's thought helps to illumine the problem that even where individuals with decision-making power wish to do the right thing, they are very likely to be drawn into sinful actions because a rut has developed; a pattern of avoiding or neglecting justice even among the best-intentioned. Getting out of that rut means exerting pressure, sometimes externally, to be sure, but often, internally, from within the institution.

The ethicist Robin Lovin has recently written of the particular difficulties the church faces in our current moment when other institutions have been stripped of moral vocabulary. How might the church speak in such a moment? Lovin draws on the Niebuhrian tradition of Christian Realism to argue that the church in our current context must become "a community of trust in which people can explore questions about their lives that they cannot yet ask in the places where those questions concretely arise" such as at work, in schools, and in neighborhoods.[18] But to become those communities of trust, we need to harness the benefits of coercion within our institutions, so that divine grace may flow through them.

4. Conclusion

My reflections here have been formed by my own work as an administrator. Certainly my participation in my school's administration has prompted me to think about these issues, about how and why injustice is either allowed to continue, or not. Indeed, when moments of critical decision have presented themselves, my administrative colleagues have been willing to transgress previously existing norms in order to see justice done. However, beyond my own experience as an administrator, this essay is the result of reflection on what I have witnessed myself not only in multiple institutions, but also in what I have heard reported from reliable

---

17. Gilkey, *Moral Man and Immoral Society*, 4.

18. Robin W. Lovin, "Reimagining Christian Realism: Church in an Amoral Time," *The Christian Century* (February 27, 2019): 29.

sources about institutions of higher education elsewhere, and indeed public accounts of what has happened outside of the educational sector, including in state and national governments. I return to the *Chronicle of Higher Education* article I mentioned at the beginning of my essay—the biggest problem facing institutions of higher education in the U.S. when it comes to gender justice, is having the courage to interrupt the "business as usual" of discriminatory negligence, and instead, follow the good policies that exist.

I want to lift up one almost cartoonish example of how pressure from within an institution can change it dramatically. Recently, a U.S. black civil rights activist, James Hart Stern, took over the leadership of a white supremacy organization, called the National Socialist Movement. Over a period of years, Mr. Stern managed to infiltrate and finally take the helm of this hate group, known for their denial of the Holocaust and their adoration of Hitler. I am sure that even now Hollywood is securing the rights to Mr. Stern's story so that the film version can be made, because truly, truth is stranger than fiction, and you cannot make this stuff up. Mr. Stern's story is even more bizarre and compelling than the story told in Spike Lee's film from last year, Black KkKlansman, in which a black police officer infiltrated the Ku Klux Klan.

Of particular interest for my purposes is that once Mr. Stern took control of the hate group, he did not dissolve it. Rather, he saw that it was a powerful institution, capable of shaping the minds of millions. Instead of simply closing up shop, Stern began to use its institutional power for different purposes. He is working now to transform the hate group's website, which attracts millions of visitors every year, into a space for Holocaust history lessons.[19] This example is extreme, no doubt, but it illustrates why paying attention to institutional power, and committing ourselves to transformation, are critical to effective social and cultural change.

Of course, it would help to address various forms of discrimination within institutions if we had more non-male, non-white people administering them. But regardless of who is in power, if Niebuhr is right, and I think he is, those who are willing to interrupt business as usual, like the Shunammite woman, will always be necessary. Constant internal pressure to follow the law where it is good is the only way that we will make significant progress on gender justice.

19. Katie Mettler, "How a Black Man Says He 'Outsmarted' a Neo-Nazi Group and Became Their New Leader," *The Washington Post*, 2 March 2019, https://www.washingtonpost.com/dc-md-va/2019/03/01/how-black-man-outsmarted-neo-nazi-group-became-their-new-leader/?utm_term=.e96bde7d2103.

Faith in our institutions is dangerously low. In order to restore trust in them, and to strengthen them for the good work that they can do, we need to people them with individuals who will act transgressively by holding their institutions accountable to their own policies. Practically speaking, it requires the presence of women and minoritized persons of all kinds within the leadership structures of these institutions in order to press for actually following policies and thus transgressing institutional norms. The argument I am making may seem banal—after all, what is transgressive about following the law? I am convinced, however, that in our current age, as in ancient Israel, pressure to uphold laws where they are good was and is a transgressive act. It is usually white male power that is upheld by disregarding good policy. Accordingly, it is white male power that must be disrupted through the persistent, creative pressure to follow the law. Interruption of business as usual is divine coercive grace at work.

Bibliography

Amit, Yairah. "A Prophet Tested Elisha, the Great Woman of Shunem and the Story's Double Message." *BibInt* 11 (2003): 279–94.

Barbour, Amy R., and Marvin E. Wickware Jr. "Breaking the Chains of Chattel Teamwork: The Future of Black Liberation Theology." *USQR* 64 (2013): 44–51.

Brueggemann, Walter. *1 and 2 Kings*. Macon, GA: Smith & Helwys, 2000.

Camp, Claudia. "1 and 2 Kings." In *The Women's Bible Commentary*, edited by Carol A. Newsom and Sharon H. Ringe, 106–8. Louisville, KY: Westminster John Knox, 1992.

Fewell, Danna N. "The Gift: World Alteration and Obligation in 2 Kings 4:8–37." In *"A Wise and Discerning Mind": Essays in Honor of Burke O. Long*, edited by Saul M. Olyan and Robert C. Culley, 109–23. Providence, RI: Brown Judaic Studies.

Fritz, Volkmar. *1 and 2 Kings: A Continental Commentary*. Translated by Anselm Hagedorn. Minneapolis, MN: Fortress, 2003.

Gilkey, Langdon B. "Introduction." In *Moral Man and Immoral Society: A Study in Ethics and Politics by Reinhold Niebuhr*, xv and 4. Library of Theological Ethics. Louisville, KY: Westminster John Knox, 1960 (orig. 1932).

Howard, Cameron. "1 and 2 Kings." In *Women's Bible Commentary*, edited by Jacqueline Lapsley, Carol Newsom, and Sharon Ringe, 166–76. 3rd ed. Louisville, KY: Westminster John Knox, 2012.

Lovin, Robin W. "Reimagining Christian Realism: Church in an Amoral Time." *The Christian Century* (February 27, 2019): 26–9.

Mettler, Katie. "How a Black Man Says He 'Outsmarted' a Neo-Nazi Group and Became Their New Leader." *The Washington Post*, https://www.washingtonpost.com/dc-md-va/2019/03/01/how-black-man-outsmarted-neo-nazi-group-became-their-new-leader/?utm_term=.e96bde7d2103.

Rice, Daniel F. "The Spirit of the Law in the Thought of Reinhold Niebuhr." *Journal of Law and Religion* 4, no. 2 (1986): 253–91.

Roncace, Mark. "Elisha and the Woman of Shunem." *JSOT* 91 (2002): 109–27.

Sabella, Jeremy Luis. "Establishment Radical: Assessing the Legacy of Reinhold Niebuhr's Reflections on the End of an Era." *Political Theology* 18, no. 5 (2017): 377–98.

Serio, Tricia. 2018. "How Colleges and Organizations Can Stop the Cycle of Faculty Sexual Abuse." *The Chronicle of Higher Education*, https://www.chronicle.com/article/How-CollegesOrganizations/243761.

Sharp, Carolyn J. "Buying Land in the Text of Jeremiah: Feminist Commentary, the Kristevan Abject, and Jeremiah 32." In *Prophecy and Power: Jeremiah in Feminist and Postcolonial Perspective*, edited by Christl M. Maier and Carolyn J. Sharp, 159–72. London: Bloomsbury T&T Clark, 2013.

Shields, Mary. "Subverting a Man of God, Elevating a Woman." *JSOT* 58 (1993): 59–69.

U.S. Equal Employment Opportunity Commission. "Promising Practices for Preventing Harassment," https://www.eeoc.gov/eeoc/publications/promising-practices.cfm.

Chapter 6

Torah as Instruction to Establish Justice: Rethinking Childbirth and Cultic Purity According to Leviticus 12*

Hendrik L. Bosman

Stellenbosch University

1. Introduction

It is estimated that more than 275,000 women die each year due to pregnancy or childbirth.[1] According to the World Health Organisation (WHO), up to 95 percent of "maternal deaths" (the death of women while pregnant or within 42 days of pregnancy and not due to accidental or incidental causes) occur in developing countries, the majority of which are located in sub-Saharan Africa.[2]

---

* This article is dedicated to Professor Elna Mouton as a token of appreciation for her creative and constructive scholarship over many years, and warm collegiality during the past two decades. Elna Mouton has indicated some interest in childbirth in the New Testament as she, in collaboration with Ellen van Wolde, identified a strand in the interpretation of 1 Tim 2:13–15 in which childbirth functioned metaphorically as motivation for moral behavior. See Elna Mouton and Ellen van Wolde, "New Life from a Pastoral Text of Terror? Gender Perspectives on God and Humanity in 1 Timothy 2," *Scriptura* 111 (2012): 583–601.

1. M. Koblinsky et al., "Maternal Mortality and Disability and Their Consequences," *Journal of Health, Population and Nutrition* 30, no. 2 (2012): 124–30.

2. World Health Organisation, "Maternal Mortality," *Fact Sheet* 348 (2014).

Childbirth is a phenomenon that is embedded in different cultures and religions across the globe. The cultural and religious processes relating to childbirth have functional and symbolic aspects that are closely interrelated. Nyambura Njoroge, an African feminist theologian, laments the plight of African women who are "groaning and languishing in labour pains…"[3] These labor pains are not to be equated with the curses and punishment related to childbirth in different cultures but might be suggestive of the pain and suffering implied by childbirth in general. Similarly, Juliana Claassens affirms that in ancient times, childbirth often caused the death of both the child and the mother—so much so that "a successful birth was celebrated as an act of deliverance in praise songs" such as Isa 42:5.[4]

2. *Torah and Justice in the Book of Leviticus*

(a) *Torah in Leviticus*

"Torah" cannot be adequately understood as "law" in the modern sense of the word as codified legislation. William Morrow reminds us that *torah* initially "meant 'instruction' or 'teaching'" and eventually "came to mean the sum total of teaching that stem from Israel's encounter with God."[5] In general terms, the Pentateuch as Torah instructed the people of Israel on how to live as a community of faith within the two broad parameters of maintaining purity and holiness (Priestly instruction), as well as justice (Deuteronomic instruction).[6] Both trajectories of the meaning of *torah* were shaped according to the example set by God and stipulated in the three legal collections (the so-called Covenant Code in Exodus; Holiness Code in Leviticus and the Deuteronomic Code in Deuteronomy).

A false juxtaposition claims that priests propagated *torah* as "law" to undergird the status quo while the prophets challenged it. One should note, however, many examples in which *torah* in the Bible was as radical as the prophets who challenged social conventions prevalent in Palestine

---

3. Nyambura Njoroge, "Groaning and Languishing in Labor Pains: But for How Long Lord?" in *Groaning in Faith*, ed. R.A. Musimbi Kanyoro and Nyambura Njoroge (Nairobi: Acton, 1996), 6.

4. L. Juliana M. Claassens, *Mourner, Mother, Midwife: Reimagining God's Delivering Presence in the Old Testament* (Louisville, KY: Westminster John Knox, 2012), 50.

5. William S. Morrow, *An Introduction to Biblical Law* (Grand Rapids, MI: Eerdmans, 2017), 3.

6. Walter Brueggemann, *Theology of the Old Testament: Testimony, Dispute and Advocacy* (Minneapolis, MN: Fortress, 1997), 187–97.

and the adjacent ancient Near East.[7] It seems Leviticus 12 could be interpreted as priestly instruction that critiqued existing cultural and religious perceptions related to childbirth.

Therefore, the following sections will consider the possibility that Leviticus 12 as instruction not only indicated how the parturient should act after childbirth, but that it also challenged certain existing norms related to childbirth in an attempt to do justice to the mother by reintegrating her back into the (postexilic) faith community.

b) *Justice in Leviticus*

According to Eckart Otto, the understanding of justice in the ancient Near East and in the Hebrew Bible highlighted the point that it is "basically one of connectivity"—not only between the people and the gods, but also between the individual and different collectives (family, clan, tribe, nation, etc.).[8] There is a longstanding and erroneous assumption that the cultic commands of the Hebrew Bible or Old Testament have been fulfilled, whilst the ethical commands must still be adhered to.[9] Recent studies of the Priestly instruction and of the Holiness Code in Leviticus 17–26 have clearly shown that purity, holiness and ethics are intimately intertwined.[10] Priestly instruction on childbirth can thus benefit from an investigation that considers the role justice played in the regulations regarding the maintenance of purity in Leviticus 12.

In general, justice, according to the Bible, is established when authoritative rules show individuals and groups how to act in specific circumstances.[11] The possibility that the instructions concerning childbirth established justice by enabling the mother of the child to remain as a fully fledged member of the Israelite or Jewish society and cultic community after forty or eighty days invites further discussion.

In particular, Mary Douglas has already viewed justice as the cornerstone of Leviticus 18–20.[12] Although Douglas initially advocated that Leviticus be read from the point of view that it primarily addressed the

---

7. Ibid., 22.

8. Eckart Otto, "Justice and Righteousness," in *Religion Past and Present: Encyclopedia of Theology and Religion, vol. 7, I, Bible*, ed. Hans Dieter Betz (Leiden: Brill, 2010), 106–7.

9. Brueggemann, *Theology*, 194.

10. Thomas Hieke, *Leviticus 1–15*, HThKAT (Freiburg: Herder, 2014).

11. Harold V. Bennett, "Justice. OT," *NIDB* 3:476–7.

12. Mary Douglas, "Justice as the Cornerstone: An Interpretation of Leviticus 18–20," *Int* 53 (1999): 341–50.

dangers of impurity as understood by priests,[13] she eventually argued that Leviticus was an example of ancient literature that focused on "the tabernacle and God's justice expressed in the covenant."[14] According to Douglas, holiness in Leviticus is much more than the strict adherence to cultic ritual, because it also entails instruction on "what God's people must do for each other in secular contexts… The ritual laws, in short, are grounded in justice."[15] Is justice served when a mother becomes ritually unclean after giving birth to a child? Adding insult to injury: why should the mother be ritually unclean for twice as long after giving birth to a girl as after the birth of a boy?[16] These questions inform the following exploration into childbirth and cultic purity in the book of Leviticus.

3. Cultic Purity in Leviticus

A brief but significant definition of impurity or ritual uncleanness comes from Mary Douglas, who describes impurity as "dirt out of place."[17] The priests had the responsibility to discern how to manage this "dirt" by means of an elaborate system of purity laws, of which Leviticus 12 forms a part. Instructions related to purity and the maintenance of cleanness are closely related to social order, which was related to "controlling boundaries, preserving hierarchies and promoting social cohesion—in a word community-making."[18] Translating *ṭâmē'* as "unclean" must be qualified as the term had little to do with the modern understanding of hygiene and sanitation, but rather with a lifestyle that allowed a person access to the religious rituals in the tabernacle and the temple in Jerusalem.[19] Dorothea Erbele-Küster makes the important observation that "purity" and "impurity" come into being as a result of gendered use of language and intersect with the societal construction of both gender and body.[20] Furthermore, I concur with Morrow that it is possible to trace this societal construction of body and gender to the priestly system of purity

---

13. Mary Douglas, *Purity and Danger: An Analysis of the Concepts of Pollution and Taboo* (London: Routledge & Kegan & Paul, 1966).
14. Douglas, "Justice," 341.
15. Ibid., 348.
16. Morrow, *Biblical Law*, 159.
17. Douglas, *Purity*, 63.
18. Morrow, *Biblical Law*, 160.
19. James L. Mays, *Leviticus. Numbers* (London: SCM, 1964), 45.
20. Dorothea Erbele-Küster, *Body, Gender and Purity in Leviticus 12 and 15*, LHBOTS 539 (London: Bloomsbury, 2017), 1.

regulations that made use of binary opposites such as "holy (*qadôš*) versus profane (*ḥôl*) or clean (*ṭāhôr*) versus unclean (*ṭāmē'*)."[21]

Children are considered a gift from God (Ps 127:3), and childbirth itself is not evil, sinful or impure. However, Leviticus 12 contains the most significant priestly instruction related to childbirth in the Pentateuch and the Hebrew Bible.[22] This instruction clearly indicates that the parturient (birthing mother) would undergo cultic impurity for up to forty days after the birth of a son and up to eighty days after the birth of a daughter.

Many reasons have been suggested to explain the collection of bodily impurities described in Leviticus 12–15, of which the instructions concerning childbirth form the introduction—sin, fear of demons, safeguarding the holiness of the Israelite sanctuaries (tabernacle, temple in Jerusalem), health reasons, enhancing priestly power and influence, and so on.[23] In partial agreement with Jacob Milgrom, this essay argues that the loss of blood during childbirth not only caused cultic impurity but also endangered life and was thus associated with death.[24] Cultic purity cannot by solely explained in terms of death or even the intertwined nature of *eros* and *thanatos*—any priestly instruction, including those linked to childbirth, must be considered against the background of establishing justice in the relationships amongst the people of God, and between the people and their God.

4. *Childbirth in Ancient Israel*

At first glance, one could say that birth stories in the Hebrew Bible usually describe extraordinary rather than routine births, and the following sequence of events can be found in most of them[25]—a barren wife desires a child, an angel announces the birth, the birth is accompanied by miracles, a hostile force or danger threatens the new born, God protects the endangered child (e.g., Moses, Samson, Samuel, etc.).

However, the many birthing rituals found in the ancient Near East as well as in Israel point to the fact that giving birth is a very ordinary

---

21. Morrow, *Biblical Law*, 160.
22. J. Roy Porter, *Leviticus*, CBC (Cambridge: Cambridge University Press, 1976), 94.
23. Jacob Milgrom, *Leviticus 1–16*, AB, 3 (New York: Doubleday, 1991), 766; Hieke, *Leviticus 1–15*, 461–5.
24. Ibid., 767–8.
25. Claudia D. Bergmann, *Childbirth as a Metaphor for Crisis: Evidence from the Ancient Near East, the Hebrew Bible and 1QH XI, 1–18*, BZAW 382 (Berlin: de Gruyter, 2008).

occurrence that affects the community in some concrete ways. Gary Beckman established in his study of Hittite birth rituals that special ceremonies were carried out to introduce the new-born and to reintegrate the new mother into the community.[26] For example, an offering was made seven days after birth, and the male baby was ritually cleansed at the beginning of the third month, while the baby girl was cleansed at the beginning of the fourth month.

Amy Kalmanofsky mentions that, on average, the limited size of houses in ancient Israel indicated relatively small families—about 4.1 pregnancies per woman with less than half (1.9) of them being live births.[27] This suggests a mortality rate of more than 50 percent for children and slightly less for the birthing mothers, indicating that childbirth in the Hebrew Bible was often considered a source of horror!

In this regard, it might be worthwhile to consider the various conceptions of childbirth in the Hebrew Bible. For instance, in Gen 3:16, childbirth is linked to suffering and not to sin. In Deut 32:18, childbirth is referred to in a figurative manner in order to describe the intimate relationship between God and Israel, as his people. And particularly in the Prophets, childbirth is used as a metaphor for crisis. For instance, in Isa 21:2–3; 26:16–21; 66:7–14 and Jer 4:31; 13:21; 22:23; 30:6; 49:24; 50:43, repeated use is made of the image or metaphor of an anguished woman giving birth to express the reaction to the judgment of God.[28] The woman in labor metaphor is used to express the "extreme vulnerability" experienced by the exiles in Babylon.[29] And lastly, in wisdom literature such as Job 38:29, childbirth is used in a figurative way to describe the creative activity of God.

Against this background, how is one to understand the reference in Lev 12:1–8 to the unclean effect of childbirth on the mother, lasting up to eighty days? In particular, given that giving birth was considered a "normal human activity" that was by no means considered sinful, this association of childbirth with unbcleanness needs to be explored further.[30]

---

26. Gary Beckman, *Hittite Birth Rituals*, 2nd ed. (Wiesbaden: Harrassowitz, 1983), 134–7.

27. Amy Kalmanofsky, "Israel's Baby: The Horror of Childbirth in the Biblical Prophets," *BibInt* 16 (2008): 60–82.

28. Bergmann, *Childbirth*, 2008.

29. L. Juliana M. Claassens, "The Rhetorical Function of the Woman in Labor Metaphor in Jeremiah 30–31: Trauma, Gender and Postcolonial Perspectives," *JTSA* 150 (2014): 67–84.

30. Morrow, *Biblical Law*, 161.

Divergent reasons have been suggested for linking "uncleanness" with childbirth.[31] In previous generations, several German scholars agreed that Leviticus 12 was added to supplement Leviticus 15 without adequately explaining why it was inserted before the instruction it was supposed to supplement.[32] More recently, however, scholars like John Sailhamer and Nobuyoshi Kiuchi have suggested that the arrangements of topics in Leviticus 11–15 correspond with the sequence of events narrated in Genesis 2–3—but that, at most, there is only an approximate fit between the events in these two texts.

5. *Justice through Reintegration in Society According to Leviticus 12*[33]

The book of Leviticus seems to have the following agenda: to instruct Israel on how to refrain from defilement and maintain purity, as well as to purge the sanctuary or temple from impurity and maintain holiness—addressed not only to priests and Levites as cultic personnel, but also to the people of God in general.[34]

Leading up to the so-called Holiness Code in Leviticus 17–26, instructions on sacrifice (Lev 1–7) and purity (Lev 11–15) are found.[35] Leviticus 11–15 forms a unit, both structurally and in terms of content. According to Vriezen and Van der Woude, the literary unity is established by corresponding introductions, "The Lord spoke to Moses [and Aaron]" in Lev 11:1; 12:1; 13:1; 14:1, 33 and 15:1, and similar concluding formulas, "This is the law [ritual]…" in Lev 11:46; 12:7; 13:59; 14:32, 54 and 15:32–33.[36]

The topics outlined in Leviticus 11–15 are uncleanness associated with animals (Lev 11), ritual defilement following childbirth (Lev 12), uncleanness caused by skin diseases (Lev 13–14), and uncleanness

---

31. Leigh M. Trevaskis, *Holiness, Ethics and Ritual in Leviticus*, HBM 29 (Sheffield: Sheffield Phoenix, 2011), 161–6.

32. These German scholars include August Dillmann (1880), Julius Wellhausen (1899), and Alfred Bertholet (1901).

33. Since this contribution is aimed at a more general audience, less attention will be given to exegetical detail.

34. Walter Brueggemann, *An Introduction to the Old Testament: The Canon and Christian Imagination* (Louisville, KY: Westminster John Knox, 2003), 68.

35. Werner H. Schmidt, *Einführung in das Alte Testament*, 2nd ed. (Berlin: de Gruyter, 1982), 94.

36. Theodorus C. Vriezen and Adriaan S. van der Woude, *Oudisraëlitische en Vroegjoodse Literatuur*, 10th ed. (Kampen: Kok, 2000), 202.

associated with reproduction and fertility (Lev 15).[37] This thematic unity is further characterized by binary combinations such as "pure versus impure," or "clean versus unclean." In this regard, one must keep in mind that being "impure" or "unclean" does not suggest hygienic cleanliness or moral purity.[38] Linda Schearing argues that it is therefore quite possible that Leviticus 12 forms part of a so-called Manual of Purity in Lev 11:1–15:33, and is "sandwiched between regulations concerning clean and unclean animals (Lev 11) and the diagnosis of skin disease (Lev 13)."[39]

Several suggestions have been made about the possible structure of Leviticus 12:[40]

a. Introductory command to Moses (v. 1);
b. Uncleanness or defilement due to birth of a son (vv. 2–4);
c. Uncleanness or defilement due to birth of a daughter (v. 5);
d. Sacrifices after the time of purification (vv. 6–7);
e. Alternative sacrifices for the poor—possible later addition (v. 8).

Leviticus 12:1 starts with the same introductory formula as the other five sections of Leviticus 11–15. One should note that in this introduction, only Moses, without Aaron, is addressed by the Lord.

In Lev 12:2, the mother is said to go through a seven-day period of uncleanness after the birth of a son and it probably entailed some form of isolation (v. 2a). According to v. 2b, the mother's uncleanness was due to her bleeding during and following childbirth and this assumption is corroborated by the comparison with menstrual uncleanness in Lev 15:19–23. There is no suggestion in this text that the mother is unclean due to childbirth as such or that childbirth was considered sinful.[41] Although circumcision was already addressed in Genesis 17, an almost incidental reference is made to the circumcision of the male child in Lev 12:3.

---

37. Gordon J. Wenham, *The Book of Leviticus*, NICOT (London: Hodder & Stoughton, 1979), 186.

38. Gerstenberger, *Leviticus*, 128.

39. Linda Schearing, "Double Time... Double Trouble? Gender, Sin, and Leviticus 12," in *The Book Leviticus: Composition and Reception*, ed. Rolf Rendtorff and Robert A. Kugler, VTSup 93 (Leiden: Brill, 2003), 430.

40. Walter C. Kaiser, "Leviticus," *NIB* 1:1084.

41. Frank Gorman, *A Commentary on the Book of Leviticus*, ITC (Grand Rapids: Eerdmans, 1997), 77.

The topic of circumcision seems to be somewhat out of place in this chapter. Some exegetes, like Erhard Gerstenberger, are of the opinion that it constituted "the primary focus" of the text and that it portrays the "male-congregational perspective."[42] On the one hand, given the general theme of cultic purity in Leviticus 11–15, it seems unlikely that circumcision is the "primary focus" of this chapter. On the other hand, circumcision was the symbol or sign of the covenantal relationship between YHWH and Israel and Leviticus 12 could be interpreted as an instruction to re-establish the relationship of the mother and the child with God and the Israelite or Jewish community.[43] It is of interest to note that circumcision is found in several ancient Middle Eastern cultures (like Egypt), forming part of the rites of passage from puberty to adulthood.[44] In Israel, however, circumcision is a sign of the covenantal relationship between a new-born child and YHWH—the child being recognized as a full-fledged member of the community of God's people.

Leviticus 12:4 stipulates that although the mother is no longer unclean after seven or fourteen days, she is required to stay at home and avoid any contact with anything holy or sacred.[45] No fewer than 33 additional days had to pass before the mother was allowed to bring the sacrifices that reintegrated her fully into the community and that made her normal participation in religious rituals possible. In South Africa, several ethnic groups such as the BaPedi and BaTsonga also quarantine the mother or parturient for prolonged periods of time.[46]

It is striking that according to Lev 12:5, the period of uncleanness was double (14 and 66 days) if the child was female. Various reasons have been offered to justify why the birth of a daughter led to a longer period of impurity. One can only speculate about the significance of the forty- and eighty-day periods of purification and about the sharp discrepancy between the two. Martin Noth provides a questionable reason for this longer period of impurity—the so-called cultic inferiority of the female sex.[47] This suggested reason probably reveals more about the presuppositions of the commentator than of the biblical text. More recently, Matthew Thiessen conducted a study of ancient embryology (Hittite, Greek, Roman, Jewish and Christian), and introduced findings that indicate that

---

42. Gerstenberger, *Leviticus*, 148.
43. Porter, *Leviticus*, 95.
44. Berend Maarsingh, *Leviticus*, POT (Nijkerk: Callenbach, 1974), 103.
45. John Hartley, *Leviticus*, WBC 4 (Dallas, TX: Word, 1992), 168.
46. Milgrom, *Leviticus 1–16*, 765.
47. Martin Noth, *Leviticus*, OTL (London: SCM, 1965), 97.

according to ancient medicine, the female developed more slowly in the uterus than the faster-growing male fetus, which consumed more fluid during the pregnancy.[48] This difference in the development, according to Thiessen, caused less lochial discharge during the birth of a male child and thus generated a shorter period of impurity.[49] This embryological explanation is similar to the speculation in the Mishna (*m. Nid.* 3, 7) that the male embryo was fully developed after 41 days, while it took 81 days for the female embryo to reach the same stage.[50] It is clear that the final word in this regard has not yet been spoken, but it seems that the difference in the duration of uncleanness or impurity for the mother after birth is gender-related.[51]

Leviticus 12:6 is another enigmatic instruction that required the mother, after the period of purification, to bring a burnt offering to the priest at the tent of meeting. The type of sacrifice was not determined by the gender of the child—a lamb for the burnt offering and a pigeon or turtledove for the sin offering. Notably, in this case, the mother and not the father was allowed to bring the offering to the priest in attendance at the sanctuary.[52]

It seems that Lev 12:7a provides a reason for this purification ritual—to cleanse the mother from the "flow of blood" that occurred during childbirth. One could well ask: why did this "flow of blood" cause impurity or uncleanness?[53]

The concluding formula, "this is the law," is found in Lev 12:7b and is peculiar to the purity instructions in Leviticus 11 to 15. It might be an indication that these chapters once functioned as an independent collection.

In Lev 12:8, there is an economic concession for the poor, as they can also comply with the requirements of this compulsory ritual by bringing two turtledoves for the burnt offering and two pigeons for a sin or

---

48. Matthew Thiessen, "The Legislation of Leviticus 12 in Light of Ancient Embryology," *VT* 68 (2018): 297–319.

49. Thiessen points out that this embryological explanation resonates with the views of Aristotle and Pliny the Elder that a male fetus develops quicker than a female fetus due to the supposed superiority of the male; see Thiessen, "Leviticus 12," 297–319. According to Gerstenberger, it is ironic that in the history of the Christian interpretation of Lev 12 the extended period of female impurity was used as an argument against the cultic equality of women; Gersternberger, *Leviticus*, 152.

50. Hieke, *Leviticus 1–16*, 453.

51. Erbele-Küster, *Body, Gender and Purity*, 138.

52. Noth, *Leviticus*, 98.

53. Norman H. Snaith, *Leviticus and Numbers*, CBC (London: Nelson, 1967), 91.

purification offering. Noth points out that the smaller sacrifice for the poor did not diminish the effectiveness of the purification.[54]

It is not entirely clear whether Lev 12:8 is a later addition due to severe economic conditions or whether this was the concluding description of the ritual process that allowed a mother to move from impurity to purity.[55] The usual closing formula in Lev 12:7 indicates, however, that v. 8 was added, while the content resonates well with the preceding verses.

In sum, the main case or instruction in Leviticus 12 is introduced by the particle *kî* ("if") in Lev 12:2b–4 (birth of a boy), while *'îm* ("then") marks the subsidiary clauses in Lev 12:5 (the birth of a girl) and Lev 12:8 (more affordable burnt offerings for poor mothers).[56]

In this shortest chapter of the book of Leviticus, the purification of the mother is not established by magic but by a sacrifice that renews the relationship between mother, God and community.[57] Furthermore, one should note that in Lev 12:6–8, the priest assists the purification of the mother afflicted by severe impurity.[58] Whereas exposure to unclean animals in Leviticus 11 caused lower level impurity, the purification can be "performed without priestly mediation" by lay people.[59]

Besides establishing justice for the birthing mother, the assertion of priestly authority cannot be ignored. Leviticus 12–15 thus highlights the central role that priests played in the purification of severe pollution or impurity. Nathan Hays argues that a postexilic redaction in Leviticus 10–16, combined with the concentrated use of terminology related to "impure" or "unclean" (*tāmē'*) and "pure" or "clean" (*ṭāhôr*), reasserted the role of the priest.[60] According to James Watts, these chapters establish

---

54. Mary, as mother of Jesus, also brought this offering that was instituted for the poor after the birth of her son, "according to the law of Moses" (Luke 2:22–24).

55. Gorman, *Leviticus*, 80.

56. Morrow, *Biblical Law*, 167–8. Cf. also Wenham, *Leviticus*, 185, who has found similar instructional patterns in Lev 1 and 4–5.

57. Walter Kornfeld, *Leviticus*, Neue Echter Bibel (Würzburg: Echter, 1983), 48–9. Although Lev 12 is the shortest chapter in the book of Leviticus, it does not only pose interpretive challenges, but also discusses highly emotive issues that have led to many a heated and emotional discussion in the past two millennia; see Hieke, *Leviticus 1–16*, 444.

58. James W. Watts, "Ritual Rhetoric in the Pentateuch: The Case of Leviticus 1–16," in *The Books of Leviticus and Numbers*, ed. Thomas Römer, BETL 215 (Leuven: Peeters, 2008), 313.

59. Ibid., 314–15.

60. Nathan Hays, "The Redactional Reassertion of the Priestly Role in Leviticus 10–16," *ZAW* 130 (2018): 175–88.

the authority of the (Aaronide?) priests to perform ritual practices that sustain life by maintaining boundaries that distinguish between pure and impure as well as between sacred and profane.[61]

6. Conclusion

According to Tamar Kamionkowski, a commentary on Leviticus with a distinctly feminist and gender interest can do the following: (a) pay attention to ignored aspects of the text; (b) identify the oppressive and problematic aspects of the texts and investigate what ideologies of power undergird them; (c) uncover the ideologies that critique patriarchal assumptions; (d) fill gaps in the texts with an informed imagination (latter day midrash?).[62] In this essay, I have argued that the aspect of justice has been neglected in the interpretation of Leviticus 12; that the role of the priests must not be forgotten as part of a male-dominated cultic praxis; that the instructions related to childbirth do not only aim to exclude or separate mothers from their faith communities, but rather to reintegrate them—resonating with an understanding of justice that is characterized by connectivity.

Perhaps more attention should be given to Claudia Bergmann's warning that "childbirth is an experience that cannot be understood and described in its totality."[63] It should therefore not come as a surprise that no conclusive or final explanation has been provided for doubling the time of uncleanness or impurity for a mother after giving birth to a girl.

With William Morrow, it is difficult to deny the influence of "androcentric values" in Leviticus 12. However, Dorothea Erbele-Küster is also correct in pointing out that in Leviticus 12, these androcentric concerns surface in the gender-specific instructions related to the supposed impurity of the mother after childbirth as articulated by the priests.[64] In distinction to the lay intervention regarding dietary laws in the preceding ch. 11, it is emphasized in Leviticus 12 that reintegration into the cultic sphere and worshipping community was mediated by (male) priests.

---

61. Watts, *Ritual Rhetoric*, 315. See also Robert Kugler, "Leviticus," in *The Pentateuch*, ed. Gale A. Yee et al., Fortress Commentary on the Bible Study Edition (Minneapolis, MN: Fortress, 2016), 192.
62. S. Tamar Kamionkowski, *Leviticus* (Collegeville, MN: Liturgical, 2018), xlvii–xlviii.
63. Bergmann, *Childbirth*, 1.
64. Morrow, *Biblical Law*, 168–9; Erbele-Küster, *Body, Gender and Purity*, 150.

Any interpretation of Leviticus 12 is challenged by inescapable ambiguity—that giving birth is dangerous to both mother and child and is perceived to threaten the holiness of religious sanctuaries; but it also indicates how amidst the above-mentioned threats, relationships with God and people can be established, re-established and maintained.[65]

The major cause of maternal death over millennia remains childbirth. Even today, childbirth continues to put the mother and the child in mortal danger.[66] Amidst the lingering androcentric impact, the instructions regarding childbirth are a telling example of the importance of life and how justice is established to safeguard mothers as the bearers of life against the forces of death that threaten during childbirth and postnatal recovery (as perceived by the authors of the Hebrew Bible more than two millennia ago).

It is significant that the instructions regarding childbirth and the period thereafter were not only about keeping birthing mothers out, but also establishing a process through which they could be reintegrated into the worshiping community.[67] Furthermore, the metaphor of the woman in labor utilized by exilic and postexilic prophets indicates that the birthing mother was seen as a symbol of vulnerability that elicited concern and not just perceived as a source of cultic impurity that had to be kept at a distance.[68] Baruch Levine also argues that the extended periods of impurity imposed on the mother are due to her perceived vulnerability.[69] One might add that the impurity instructions only excluded the mother on a temporary basis to ensure longer term inclusion in the community and access to the sanctuaries.

Leviticus 12 thus combines concerns for the maintenance of purity, cleanness and holiness with the responsibility of safeguarding justice by re-establishing connectivity between mother and community. The mentioning of circumcision is a further indication that not only the

---

65. Maarsingh, *Leviticus*, 105.
66. Morrow, *Biblical Law*, 168–9.
67. Schearing, "Leviticus 12," 450, points out that the purity instructions in Lev 12 have influenced both Jewish and Christian readers over two millennia to exclude mothers from faith communities by means of numerous practices, making it all the more important to rethink how these instructions could lead to justice.
68. Claassens, "Woman in Labor," 67–84. Bergmann, *Childbirth*, 1, also points out that childbirth was perceived to be a symbol of courage and heroism and that warriors in battle were compared to women giving birth—see Jer 48:41; 49:22.
69. Baruch Levine, *Leviticus*, JPS Torah Commentaries (Philadelphia, PA: Jewish Publication Society, 1989), 249.

mother, but also the new-born child is seen as part of the covenantal relationship between YHWH and Israel. Leviticus 12 also suggests that the so-called Priestly Torah was not only interested in priestly matters but also took into consideration the mothers and children that formed an integral part of the people of God.

This essay has attempted to dig "deeper than the topsoil of Israel's purity system" and has suggested that justice is part of the "bedrock" of all priestly *torah* or instruction.[70] Justice is served when the establishment of religious (covenantal) relationships are confirmed by the instruction in Leviticus 12; for the first time in the case of the new-born child, and re-established in terms of the mother.[71] Cultic ritual related to childbirth and impurity in Leviticus 12 is not merely a "blunt instrument" of priestly control, but is grounded in justice and it enables the enactment of the instruction that pointed to the reintegration of the mother in society.[72] This creative intervention becomes clear when one considers that Leviticus 12 entails both a "separation ritual" of seven or fourteen days (vv. 2 and 5) due to the impurity caused by the childbirth, and a transformation ritual

---

70. Schearing, "Leviticus 12," 450.

71. There must be a clear distinction made between "justice" as a forensic or legal concept concerned with enabling justifiable relationships and "righteousness" as a moral concept that is often related to being "clean" and "unclean" or "pure" and "impure." Although all these concepts are related, the former is emphasized in this discussion. Reflecting on the distinction between "justice" and "righteousness" one must also keep Milgrom's comment in mind that the basic values of Israelite priests are "ensconced in the rituals prescribed by the priestly texts of the Pentateuch"; see Jacob Milgrom, "Seeing the Ethical within the Ritual," *Bible Review* (August 1992): 6, 13. Although Hieke, *Leviticus 1–16*, 449, is correct that the instructions regulating the impurity emanating from childbirth is "*keinerlei moralischer Makel*," how these instructions were applied had implications for the establishment of justice as justifiable relationships. To quote Hieke, *Leviticus 1–16*, 462, again: "*Eine zentrale Aufgabe des Rituals wiederum ist es, derartige Verunsicherung aufzufangen und so den/die einzelne/n und die Gemeinschaft zu stabilisieren.*"

72. Jonathan Klawans, "Review Essay. Rethinking Leviticus and Rereading Purity and Danger," *AJS Review* 27 (2003): 89–102. Musimbi Kanyoro, "Where Are the African Women in the Theological Debate?" *Journal of Constructive Theology* 6, no. 2 (2000): 3–20, describes how the struggle against colonialism and imperialism in Africa has led to the lamentable position that the "quest for justice for women is trivialised in favour of 'larger' issues such as national liberation, famine, disease, war, poverty etc." She further points out, "Many women in Africa testify to the Churches' fears and suspicions of women's sexuality and therefore sexuality is given as an excuse for denying ordination to women…and because of that, women are seen to be unacceptable for church leadership." Kanyoro, "African Women," 16–17.

lasting 33 or 66 days indicated as purification by blood.[73] The latter goes beyond mere exclusion and patriarchal control, as it clearly facilitates the reintegration of the mother into the society—ensuring that the mother again becomes part of the larger community that forms an essential part of justice as societal connectivity.

Rethinking childbirth has opened up new interpretive options to consider how the instructions in Leviticus 12 furthered justice amidst and despite priestly and patriarchal control. Purity and holiness do not only relate to the cult and the sanctuary in particular,[74] but are also pertinent to the enactment in relation to the body of the mother—this "embodiment" of justice invites more attention and research in future.[75]

Finally, in dialogue with Elna Mouton and Ellen van Wolde,[76] one may end with the question: "how do we respect the text as a product of its time and at the same time allow it to inform and transform our own rhetoric and praxis, so that the integrity of God's justice seeking new creation… will likewise be recognised by all?" Is Leviticus 12, in the words of Mouton and Van Wolde, "irretrievably patriarchal"?[77] This essay argues that we can read against the patriarchal and priestly grain and allow the text to speak for justice, not only then (postexilic Yehud and the Jewish diaspora) but also now (in our various twenty-first century contexts). By means of such creative interventions, transgression indeed may lead to transformation.

Bibliography

Beckman, Gary. *Hittite Birth Rituals.* 2d ed. Wiesbaden: Harrassowitz, 1983.
Bennett, Harold V. "Justice. OT." *NIDB* 3:476–7.
Bergmann, Claudia D. *Childbirth as a Metaphor for Crisis: Evidence from the Ancient Near East, the Hebrew Bible and 1QH XI, 1–18.* BZAW 382. Berlin: de Gruyter, 2008.
Bertholet, Alfred. *Leviticus.* KHC. Tübingen: Mohr, 1901.
Brueggemann, Walter. *Theology of the Old Testament: Testimony, Dispute and Advocacy.* Minneapolis, MN: Fortress, 1977.

---

73. Erbele-Küster, *Body, Gender and Purity*, 39.
74. Ibid., 151, 162.
75. Meyer argues persuasively that although bodily impurity and ritual impurity can be distinguished from one another in Leviticus, one should also keep in mind that that both were integrated into one cultic system. It is this comprehensive cultic system that not only separated the mother from her community but that also reintroduced her back into the community. Esias E. Meyer, "Liggaamlike en morele onreinheid in Levitikus: 'n geïntegreerde reinigingsisteem," *LitNet Akademies* 16, no. 3 (2019): 393.
76. Mouton and van Wolde, "1 Timothy 2," 596.
77. Ibid., 597.

Brueggemann, Walter. *An Introduction to the Old Testament: The Canon and Christian Imagination*. Louisville, KY: Westminster John Knox, 2003.
Claassens, L. Juliana. *Mourner, Mother, Midwife: Reimagining God's Delivering Presence in the Old Testament*. Louisville, KY: Westminster John Knox, 2012.
Claassens, L. Juliana. "The Rhetorical Function of the Woman in Labour Metaphor in Jeremiah 30–31: Trauma, Gender and Postcolonial Perspectives." *JThSA* 150 (2014): 67–84.
Dillmann, August. *Die Bücher Exodus und Leviticus*. KEH. Leipzig: Hirzel, 1880.
Douglas, Mary. "Justice as the Cornerstone. An Interpretation of Leviticus 18–20." *Int* 53 (1999): 341–50.
Douglas, Mary. *Purity and Danger: An Analysis of the Concepts of Pollution and Taboo*. London: Routledge & Kegan Paul, 1966.
Erbele-Küster, Dorothea. *Body, Gender and Purity in Leviticus 12 and 15*. LHBOTS 539. London: Bloomsbury, 2017.
Gerstenberger, Erhard S. *Leviticus*. OTL. Louisville, KY: Westminster, 1996.
Gorman, Frank H. *A Commentary on the Book of Leviticus*. ITC. Grand Rapids, MI: Eerdmans, 1997.
Hartley, John E. *Leviticus*. WBC 4. Dallas, TX: Word, 1992.
Hays, Nathan. "The Redactional Reassertion of the Priestly Role in Leviticus 10–16." *ZAW* 130 (2018): 175–88.
Hieke, Thomas. *Leviticus 1–15*. HThKAT. Freiburg: Herder, 2014.
Kaiser Jr., Walter C. "Leviticus." *NIB* 1:985–1191.
Kalmanofsky, Amy. "Israel's Baby: The Horror of Childbirth in the Biblical Prophets." *BibInt* 16 (2008): 60–82.
Kamionkowski, S. Tamar. *Leviticus*. Wisdom Commentary 3. Collegeville: Liturgical, 2018.
Kanyoro, Musimbi R. A. "Where Are the African Women in the Theological Debate?" *Journal of Constructive Theology* 6, no. 2 (2000): 3–20.
Kiuchi, Nobuyoshi. *Leviticus*. Apollos. Leicester: IVP, 2007.
Klawans, Jonathan. "Review Essay. Rethinking Leviticus and Rereading *Purity and Danger*." *AJS Review* 27 (2003): 89–102.
Koblinsky, M. et al. "Maternal Mortality and Disability and Their Consequences." *Journal of Health, Population and Nutrition* 30, no. 2 (2012): 124–30.
Kornfeld, Walter. *Leviticus*. Neue Echter Bibel. Würzburg: Echter, 1983.
Kugler, Robert. "Leviticus." In *The Pentateuch: Fortress Commentary on the Bible Study Edition*, edited by Gale A. Yee et al., 179–209. Minneapolis, MN: Fortress, 2016.
Levine, Baruch E. *Leviticus*. JPS Torah Commentaries. Philadelphia, PA: Jewish Publication Society, 1989.
Maarsingh, Berend. *Leviticus*. POT. Nijkerk: Callenbach, 1974.
Mays, James L. *Leviticus. Numbers*. London: SCM, 1964.
Meyer, Esias E. "Liggaamlike en morele onreinheid in Levitikus: `n geïntegreerde reinigingsisteem." *LitNet Akademies* 16, no. 3 (2019): 393–422.
Milgrom, Jacob. *Leviticus 1–16*. AB 3. New York: Doubleday, 1991.
Milgrom, Jacob. "Seeing the Ethical within the Ritual." *Bible Review* 8, no. 4 (1992): 6, 13.
Morrow, William S. *An Introduction to Biblical Law*. Grand Rapids, MI: Eerdmans, 2017.
Mouton, Elna, and Ellen Van Wolde. "New Life from a Pastoral Text of Terror? Gender Perspectives on God and Humanity in 1 Timothy 2." *Scriptura* 111 (2012): 583–601.

Njoroge, Nyambura. "Groaning and Languishing in Labour Pains: But for How Long Lord?" In *Groaning in Faith*, edited by Musimbi R. A. Kanyoro and N. Njoroge, 3–15. Nairobi: Acton, 1996.

Noth, Martin. *Leviticus*. OTL. London: SCM, 1965.

Otto, Eckart. "Justice and Righteousness I. Bible." In *Religion Past and Present: Encyclopedia of Theology and Religion, vol. 7, I. Bible*, edited by Hans Dieter Betz, 106–7. Leiden: Brill, 2010.

Porter, J. Roy. *Leviticus*. CBC. Cambridge: Cambridge University Press, 1976.

Sailhamer, John H. *The Pentateuch as Narrative.* Grand Rapids, MI: Zondervan, 1992.

Schearing, Linda. "Double Time… Double Trouble? Gender, Sin, and Leviticus 12." In *The Book Leviticus: Composition and Reception*, edited by Rolf Rendtorff and Robert A. Kugler, 429–50. VTSup 93. Leiden: Brill, 2003.

Schmidt, Werner H. *Einführung in das Alte Testament.* 2d ed. Berlin: de Gruyter, 1982.

Snaith, Norman H. *Leviticus and Numbers*. CB. London: Nelson, 1967.

Thiessen, Matthew. "The Legislation of Leviticus 12 in Light of Ancient Embryology." *VT* 68 (2018): 297–319.

Trevaskis, Leigh M. *Holiness, Ethics and Ritual in Leviticus*. HBM 29. Sheffield: Sheffield Phoenix, 2011.

Vriezen, Theodorus C., and Adriaan S. Van der Woude. *Oudisraëlitische en Vroegjoodse Literatuur*. 10th ed. Kampen: Kok, 2000.

Watts, James W. "Ritual Rhetoric in the Pentateuch. The Case of Leviticus 1–16." In *The Books of Leviticus and Numbers*, edited by Thomas Römer, 305–18. BETL 215. Leuven: Peeters, 2008.

Wenham, Gordon J. *The Book of Leviticus*. NICOT. London: Hodder & Stoughton, 1979.

Wellhausen, Julius. *Die Composition des Hexateuchs und der historischen Bücher des Alten Testaments*. Berlin: Reimer, 1899.

World Health Organisation. "Maternal Mortality." *Fact Sheet* 348 (2014).

Part II

Transgressive Methodologies

Chapter 7

Excavating Trauma Narratives: Haunting Memories in the Story of Lot's Daughters*

L. Juliana Claassens

Stellenbosch University

Lot's Daughters—Genesis 19

I

At first—a leering mob circling
the house, jeering, dancing naked,
taunting the guests with their sex—
the daughters thought their father brave
to step outside, lock the door behind him,
stretch his arms out in protection.

---

* Part of this essay fed into one of the chapters of my monograph *Writing/Reading to Survive: Biblical and Contemporary Trauma Narratives in Conversation* (Sheffield: Sheffield Phoenix Press, 2020). In addition to offering a theoretical framework for considering aspects of the text production and reception of biblical and contemporary trauma narratives, this monograph offers a number of examples of such creative engagements between biblical stories of especially women's secret or hidden traumas and a number of contemporary trauma novels. In the monograph, I bring the story of Lot's daughters into conversation with the novel *The Bookshop* by Penelope Fitzgerald.

But then, even he offered them up,
a sacrifice to protect strangers,
their father, the only
"righteous man" in a city destined for flames,
"Do with them what you like.
But don't do anything to these men."

Then their eyes were like Isaac's
below the knife,
the ram not yet in the bush,
the blade gleaming.

II

What dread dug in the daughters'
betrayed hearts before the rioters—
struck blind—stumbled and fell,
unable to find the door,
Lot tugged back safely to the house?

Eyes straight toward Zoar,
did they hear their mother turning,
nostalgia sliced mid-sentence?
That life left behind,
what fixed their gaze away
from home—their father's almost-sacrifice,
or the intervention?

III

No mention of mourning.
Their mother's unbelief behind them.
Too many miles.
The sun hot as horror.

IV

When they fled to the cave
with no hope for heirs,
ashen cities behind them,
mercy was an unremembered flame.

This time, they sacrificed themselves,
holding out wine, lifting their dresses
to lure their father.

He twirled a drunken dance,
love or revenge spinning,
blurring vision.

"Rewarded" with sons,
they named them From Father
and Son of My People,
sang lullabies of fear and fire,
of what it means to wander,
to exile yourself,
to dream of salt and sand.[1]

1. Introduction

It is a disturbing story no matter which way you look at it. Two young betrothed women come close to being raped when their father volunteers to hand them over to an angry mob that wants to have its way with the visitors. Those same women, after seeing their city, including their husbands-to-be, destroyed, and losing their mother who turned into a pillar of salt after looking back, conceive a plan to get their likely traumatized father drunk, and then sleep with him in order to conceive children in this post-cataclysmic world in which they find themselves. The offspring of this incestuous relationship is said to be Moab (meaning, "of my father") and Ammon (meaning, "of my kinsmen")—the ancestors of Israel's longstanding, and much despised, enemies.[2]

This very strange story inevitably evokes some strong emotions in those who hear it, as was also surely the case for the original audience, but possibly also contemporary readers would recoil in disgust when hearing about daughters sleeping with their father. Or if one thinks of it, perhaps also at the thought that a father would callously throw his young virgin daughters to the wolves to be savaged by a horde of menacing assailants.

---

1. Marjorie Maddox, "Lot's Daughters," previously published in *What She Was Saying* (Fomite Press, 2017) and *Christian Century* (6 September, 2005) and *Adam, Eve, & the Riders of the Apocalypse: 59 Contemporary Poets on the Characters in the Bible* (Cascade Books, 2017). Copyright © 2005 by the Christian Century. Lot's Daughters by Marjorie Maddox is reprinted by permission from the September 6, 2005 issue of the *Christian Century*. Used with permission by the Poet.

2. Katherine B. Low, "The Sexual Abuse of Lot's Daughters: Reconceptualizing Kinship for the Sake of Our Daughters," *Journal of Feminist Studies in Religion* 26, no. 2 (2010): 48.

The poem by Marjorie Maddox cited in the beginning of this essay helps us to view this story for what it is—a trauma narrative reflecting multiple layers of pain deriving from a range of exceedingly traumatic experiences that has been instrumentalized further to inflict even more pain and suffering on Israel's neighbors. In this essay, I will consider what difference it makes to read the story of Lot's daughters as a trauma narrative. In conjunction with such approaches as feminist and postcolonial interpretation, trauma hermeneutics is a helpful tool in interrogating, or one could say, excavating the multiple, intersecting levels of traumatic memories of Israel and her neighbors that continue to haunt Israel as she seeks to make sense of her place in the world. By learning to appreciate the various levels of traumatic memories within trauma narratives, we also may be more cognizant of the incredibly complex, multifaceted stories in which we ourselves are actors.

2. Traumatic Memories I: A World Comes Undone

Feminist biblical interpreters have helped us become more attentive to the stories within stories. So Jacqueline Lapsley, in her classic book *Whispering the Word*, speaks about the importance of "enter[ing] the moral complexity of the worlds," which female characters such as Rachel, the unnamed rape victim of Judges 19, the women of Exodus 1–4, Ruth and Naomi occupy.[3] In this encounter, one might indeed find the "extremely subtle," "the deftly nuanced," the gently reflected words and values that whisper in the biblical text.[4] Read this way, one unearths, in the episode of Lot's daughters, a greatly traumatic story hidden just below the surface. Feminist interpretation in conjunction with trauma hermeneutics thus helps us to excavate a different story of pain and trauma that has inflicted deep wounds and will continue to haunt the descendants of Moab as well as of Israel at the points where their stories intersect.

In this regard, it is important to recognize that the topic of incest is greatly traumatizing in itself. Several feminist scholars have identified some of the classic elements of incest in this story that include for instance the "timid perpetrator,"[5] the mother who looks away,[6] the presence of

---

3. Jacqueline E. Lapsley, *Whispering the Word: Hearing Women's Stories in the Old Testament* (Louisville, KY: Westminster John Knox, 2005), 11.

4. Ibid., 18.

5. Low, "Sexual Abuse of Lot's Daughters," 45.

6. Ilona Rashkow, "Daddy-Dearest and the 'Invisible Spirit of Wine'," in *Genesis: A Feminist Companion to the Bible*, ed. Athalya Brenner, FCB 1, 2nd Series 1 (Sheffield: Sheffield Academic, 1998), 82; Rashkow argues that "Mrs Lot could be

alcohol abuse,[7] the involvement of more than one daughter with "the incestuous father commonly mov[ing] from older to younger daughters."[8] However, Katharine Low reads the story of incest as represented in the story of Lot's daughters through the traumatic memories of what her own mother had experienced from Low's grandfather.[9]

The traumatic nature of this aspect of the text, though, is not recognized by all. Ilona Rashkow highlights the fact that there is no narrative judgment in the text regarding the incestuous relationship between Lot and his daughters; "It's not treated in the text as 'wrong.' Indeed, it goes unpunished and without further narrative comment."[10] Moreover, a number of scholars join the Rabbis in commending the daughters for their agency in securing a future for themselves.[11] For instance, Melissa Jackson, who reads the story of Lot's daughters as trickster narrative, emphasizes the daughters' cleverness, describing them as "underdog protagonists" who "are flexible, pragmatic and sexual."[12] Jackson describes this story as comedic in nature, as it serves the purpose of giving its readers hope and the impetus to imagine new possibilities.[13] Jackson argues that these two daughters, "mothers of nations and foremothers of royalty," whom she

---

viewed, in effect, as having 'looked away' from what was going on between father and daughters, a behavior common in clinical incest" (p. 105). Cf. also Low who speaks of the absent mothers in archetypal incest stories like that of Lot's wife, who is "dead, punished by God"; Low, "Sexual Abuse of Lot's Daughters," 42. Low offers, though, an alternative reading of the image of Lot's wife turning into a pillar of salt, reading it as a memorial of past memories of trauma that offers future generations the opportunity to respond differently. She writes: "For me, Lot's wife represents my mother and her standing strength to look back and remember her past. Because my mother looked back and shared her guiding narrative of sexual abuse with me, I am able to enter into it, subvert, and destabilise it"; ibid., 43.

7. Rashkow, "Daddy-Dearest," 82.
8. Ibid., 104.
9. Low, "Sexual Abuse of Lot's Daughters," 37–8.
10. Rashkow, "Daddy-Dearest," 104.
11. Ruth Tsoffar remarks that the rabbis speak of the transformation of the daughters to mothers in a positive way, calling them "agents of history." She argues that, "their incestuous act was not motivated by libidinal desire but by an altruistic urge to rescue humankind"; Ruth Tsoffar, "The Trauma of Otherness and Hunger: Ruth and Lot's Daughters," *Women in Judaism: A Multidisciplinary Journal* 5, no. 1 (2007): 7, 8.
12. Melissa Jackson, "Lot's Daughters and Tamar as Tricksters and the Patriarchal Narratives as Feminist Theology," *JSOT* 26 (2002): 39.
13. Ibid., 45. Jackson characterizes some of the feminist interpretations of this story also cited in this article as painting a "dark and sinister picture"; ibid., 43.

describes as the "first feminist theologians," "question the basic assumptions of the social order and envision a completely inverted reality."[14] Given the disturbing nature of incest and the long-lasting effects on children and families as a whole, however, such an interpretation, I would say, is rather problematic, and even dangerous as it normalizes something that is rooted in a great abuse of power and trust.

I find more helpful Ruth Tsoffar's interpretation of the story of Lot's daughters, which reads this text from the perspective of trauma theory. Tsoffar helps to draw our attention beyond the incident of incest to the greatly traumatizing context that precedes the event in the cave at Zoar. She reflects on the "symbolic wound and the traumatic history" that marks Moabite and Ammonite identity in the sense that, "These nations emerged from an ultimate threat to humankind which was fully internalized by Lot's daughters; namely the fear of apocalyptic *kilayon*, or annihilation."[15]

Indeed, the entire narrative of Genesis 19 is marked by threat and fear. The destruction of Sodom with the proverbial fire and brimstone is coupled not only with the narrow escape of Lot's family but also with the extreme difficulty of letting go of the past. Tsoffar notes that the heavenly visitors literally have to take the hands of Lot, his wife and daughters to lead them out of city (v. 16). Fear also marks the journey, with Lot being afraid of the long journey ahead and asking to go to the city of Zoar that is nearby (v. 19). And because even Zoar is deemed unsafe, the family ends up in a cave in the hills above the city (v. 30). The tremendous loss of the city and the lives they had before is coupled with the loss of Lot's wife, the daughters' mother, who is said to turn into a pillar of salt due to looking back at her hometown in ruins.[16]

But even these traumatic events outlined by Tsoffar are not the full story. Prior to the escape from the burning city, the two daughters came close to being raped by a gang of agitated men threatening the safety of the visitors who were spending the night in their home. Even more

14. Ibid., 46. Cf. also Kenneth Stone who makes a similar argument with reference to the story of Tamar who tricked her father-in-law into sleeping with her in order to secure her future by bringing a child into the world. Stone argues that Tamar's "sexual actions, like those of many of us, stand outside accepted conventions of her society, and at one point bring her quite close to being killed." In this respect, Stone proposes that Tamar "offers a biblical, 'Canaanite,' position from which a 'queering' of theology, biblical interpretation, and the conceptualization of religious 'identity' might usefully commence"; Kenneth Stone, *Practicing Safer Texts: Food, Sex and Bible in Queer Perspective* (London: T&T Clark, 2005), 67.

15. Tsoffar, "The Trauma of Otherness and Hunger," 6.

16. Ibid., 7.

troubling is the fact that it was their own father who offered his daughters in exchange for the guests, thus, clearly communicating that hospitality towards men is more important than the welfare and safety of women.[17] Low recognizes the terrible thing that almost happened to these two daughters:

> For me, the repulsion I feel comes much earlier in the story, when Lot assumes that his daughters' sexuality remains at his disposal, even to dispense their bodies to the angry mob. Lot disregards his daughters' feelings, claiming control over their sexual destiny.[18]

What is compelling about Tsoffar's interpretation is that she ascribes the description of the incest between Lot and his daughters in Gen 19:30–38 to a direct outflow of the extreme trauma these survivors had lived through—the crisis of the obliteration of their entire world followed by the loss of their mother, in addition to coming close to being gang-raped, forcing yet another crisis. As she writes, "The daughters interpret their reality according to the psychological impact and magnitude of their trauma. They perceive the destruction far more extensive than just the city."[19] Thus, even though the family successfully escaped the destruction of their city, "the psychological impact of the trauma of experiencing the disintegration of the world as they know it" is, according to Tsoffar, responsible for the fact that "whatever sense they may have entertained about the future" is completely destroyed.[20] Truly believing that there are no men left who would make suitable marriage partners, and that their father is their only hope for conceiving a child, the traumatized daughters act in a way that secures what they perceive to be the only future open to them, so serving as a "living testimony of the historical trauma" their family had lived through.[21]

---

17. Lyn M. Bechtel, "A Feminist Reading of Genesis 19:1–11," in Brenner (ed.), *Genesis*, 111. Bechtel notes that this part of the story is typically overlooked or ignored by interpreters. Further, "the apparent disregard for women in his offer violates the assumption of protection of women as the producers of life that characterises ancient society"; ibid., 122.

18. Low, "Sexual Abuse of Lot's Daughters," 39–40.

19. Tsoffar, "The Trauma of Otherness and Hunger," 7.

20. Ibid, 8.

21. Ibid. Tsoffar also highlights the isolation suggested by the setting of the mountain cave, which is responsible for "the daughters' sense of total annihilation which justifies their desperate act of survival"; ibid.

Moreover, as Tsoffar rightly reminds us, "incest as a form of violence is as much a crisis in itself as it is a remedy for their perceived crisis."[22] And by not judging the acts of incest, it "blur[s] the distinction between the crisis itself and its resolution," but even more disconcerting, "it also legitimizes his incestuous act."[23] Tsoffar's interpretation, which takes seriously the traumatic origins of the story of Lot's daughters, serves as an important reminder of the very real consequences of failing to recognize something for the trauma that it is, and the distinct ways in which such traumatic events impact the behavior of individuals (and of their descendants) for years to come. Thus, instead of viewing the behavior of Lot's daughters "as a symptom of pathology, a given crisis [that] becomes the very essence or main aspect of representation," Tsoffar argues that "this initial story of trauma comes to be associated with Moab and Ammon's stories of origin." She argues that, "if such a crisis is the founding moment of certain realities—an ordeal, a test, a proof, a lesson—it is soon identified as the main aspect of identity."[24]

This brings us to yet another layer of traumatic memories embedded within this story. If one excavates further, one encounters another whole level of trauma associated with Israel's troubling relationship with its neighbors.

3. Traumatic Memories II: The Fragile Boundaries of Israel's Self

Postcolonial biblical criticism has been particularly helpful in making readers cognizant of the way in which the Other is constructed. In this regard, Judith McKinlay highlights the role of power in defining and representing the Other, which is a central feature of postcolonial biblical interpretation, and in particular, of how such portrayals are utilized to exercise control of the Other.[25]

---

22. Ibid.
23. Ibid.
24. Ibid.
25. Judith McKinlay, "Challenges and Opportunities for Feminist and Postcolonial Biblical Criticism," in *Prophecy and Power: Jeremiah in Feminist and Postcolonial Perspective*, ed. Christl M. Maier and Carolyn J. Sharp, LHBOTS 577 (London: Bloomsbury T&T Clark, 2013), 22. Cf. also Fernando Segovia, who asks the following questions: (1) "How do the margins look at the 'world'—a world dominated by the reality of empire? (2) How does the center regard and treat the margins in the light of its own view of the 'world' and life in that world? (3) What images and representations of the 'other' arise from either side? (4) How is history

Within this process of identity formation of the Self and the Other, the work of Julia Kristeva on the abject has been of particular importance. Julia Kristeva demonstrates, from a psychoanalytic point of view, how this process of what she calls abjection is an important part of identity formation in which the "I" explores the boundaries of the self, and deems objectional that which does not fit into the vision of what constitutes the borders of the "I" and the "We."[26] She begins her essay on abjection as follows:

> There looms, within abjection, one of those violent, dark revolts of being, directed against a threat that seems to emanate from an exorbitant outside, ejected beyond the scope of the possible, the tolerable, the thinkable. It lies there, quite close, but it cannot be assimilated. It beseeches, worries, and fascinates desire, which, nevertheless, does not let itself be seduced. Apprehensive, desire turns aside; sickened, it rejects.[27]

According to Kristeva, the "abject" can be said to refer to that which is discharged from the body—spewed out, vomited out, defecated out. However, from vomit and excrement, Kristeva moves on to other elements and, more significantly, to individuals that are considered other or alien, and hence threatening to the self. Thus, on a metaphorical level, whatever, or often also whoever, is deemed abhorrent to the other is cast out, rejected, or in an extreme fashion, annihilated.[28]

Several biblical scholars have picked up on Julia Kristeva's notion of the abject as important for dialogue on Israel's process of identity formation particularly as it pertains to Israel's relationship to her neighbors. For instance, Cheryl Exum, in an article titled, "Hagar *en procès*: The Abject in Search of Subjectivity," shows that Ishmael and his Egyptian mother Hagar threaten the fragile boundaries of Israel's emerging self. In the various stories of Hagar's expulsion, the quintessential abject, in Kristevian words, is cast away, so serving as evidence of "a difficult and

---

conceived and constructed by both sides? (5) What conceptions of oppression and justice are to be found?" Fernando Segovia, "Biblical Criticism and Postcolonial Studies: Toward a Postcolonial Optic," in *The Postcolonial Biblical Reader*, ed. R. S. Sugirtharajah (Malden, MA: Blackwell, 2006), 38.

26. Julia Kristeva, *Powers of Horror: An Essay on Abjection* (trans. Leon S. Roudiez; New York: Columbia University Press, 1982), 5–6.

27. Ibid., 1.

28. Kristeva remarks that "the abjection of Nazi crime reaches its apex when death…interferes with what, in my living universe, is supposed to save me from death: childhood, science, among other things"; ibid., 4.

traumatic process," that "reveals the struggle the subject-in-process Israel has in drawing boundaries."[29]

And yet, Exum notes that "Ishmael, the abject, does not go away." Rather Ishmael and his descendants are said to hover "at the edges of Israel's consciousness, a reminder of the unstable boundaries of the self that is Israel, and a threat to borders, system, and order."[30] The reason for this is that "the subject is always in process, never finished, never complete and never able to create stable boundaries between itself and the world around it, the abject remains a threat to subjectivity against which the subject must maintain vigilance."[31] This is particularly evident given the close familial relationship, with Ishmael being Abraham's own flesh and blood and hence representing the stranger within.

Also, Carolyn Sharp, in her consideration of the value of feminist and postcolonial biblical interpretation for the book of Jeremiah, describes the notion of the abject as those attempts to expel, forbid, and even exterminate elements of "impurity, foreignness, illness, offal, and death from the boundaries of the (constructed) viable subject." Ironically though, these attempts have the adverse effect of "ensur[ing] that the threat remains present, for revulsion can come only from the continued (implied) presence of that which is compelling disgust."[32] The process of identity formation is thus never fully completed with the subject continuously having to create distance between the Self and the Other in order to protect itself.[33]

In this regard, Kenneth Stone has demonstrated how food and sex both can be said to play a role in creating and maintaining boundaries between Israel and her neighbors. Especially in Leviticus, many of the laws have to do with the distinction between clean/unclean, pure/impure, permitted/forbidden foods and sexual partners that were considered to be crucial in delineating Israel's identity over against the other nations. For instance, in Lev 20:22, at the end of the section outlining forbidden sexual relationships, one finds the commandment to keep all the statues and

---

29. J. Cheryl Exum, "Hagar *en procès*: The Abject in Search of Subjectivity," in *From the Margins 1: Women of the Hebrew Bible and Their Afterlives*, ed. Peter S. Hawkins and Lesleigh Cushing Stahlberg (Sheffield: Sheffield Phoenix, 2009), 4.

30. Ibid., 12.

31. Ibid., 1.

32. Carolyn Sharp, "Buying Land in the Text of Jeremiah: Feminist Commentary, the Kristevan Abject, and Jeremiah 32," in Maier and Sharp (eds.), *Prophecy and Power*, 158.

33. As Sara Ahmed poignantly states, "Borders needed to be threatened in order to be maintained"; Sara Ahmed, *The Cultural Politics of Emotion* (Edinburgh: Edinburgh University Press, 2004), 87.

commandments so that the land in which you live "does not vomit you out"—the act of vomiting is closely associated with the act of casting out, or one could say, abjection. The divine commandment further calls upon the people to separate themselves from the other unclean, or, one could say, disgusting nations so that they may be holy as God is holy (Lev 20:26).[34]

This obsession regarding sex, which exhibits strong connotations with disgust, is frequently used to demonize the vile sexual practices of the Other. This point has compellingly been made by Randall Bailey, who shows how sexual rhetoric is used to stigmatize and to mark as repulsive members of other ethnic groups including the Canaanites, Moabites and Ammonites.[35] Stone notes that such stereotypical representations are not always rooted in any real observations, but rather in pre-existing ideas and feelings of hatred and resentment regarding the other.[36]

Nevertheless, such representations, void of reality as they may be, are incredibly strong in justifying acts of abjection. So one finds that in the story of Lot's daughters, which narrates the origins of the Moabites and the Ammonites, the close association between sex and disgust becomes a way of demonizing and discrediting the others in Israel's midst whose presence has become threatening to the fragile boundaries of the self. Citing the work of Jonathan Smith, Johnny Miles puts it as follow: "The real problematic emerges when the 'other' is 'TOO-MUCH-LIKE-US, or when he claims to BE-US.'"[37]

---

34. Stone, *Practicing Safer Texts*, 50. A similar tendency is seen also in Num 25:1–3, where God is portrayed as furious with the people of Israel who "defiled themselves" in terms of their sexual liaisons with Moabite women and their suspicious food practices that involved eating and bowing down before Baal of Peor; ibid., 53.

35. Randall Bailey, "They're Nothing but Incestuous Bastards: The Polemical Use of Sex and Sexuality in Hebrew Canon Narratives," in *Reading from This Place*. Vol. 1, *Social Location and Biblical Interpretation in the U.S.*, ed. Fernando F. Segovia and Mary Ann Tolbert (Minneapolis, MN: Fortress, 1995), 123–4. Stone notes that William Albright was quite influential in cementing the notion of the wicked Canaanites, particularly in terms of their "sexual abominations," when it comes to justifying their extermination. Stone, *Practicing Safer Texts*, 63.

36. Ibid., 51. Stone, drawing on the work of anthropologist Lila Abu-Lughod, writes that "beliefs about the shameless sexual behaviors of others are put forward even when opportunities for the actual observation of such persons and practices are absent."

37. Johnny Miles, *Constructing the Other in Ancient Israel and the USA*, BMW 32 (Sheffield: Sheffield Phoenix, 2011), 14; Jonathan Z. Smith, "What a Difference a Difference Makes," in *"To See Ourselves as Others See Us": Christians, Jews, 'Others' in Late Antiquity*, ed. Jacob Neusner and Ernest S. Frerichs, SPSH (Chico,

The story of Lot's daughters thus, on a deeply existential level, expresses Israel's struggle with the Other in her midst—the near descendants of Abraham's nephew Lot presented as being born out of repulsive sexual union and hence worthy of being abjected as evident in the harsh laws in Deut 23:2–3. From the prohibition in Deut 23:2 that expels the offspring of an "illicit union," which in Hebrew specifically pertains to incest, from the *qĕhal yhwh*, it is evident though that, as in the closely associated story of Genesis 19, the connection that is drawn between sex, disgust and abjection is central to the process of forging boundaries between Israel and her neighbors.[38] Through this narrative, one sees how boundaries are drawn in terms of revolting sexual practices—incest being particularly offensive in nature.[39] It thus seems that precisely because there did not exist clear demarcations between Israel and Canaan, or between Israel and Moab/Ammon, one finds the conscious or subconscious attempts in Israel's legal and narrative traditions to alleviate what Stone, drawing on the work of Marion Young, characterizes as "border anxiety."[40] It is this anxiety regarding fragile boundaries that is responsible for the drive to create clear boundaries between us and them by labelling, as Bailey has suggested, "within the consciousness of the reader the view of these nations as nothing more than 'incestuous bastards.'"[41]

In this process, quite often, the focus falls on only one real or perceived trait that is deemed objectionable, which has the effect of turning the Other into a stereotype. Miles describes the role of stereotypes in solidifying boundaries as follows:

> They as Other are always objectified being constructed by and for the benefit of the subject to achieve masterful self-definition. Stereotyping the Other becomes a means to knowing oneself, to have a certain legitimacy by the symbolic exclusion of the Other. This is 'us' here; that is 'them' there. By naming and defining the characteristics of the Other, the dominant self denies 'others' their right to name and define themselves.[42]

CA: Scholars Press, 1985), 47. Cf. also Miles' careful examination of what it is we do know regarding the history and culture of the Moabites; Miles, *Constructing the Other*, 139–55.

38. Bailey, "They're Nothing but Incestuous Bastards," 130–1.

39. A contemporary example of how the association between sex and disgust functions in creating boundaries between us and them is the slur that members of one gang would call another: "You are Motherf#$%@$rs!!" In the case of the story of Lot, it would be expressed in terms of viewing the Moabites as "Fatherf#$%@$rs!!"

40. Stone, *Practicing Safer Texts*, 58–67.

41. Bailey, "They're Nothing but Incestuous Bastards," 131.

42. Miles, *Constructing the Other*, 32.

In this regard, one should also be mindful of the performative nature of such speech acts. Drawing on Judith Butler's notion of "performativity," Ahmed writes about "the power of discourse to produce effects through reiteration."[43] Thus, it is by repeating expressions of disgust in laws and in narratives that a certain representation of a particular group is fixed and perpetuated. If one tells it often enough, people, even the teller of the story, starts to believe it.[44]

Finally, such stereotypical representations can be described as a form of violence on a physical, figural and emotional level. In this regard, Regina Schwartz has argued that the very act of naming and constructing the Other in itself as part of a process of identity formation constitutes "acts of violence."[45] And one should be mindful that in the biblical text, there are numerous examples of how literary violence is but one step away from actual violence, as evident in the case of the *ḥerem* laws that take abjection to its utmost extent.[46]

4. *Conclusion—Reading with Compassion?*

To read the troubling story of Lot's daughters as a trauma narrative yields a number of perspectives that are important for our ongoing task of deconstructing and reconstructing meaning with an eye toward transformation. In the first instance, it is important to hold in tension the multiple intersecting levels of trauma that are embedded in this story and

---

43. Ahmed, *Cultural Politics of Emotion*, 92. Cf. also Judith Butler, *Gender Trouble: Feminism and the Subversion of Identity* (New York: Routledge, 1993), 33.

44. According to Ahmed, "[t]o name something as disgusting—typically, in the speech act, 'That's disgusting!'—is performative. It relies on previous norms and conventions of speech, and it generates the object that it names (the disgusting object/ event). To name something as disgusting is not to make something out of nothing. But to say something is disgusting is still to 'make something'; it generates a set of effects, which then adhere as a disgusting object"; ibid., 93.

45. Regina Schwartz, *The Curse of Cain: The Violent Legacy of Monotheism* (Chicago, IL: The University of Chicago Press, 1997), 5, cited in Tsoffar, "The Trauma of Otherness and Hunger," 4. Cf. also Miles, who writes from his own context of Hispanic Americans in the United States that "to privilege one ethnic group by denying the 'other' its identity, suppressing its voice and, simultaneously, that nation's own origins" may contribute to a form of cultural amnesia. As Miles has rightly said, "[F]orgetting results in dismembering"; Miles, *Constructing the Other*, 138.

46. Eric Seibert, *The Violence of Scripture: Overcoming the Old Testament's Troubling Legacy* (Minneapolis, MN: Fortress, 2012), 16–18. Cf. also L. Juliana Claassens, "God and Violence in the Prophets," in *Oxford Handbook to the Prophets*, ed. Carolyn J. Sharp (New York: Oxford University Press, 2016), 334–49.

its reception. On an individual level, trauma hermeneutics coupled with feminist biblical interpretation may help one to read with compassion, that is, to grow in empathy with the characters in pain, who have to act within an exceedingly difficult situation that is marked by the constant fear of annihilation. This ranges from the visceral threat of being raped by a mob of angry men, to their city and everything they know going up in flames, to losing their mother, who metaphorically, if not literally, gets stuck in the past.

However, postcolonial criticism intersecting with trauma hermeneutics also shows how this individual story of trauma can be put into the context of collective trauma. Hence, if one digs deeper, one would find that this story of trauma represents age-old resentments and ancient feuds. It is significant to note that in Deut 23:4, the real reason for the abjection reflected in the laws cited earlier that prohibit any Moabite or Ammonite from becoming part of the Israelite community (Deut 23:1–2) is, "because they did not meet you with food and water on your journey out of Egypt, and because they hired against you Balaam son of Beor, from Pethor of Mesopotamia, to curse you." Thus, even though one could say that the revulsion regarding particular sexual practices is responsible for deeming the subject to be worthy of abjection, the real reason for the abjection of Moab seems to go back to some prior resentment that has nothing to do with sex. The people of Israel continue to harbor great bitterness against Moab for not giving them food and water when they were in a precarious position during their flight from Egypt.[47] This point corroborates Ahmed's argument that the emotion of disgust is always rooted in some other (prior) resentment or loathing for the Other.[48] The potentially traumatizing effects of literary violence spilling over into actual violence, both symbolic but in too many instances, and on a literal level, underscore the importance of what we do as feminist and postcolonial biblical interpreters.

Can it be different? Is it possible for feminist and postcolonial biblical interpreters to play some role in helping individuals and groups face traumatic memories that do so much harm to them on both an individual and collective level? Could the biblical texts that we read through the lens of feminist, queer and postcolonial biblical interpretation conceivably offer a safe space for dealing productively with, and perhaps even overcoming, those traumatic memories that continue to haunt individuals and communities? In addition, could this act of reading the multiple layers of trauma

47. Tsoffar, "The Trauma of Otherness," 4. Tsoffar explains that "this tense encounter around food and feeding positioned Moab as the ultimate other in the collective memory of Israel"; ibid.
48. Ahmed, *Cultural Politics of Emotion*, 92–3; Stone, *Practicing Safer Texts*, 51.

narratives ultimately assist trauma survivors to once more live productive lives where they move beyond merely surviving, and start to actually flourish or thrive? It is these questions that fuel the ongoing commitment to read in such ways that may be labelled as transgressive, but which one ultimately hopes will result in transformation.

Bibliography

Ahmed, Sara. *The Cultural Politics of Emotion.* Edinburgh: Edinburgh University Press, 2004.
Bailey, Randall. "They're Nothing but Incestuous Bastards: The Polemical Use of Sex and Sexuality in Hebrew Canon Narratives." In *Reading from This Place*. Vol. 1, *Social Location and Biblical Interpretation in the U.S.*, edited by Fernando F. Segovia and Mary Ann Tolbert, 123–31. Minneapolis, MN: Fortress, 1995.
Bechtel, Lyn M. "A Feminist Reading of Genesis 19:1–11." In *Genesis: A Feminist Companion to the Bible*, edited by Athalya Brenner, 108–28. FCB 1. 2nd Series. Sheffield: Sheffield Academic, 1998.
Butler, Judith. *Gender Trouble: Feminism and the Subversion of Identity*. New York: Routledge, 1993.
Claassens, L. Juliana. "God and Violence in the Prophets." In *Oxford Handbook to the Prophets*, edited by Carolyn J. Sharp, 334–49. New York: Oxford University Press, 2016.
Claassens, L. Juliana. *Writing/Reading to Survive: Biblical and Contemporary Trauma Narratives in Conversation.* Sheffield: Sheffield Phoenix, 2020.
Exum, J. Cheryl. "Hagar *en procès*: The Abject in Search of Subjectivity." In *From the Margins 1: Women of the Hebrew Bible and Their Afterlives*, edited by Peter S. Hawkins and Lesleigh Cushing Stahlberg, 4–12. Sheffield: Sheffield Phoenix, 2009.
Jackson, Melissa. "Lot's Daughters and Tamar as Tricksters and the Patriarchal Narratives as Feminist Theology." *JSOT* 26 (2002): 29–46.
Kristeva, Julia. *Powers of Horror: An Essay on Abjection.* Translated by Leon S. Roudiez. New York: Columbia University Press, 1982.
Lapsley, Jacqueline E. *Whispering the Word: Hearing Women's Stories in the Old Testament*. Louisville, KY: Westminster John Knox, 2005.
Low, Katherine B. "The Sexual Abuse of Lot's Daughters: Reconceptualizing Kinship for the Sake of Our Daughters." *Journal of Feminist Studies in Religion* 26, no. 2 (2010): 37–54.
Maddox, Marjorie. 2005. "Lot's Daughters." *Christian Century*, https://www.christiancentury.org.
McKinlay, Judith, E. "Challenges and Opportunities for Feminist and Postcolonial Biblical Criticism." In *Prophecy and Power: Jeremiah in Feminist and Postcolonial Perspective*, edited by Christl M. Maier and Carolyn J. Sharp, 19–37. LHBOTS 577. London: Bloomsbury T&T Clark, 2013.
Miles, Johnny. *Constructing the Other in Ancient Israel and the USA.* BMW 32. Sheffield: Sheffield Phoenix, 2011.
Rashkow Ilona. "Daddy-Dearest and the Invisible Spirit of Wine'." In *Genesis: A Feminist Companion to the Bible*, edited by Athalya Brenner, 82–107. FCB 1. 2nd Series. Sheffield: Sheffield Academic, 1998.

Schwartz, Regina M. *The Curse of Cain: The Violent Legacy of Monotheism*. Chicago, IL: The University of Chicago Press, 1997.

Segovia, Fernando. "Biblical Criticism and Postcolonial Studies: Toward a Postcolonial Optic." In *The Postcolonial Biblical Reader*, edited by Rasiah S. Sugirtharajah, 33–44. Malden, MA: Blackwell, 2006.

Seibert, Eric. *The Violence of Scripture: Overcoming the Old Testament's Troubling Legacy*. Minneapolis, MN: Fortress, 2012.

Sharp, Carolyn J. "Buying Land in the Text of Jeremiah: Feminist Commentary, the Kristevan Abject, and Jeremiah 32." In *Prophecy and Power: Jeremiah in Feminist and Postcolonial Perspective*, edited by Christl M. Maier and Carolyn J. Sharp, 150–72. LHBOTS 577. London: Bloomsbury T&T Clark, 2013.

Smith, Jonathan Z. "What a Difference a Difference Makes." In *To See Ourselves as Others See Us: Christians, Jews, "Others" in Late Antiquity*, edited by Jacob Neusner and Ernest S. Frerichs, 3–48. Chico, CA: Scholars Press, 1985.

Stone, Ken. *Practicing Safer Texts: Food, Sex and Bible in Queer Perspective*. London: T&T Clark, 2005.

Tsoffar, Ruth. "The Trauma of Otherness and Hunger: Ruth and Lot's Daughters." *Women in Judaism: A Multidisciplinary Journal* 5, no. 1 (2007): 1–13.

Chapter 8

Normative Masculinities Turned Upside Down? Reading Genesis 19:30–38 Side by Side with Selected African Proverbs

Madipoane Masenya (Ngwan'a Mphahlele)
UNISA

1. Introduction

The reading of Gen 19:30–38 as reflected in the present essay is transgressive, that is, it deviates from the norm. First, it privileges African proverbs by using them as a lens to engage a biblical text. Within the fields of Bible and Theology, where the American-Eurocentric frameworks and knowledge systems remain the norm, bringing African knowledge to bear on one's reading of the Bible remains not only a pertinent task, but an act of justice in a scholar's commitment to the positive transformation of our contexts. Such a venture is made even more urgent in a historical context in which the same Bible was used to perpetuate colonialism and apartheid.

Second, as implied from the first part of the title of this essay, normative notions of manhood—such notions that resist the transformation of the patriarchal status quo both in the biblical and African contexts—will be challenged and resisted in the present work. It is hoped that in the process, the end product will be helpful in deconstructing problematic notions of femininities and masculinities, and in efforts towards the positive transformation of our contexts.

2. *Masculinity and Virility: Bed Fellows?*

In many an African context, dare one say even in other global contexts,[1] to be a real man is not to be a woman. Paul Leshota thus argues that,

> [I]n a man's world, nothing could be as ill-omened [as] being and behaving as a woman... For a man to be portrayed as a woman is demeaning and contemptuous. This is simply because a man can only become a man by not becoming a woman, who is fainthearted, powerless, emotional and weak.[2]

In such cultures, a clear demarcation is perceived to exist between notions of femininity and masculinity; between features which are claimed to typify what ideal manhood and womanhood should entail. One of the features which typify ideal masculinity in many a culture, including both the African and biblical cultures, was/is virility or sexual prowess; hence, the Rundi proverb, "Virility gone, one might as well be woman." This proverb is cited by one (read: a man) who is conscious of his decay, downfall, uselessness and impotence.[3] It occasions no surprise then that Mieke Schipper would argue that the polygynous inclinations of men appear natural in African contexts.[4] In that category, one may include married men's age-old tendencies to accept the proverbial legitimation of sharing their bodies with other women extra-maritally. A woman who dares to be a man (read: exercise high levels of sexual prowess) is sure to attract unpalatable names and designations.

In African and biblical cultures, therefore, sexual prowess is almost always linked to men rather than to women. In the case of the Hebrew Bible, Stephen Wilson, for example, observes that fertility and the virile production of children contribute in a significant way to the portrait of

---

1. For example, Connell argues that "masculinity does not exist except in contrast to femininity." R. W. Connell, *Masculinities* (Cambridge: Polity, 1998), 68, as quoted by Stephen M. Wilson, "Biblical Masculinity Studies and Multiple Masculinities Theory: Past, Present and Future," in *Hebrew Masculinities Anew*, ed. Ovidiu Creangă (Sheffield: Sheffield Phoenix, 2019), 19–40 (27).

2. Paul Leshota, "Under the Spell of Discrete Islands of Consciousness: My Journey with Masculinities in the Context of HIV and AIDS," in *Redemptive Masculinities: Men, HIV and Religion*, ed. Ezra Chitando and Sophie Chirongoma (Geneva: WCC, 2012), 147–70 (153).

3. Mieke Schipper, *Source of Evil: Proverbs and Sayings on Women* (Chicago, IL: Ivan R. Dee, 1991), 90.

4. Ibid., 5.

idealized hegemonic masculinity in the Hebrew Bible.[5] Exercising virility and the production of children were supposed to be done within certain confines in order to produce heirs who would be legitimate. So, fertility (read: virility) needs to happen within the context of self-control, hence, continues Wilson, "The goal of male sexual virility in the Hebrew Bible is to produce legitimate heirs by (ideally Israelite) wives, and not to heedlessly father many children by multiple random women..."[6]

What is it that attracts me to this less researched and "notorious" text of the narrative of Lot and his daughters in the last episode of Genesis 19, that is, Gen 19:30–38? I do not seek to focus on issues of the historicity of the episode in question;[7] neither am I concerned with the perspectives (Israelite/Moabite/Ammonite) which may have originally informed the episode. As already noted, in my efforts to transgress the Eurocentric way of reading the biblical text, and informed by selected African (Northern Sotho) proverbs on ideal manhood/masculinity, especially those pertaining to men's sexual prowess, I seek to establish the kind of findings which might emerge if the characters that feature in Gen 19:30–38 are re-read side by side with selected African proverbs on masculinity and male virility. Do notions of masculinity (and to an extent, femininity) as revealed in Gen 19:30–38 resonate with some masculinity constructions in selected African proverbs?

3. Analysis of Selected Northern Sotho Proverbs on Masculinity and Virility

Let us revisit the preceding quote by Paul Leshota on how masculinity is defined in contrast to femininity[8] in African contexts. Femininity is linked

---

5. Wilson, "Biblical Masculinities," 27. Haddox also argues that an ideal Israelite man was supposed to have children, especially sons. Susan E. Haddox, "Masculinities Studies of the Hebrew Bible: The First Two Decades," *CBR* 14, no. 2 (2016): 176–206.

6. Ibid.

7. See George W. Coats. *Genesis with an Introduction to Narrative Literature* (Grand Rapids, MI: Eerdmans, 1983), 146. For an elaborate description of the various interpretations of the text of Gen 19:30–38 through the years, see Carol Smith, "Challenged by the Text: Interpreting Two Stories of Incest in the Hebrew Bible," in *A Feminist Companion to Reading Bible: Approaches, Methods and Strategies*, ed. Athalya Brenner and Carole Fontaine (Sheffield: Sheffield Academic, 1997), 115–35.

8. Leshota argues that "in a man's world, nothing could be as ill-omened as being and behaving as a woman... For a man to be portrayed as a woman is demeaning and

with faintheartedness, powerlessness, inability to control one's emotions and weakness, which are viewed as traits that can never or rather must never typify a man or ideal masculinity. It may not be an exaggeration to argue that female weakness can also be revealed in the perceived absence(?) of female sexual prowess. The Rundi proverb quoted earlier points to the notion of an impotent man who is then compared to a woman: "Virility gone, one might as well be a woman." It thus occasions no surprise that there are hardly any Northern Sotho proverbs (only one proverb emerged from my research) that celebrate female sexual prowess. For example, the Northern Sotho expression, "*O lomilwe ke mmutla*" (He has been beaten by a rabbit) is gendered. It can only be used in the context of male anatomy. The saying depicts a man (male) who is impotent; one who cannot easily mix with females with the aim of expressing his masculinity (read: virility) through sexual advances and/or performance. Ezra Chitando and Sophie Chirongoma capture this obsession with the male ego and sexual prowess succinctly as follows:

> Unfortunately, many men strive to live up to the ideal of competence and conquest in the area of sexuality. Most men do not invest in intimacy. They regard sex as a form of entertainment wherein they must be the ones who derive maximum satisfaction. Men have been pampered to believe that their egos must be massaged, and that they must always have things their own way.[9]

In the preceding culture, no man will celebrate the thought or "reality"(?) of metaphorically being beaten by a rabbit. The proverbial expression, "*Go longwa ke mmutla*" is quite loaded in itself. The object of the rabbit's bite is so weak (read: feminine) that she could be beaten by a harmless animal like a rabbit! This Northern Sotho idiom shows just how intolerable the absence of male virility is in many African cultures.

The following two African (Northern Sotho) proverbs further demonstrate the same point. In both proverbs, a human being (read: woman and man) is compared to a baboon (*tšhwene*). The second stichos of the proverbs mention the hands (read: genitals) of either a man or a woman.

---

contemptuous. This is simply because a man can only become a man by not becoming a woman, who is *fainthearted, powerless, emotional and weak*" (italics added). Leshota, "Under the Spell of Discrete Islands," 153.

9. Ezra Chitando and Sophie Chirongoma, "Challenging Masculinities: Religious Studies, Men and HIV in Africa," *Journal of Constructive Theology* 14, no. 1 (2008): 55–69.

Proverb 1: Mosadi ke tšhwene, o lewa mabogo: "*A woman is a baboon; her hands are eaten.*"

The tenor of the proverb reveals that a married woman must be diligent in taking care of the needs of her family, including her husband's sexual needs. Noteworthy is the passive form of the verb in the second stichos, *o lewa* (eaten) *mabogo* (her hands are *eaten*). If we apply the second *stichos* to the expectation that a married woman's diligence should also be reflected in her responsibility to meet her husband's sexual needs, it may not be far-fetched to see an analogy between female hands and female genitals. In that case, the (sexually) passive female, has her hands eaten by the sexually (read: virile) active male. An interesting difference is noticeable when we turn to the following proverb.

Proverb 2: Monna ke tšhwene, o ja ka matsogo a mabedi: "*A man is a baboon, he eats with two hands.*"

This proverb's tenor reveals that though a man may be married, he can share his body with other women outside the marriage. The presumed male sexual prowess is revealed in the legitimacy granted to a man to have sexual partners even outside the confines of his household. Unlike in Proverb 1 above, the verb used to describe what a man who is like a proverbial baboon does is in the active form (*o ja*, "he eats'). The male proverbial baboon eats with both hands.[10] The stichos thus shows men's insatiable hunger for sex. Being stared in the face by high levels of virility, a man cannot afford to eat with one hand! Both proverbs compare two human beings (male and female) with a baboon, possibly in terms of hard work. In the case of the female, part of her hard work would be celebrated as she meets the needs of one who possesses sexual prowess (read: a male/man). In the case of a man, his hard work is revealed when he extends his virility even beyond the confines of his household. Masculinity and sexual prowess (read: virility) go hand in glove in many a culture, not excluding the cultures of Africa.

At this point, our discussion will benefit from an engagement with a few proverbs that not only celebrate male sexual prowess, but which also appear to legitimate the observation that married men's bodies can be shared with those of other women outside of marriage. What is also noteworthy is that each proverb starts with the expression *Monna ke*,

---

10. The preceding active form (*ja*, "eats") used in the case of a man as subject, stands in stark contrast to *lewa* ("eaten"), which is used in the case of a woman as a proverbial baboon.

literally, "A man is," an expression pointing to man's identity, one that sheds light on what ideal masculinity should entail in the preceding culture.

Proverb 3: Monna ke phoka o wa bošego: "A man is fog, he falls in the night."

Noteworthy in this proverb is the fact that in real life a fog usually spreads freely over vast areas of the land.[11] Moreover, the active verb (*go wa*, "to fall") reveals the activity of a man in the whole process. Finally, the last stichos seems to point to the problematic side of the male action. Why is this so? The exercise of male virility happens outside the legitimate confines of his household; hence, the falling of the fog not in the day but in the night—the latter entails darkness, invisibility, shame(?), secrecy, and obscurity among others. If an element of self-control is allowed to feature in this context, it would be that male sexual virility must happen in a contained environment and in the night. Male virility thus can be exercised anywhere as long as it happens under the cover of the night according to the proverb.

The next proverb that links masculinity with male sexual prowess reads:

Proverb 4: Monna ke selepe o lala a louditšwe: "A man is an axe, sharpened in the night."

A man's intense virility is likened to the sharpness of an axe. What is interesting, though, is the thought conveyed in the second stichos of the proverb. The expression *o lala a louditšwe*, "he gets sharpened in the night," is cast in the passive form. Although the proverb is meant to celebrate male virility, there appears to be a reversal in terms of an active partner as the one who sharpens male virility (male genitals?), which naturally would be the female Other in African heterosexual contexts. Noteworthy is the fact that the element of the night (darkness, obscurity, containment) also features in the present proverb. The verb *lala* entails sleep and/or that which happens in the night.[12]

---

11. The idea of spreading (everywhere—wherever he likes) is also conveyed by the proverb, *Monna ke thaka o a naba*, "A man a pumpkin plant, he spreads."

12. Why the cover of the night we may ask? It reveals that in traditional African cultures, the practice of adultery (even by males) was not tolerated. That is why young female adults who had children before marriage would undergo a shaming ritual, but one is not aware that the same penalty measures are meted out on the "owners" of the pregnancies.

The notion of female agency (read: sexual prowess), alluded to in the preceding proverb, is expressed clearly in the following proverb:

Proverb 5: Monna ke lepai, re a gogelana: "A man is a blanket; we (women) wrap him around our bodies."

As Proverb 5 appears to celebrate female sexual prowess, it probably originated from a female space and thus was coined by women. However, like the preceding male-identified proverbs, it starts with the expression, *monna ke...* ("a man is") instead of *mosadi ke* ("a woman is"). Or could it be that even this proverb was coined by men to fit their own agenda? An affirmative answer may not be farfetched. The tenor of the proverb shows that just like a blanket that is shared by several people in our communal family-oriented African contexts, a man can be shared by several women. As already noted, this is the only proverb that seems to endorse extra-marital relations by women, one that indirectly points to female sexual prowess. A passive blanket (read: male) is acted upon by women—literally, they wrap him around like a blanket. A reversal of roles happens here as a conventional subject is objectified by a conventional subject.

By way of bringing the preceding discussion to a close, a fitting question, also in line with Gen 19:30–38, would be: In which context did the proverbial axe, fog, baboon and pumpkin plant exercise its virility? Whatever it was, it would not have been a conventional familial context. As heterosexual marriage was and continues to be the norm in many an African context,[13] it was/is celebrated and its integrity respected.[14] It can be argued that such sexual encounters happened in shady, contained,

---

13. Madipoane Masenya (Ngwan'a Mphahlele) and Marthe Maleke Kondemo, "What of the Problematic Norm? Rereading the Book of Ruth within the Mongo Women's Context," in *Navigating African Biblical Hermeneutics: Trends and Themes from our Pots and Our Calabashes*, ed. Madipoane Masenya (Ngwan'a Mphahlele) and Kenneth N. Ngwa (Cambridge: Cambridge Scholars Publishing, 2018), 122–36.

14. Mercy Oduyoye thus rightly argues that, "The language of marriage proverbs indicates that a wife only reflects the stage of the marriage and a man's competence as a husband... *Society demands that she stays married, because a woman has no dignity outside marriage*" (italics added). Mercy A. Oduyoye, *Daughters of Anowa: African Women and Patriarchy* (Maryknoll, NY: Orbis, 1995), 68. The expectation for humans, both male and female, to enter into a heterosexual marriage relationship is also noted by Mbiti, who reasons that, "To die without getting married and without children, is to be completely cut off from the human community...to become an outcast and to lose all links with mankind [*sic*]. Everybody therefore must get married and bear children: that is the greatest hope of the individual for himself [*sic*] and of the community for the individual." John S. Mbiti, *African Religions and Philosophy* (Oxford: Heinemann, 1969), 131.

hidden extra-marital spaces, possibly with the wives of other men, as the phenomenon of single parented families is a fairly recent one in many African (and possibly some other) contexts today. Worth noting, especially in the context of what some scholars designate as an incestuous[15] connection between Lot's daughters and their father, is the presence of wives in endogamous marriages. Such forms of marital relationships were also typical within the period of the patriarchs in the Hebrew Bible.[16]

With this background in mind, we now turn to the rereading of the story of Lot's daughters through the lens of selected African proverbs. The Northern Sotho proverb, *Tša etwa ke ye tshadi pele, di wela ka leope* is translated, "If they are led by a female one, they will fall into a donga." Its tenor reveals the challenge that is supposedly posed by female leadership. In the Northern Sotho culture, as in many other African cultures, women do not lead. However, the episode of Gen 19:30–38 seems to transgress the status quo by pointing to a different reality, hence, the proverbial heading below.

4. *Being Led by a Female One with a Donga as a Certain Destination? Reading Genesis 19:30–38 through an African Proverbial Lens*

One of the central writings on typical features of biblical masculinity is the monograph *Play the Man! The Masculine Imperative in the Bible* by David J. A. Clines.[17] What is interesting for our present discussion is that among the typical features of masculinity cited by Clines, virility is not mentioned. As a matter of fact, a typical male is portrayed as womanless, according to Clines. However, irrespective of the gendered spaces of biblical Israel (cf. the public male sphere and the private female sphere), the preceding feature does not problematize the expectation of virility for an ideal Israelite man in a heterosexual space. That space also includes the celebration of women's motherhood role in ancient Israelite society. Is it any wonder that the daughters of Lot in Gen 19:30–38, possibly having been persuaded of their female responsibility to mother sons, would have

---

15. Coats, *Genesis*, 146.

16. For an elaborate exposition of the topic of incest in the Hebrew Bible, see the essay by Athalya Brenner, "On Incest," in *A Feminist Companion to Exodus to Deuteronomy*, ed. Athalya Brenner (Sheffield: Sheffield Academic, 1994), 113–38.

17. See David J. A. Clines, *Play the Man! The Masculine Imperative in the Bible* (Sheffield: Sheffield Phoenix, 2013), 215–28. According to Clines, the following elements typifies manhood in the David story: (1) the fighting male; (2) the persuasive male; (3) the beautiful male; (4) the bonding male; (5) the womanless male; and (6) the musical male.

become agentic in ensuring that the human race is perpetuated, even at all costs?

Susan E. Haddox, one of the most important scholars of masculinity in the Hebrew Bible, identifies features that in her view typified masculinity in ancient Israel as military might, bodily integrity, honor, virility, provisioning and spatiality.[18] In Haddox's view, an ideal Israelite man was supposed to be able to have children, especially sons.

It will be in order at this stage to revisit the questions we asked earlier: If the episode of Gen 19:30–38 is re-read side by side with selected African proverbs on masculinity and male virility, which insights would emerge? Do notions of masculinity (and to an extent, femininity), as revealed in Gen 19:30–38, resonate with those which feature in selected African (Northern Sotho) proverbs?

The Northern Sotho proverb, *Tša etwa ke ye tshadi pele, di wela ka leope*, "If they (cattle) are led by a female one, they will fall into a donga," comes to mind when one attempts to read Gen 19:30–38 through the lens of African proverbs. Females, especially as the neglected category in the Hebrew Bible, that is, the category of daughters, take center stage in the text under investigation.

After being saved from the destruction of Sodom and Gomorrah, Lot requests the angels to be sent to Zoar, the little city he confidently assumes would offer safety (Gen 19:18–20). He settles together with his two daughters in the cave. The announcement of a secluded contained space in which two females, albeit with a problematic and precarious status in that specific context, and an elderly male are thrown together, may already prepare a reader for a possibility, a temptation, a sense of responsibility, a sense of obligation for intimacy. The episode appears to present a transgression of the patriarchal status quo, as the active characters are ironically younger females in the presence of an elderly passive male character. It thus becomes fitting to engage first the only proverb that appears to endorse female virility, *Monna ke lepai, re a gogelana*, "A man is a blanket, we wrap him around our bodies." One could ask whether Lot's daughters and what they did to their father's body resonate with this proverb. Could this proverb, which reveals a reversal of male virility claims, enable the readers of Gen 19:30–38 to make sense of the actions of Lot's daughters towards their basically passive father?[19]

---

18. Haddox, "Masculinities Studies."

19. Susan Niditch notes something about the passivity of the men within the women's narratives in patriarchal history. She asks, "Would not women authors and audiences take special pleasure in Rebekah's fooling her dotty old husband or in Rachel using men's attitudes to menstruation to deceive her father Laban, or in

Being persuaded that they were the only human beings left on earth after the destruction of the cities of Sodom and Gomorrah, the firstborn daughter assumes leadership role, displayed female virility and acted "so that we may preserve offspring through our father" (Gen 19:34). Elsewhere in the book of Genesis, humans have been commanded to be fruitful and replenish the earth (Gen 1:22, 28; 8:17; 9:1, 7; 17:6, 20; 26:22; 28:3; 35:11). In a sense, argues Eli Kohn, in Gen 19:30–38, Lot's daughters were in a way responding to the already known tradition of "replenishing the earth" because they are depicted as saying, "that we may preserve the offspring from our father" (Gen 19:32). The two females are therefore credited with not having had improper motives as they schemed to conceive and have children through their father.[20]

Such commentators would argue that the episode is not about sex. If we use Proverb 5 above as a lens through which to engage the text, a different reading might emerge—a man is a blanket, we (women) wrap him around our bodies. Although the women (most probably not the daughters of the men involved, but the wives of other husbands) who mouth this proverb in the African context are well aware of the possibility of conception, and the important role which women play as mothers of sons, they are propelled first and foremost by their desire to engage in intimacy with men. The move by the daughters of Lot appears to be as calculated as the one by those who are persuaded (by the scarcity of men?) that men must be shared amongst women.

Not only does the older daughter choose to share her father's body with her younger sister, but the move appears to be well calculated. The plan to get their father drunk[21] formed part of a calculated strategy that would not only provide fertile soil (a fitting sensual atmosphere?) in

---

Tamar's more directly and daringly using her sexuality to obtain sons *through Judah? Like Adam, the men in many of the women's stories of Genesis are bumbling, passive and ineffectual*" (emphasis added). Susan Niditch, "Genesis," in *The Women's Bible Commentary*, ed. Carol. A. Newsom and Sharon H. Ringe (Louisville, KY: Westminster John Knox, 1992), 33.

20. Eli Kohn, "Drunkenness, Prostitution and Immodest Appearances in Hebrew Biblical Narrative, Second Temple Writings and Early Rabbinic Literature: A Literary Rhetorical Study" (PhD diss., Bloemfontein: University of the Free State, 2006), 138.

21. In the ancient Near East, the culture of getting drunk after drinking "fermented" wine was not reprehensible. Scholars acknowledge Ugaritic sources which did not see any "inherent problems with the idea that the supreme god was, on occasion, completely drunk that he needed the help of junior gods to escort him back to his throne room." See Victor P. Hamilton, *The Book of Genesis: Chapters 1–17*, NICOT (Grand Rapids, MI: Eerdmans, 1990), 321–3. Claus Westermann, *Genesis: A Commentary*

which the active females would become intimate with their father, but their hope was that their sexual relationship with their father would also lead to the conception of male children. As the actors on the scene, they are portrayed as the ones who act on the proverbial axe, *Monna ke selepe o lala a louditšwe*. As the proverbial axe, a man is indeed sharpened in the night. As they take total control of the situation, they also would have in all probability made sure that the proverbial baboon does not get too intoxicated, since he would then struggle to eat with two hands, leading to failure to accomplish their mission.

As the females who feature in the present episode are the ones who think, plan, act and take full control of the situation, the reader cannot but safely conclude that the masculinity practiced by the character of Lot in the episode is of a different kind because male virility is challenged, patriarchy mocked, while the mission of those whose power is not legitimated by patriarchy gets accomplished.

5. *Conclusion*

First, in our efforts to decolonize biblical scholarship and thus transgress the norm, even in our commitment to the positive transformation of our contexts, African ways of knowing need not only be acknowledged, but also allowed to form an integral part of scholarship as the present engagement with the text shows. The recognition of the end products of such endeavors may assist global biblical scholarship to have the courage to consume that which has been produced especially in the marginal parts of the globe, that is, the global South, not excluding African contexts.

Second, re-reading the text of Gen 19:30–38 side by side with selected African proverbs on masculinity and male virility enabled us to note some points of resemblance between the African and the biblical context about conventional notions of masculinity and virility. In the process, problematic notions of masculinity, especially as embedded in African proverbs, were mocked and problematized. The resultant reading, enabled a revision (read: re-invention?) of the key proverbs as in the following:

(Minneapolis, MN: Augsburg, 1984), 488, cited in Kohn, "Drunkenness, Prostitution and Immodest Appearances," 18. There are a number of narratives in the Hebrew Bible which deal with seemingly inappropriate behaviors, such as drunkenness and prostitution. For example, Isa 51:17–18 pictures Zion as a mother who is drunk, while her sons whom she has brought up do not hold her hand to support her (see Kohn, "Drunkenness, Prostitution and Immodest Appearances," 7, 36).

Monna ke phoka o wa bošego, "A man is a fog, he falls in the night," becomes *Monna ke phoka, o wa bošego **eupša mo go ratago basadi***, "A man is a fog he falls in the night, **only within the territory designated by women**."

Monna ke tšhwene o ja ka matsogo a mabedi, "A man is a baboon, he eats with two hands," becomes *Monna ke tšhwene, o ja ka matsogo a mabedi **ge go kgahla basadi***, "A man is a baboon, he eats with two hands, **only when women have allowed it**."

Monna ke selepe, o lala a louditšwe, "A man is an axe, he is sharpened in the night," becomes *Monna ke selepe, o lala a louditšwe **ke basadi***, "A man is an axe, he is sharpened in the night **by women**."

Hence, in order for a positive transformation of our contexts to happen, we need to problematize certain stereotypes, including those about notions of femininity and masculinity. We may shudder to discover that those long held and cherished stereotypes do not tell us the full truth, if at all they tell any.

Bibliography

Brenner, Athalya. "On Incest." In *A Feminist Companion to Exodus to Deuteronomy*, edited by Athalya Brenner, 113–38. Sheffield: Sheffield Academic, 1994.

Chitando, Ezra, and Sophie Chirongoma. "Challenging Masculinities: Religious Studies, Men and HIV in Africa." *Journal of Constructive Theology* 14, no. 1 (2008): 55–69.

Clines, David, J. A. *Play the Man! The Masculine Imperative in the Bible*. Sheffield: Sheffield Phoenix, 2013.

Coats, George W. *Genesis with an Introduction to Narrative Literature*. Grand Rapids, MI: Eerdmans, 1983.

Connell, R. W. *Masculinities*. Cambridge: Polity, 1998.

Haddox, Susan E. "Masculinities Studies of the Hebrew Bible: The First Two Decades." *CBR* 14, no. 2 (2016): 176–206.

Hamilton, Victor P. 1990. *The Book of Genesis: Chapters 1–17*. NICOT. Grand Rapids, MI: Eerdmans.

Kohn, Eli. "Drunkenness, Prostitution and Immodest Appearances in Hebrew Biblical Narrative, Second Temple Writings and Early Rabbinic Literature: A Literary Rhetorical Study." PhD diss., University of the Free State, 2006.

Leshota, Paul. "Under the Spell of Discrete Islands of Consciousness: My Journey with Masculinities in the Context of HIV and AIDS." In *Redemptive Masculinities: Men, HIV and Religion*, edited by Ezra Chitando and Sophie Chirongoma, 147–70. Geneva: WCC, 2012.

Mbiti, John, S. *African Religions and Philosophy*. Oxford: Heinemann, 1969.

Masenya (Ngwan'a Mphahlele), Madipoane, and Marthe Maleke Kondemo. "What of the Problematic Norm? Rereading the Book of Ruth within the Mongo Women's Context." In *Navigating African Biblical Hermeneutics: Trends and Themes from Our Pots and Our Calabashes*, edited by Madipoane Masenya (Ngwan'a Mphahlele) and Kenneth N. Ngwa, 122–36. Cambridge: Cambridge Scholars Publishing, 2018.

Niditch, Susan, "Genesis." In *The Women's Bible Commentary*, edited by Carol A. Newsom and Sharon H. Ringe, 10–25. Louisville, KY: Westminster John Knox, 1992.

Oduyoye, Mercy A. *Daughters of Anowa: African Women and Patriarchy.* Maryknoll, NY: Orbis, 1995.

Schipper, Mieke. *Source of Evil: Proverbs and Sayings on Women.* Chicago, IL: Ivan R. Dee, 1991.

Smith, Carol. "Challenged by the Text: Interpreting Two Stories of Incest in the Hebrew Bible." In *A Feminist Companion to Reading Bible: Approaches, Methods and Strategies*, edited by Athalya Brenner and Carole Fontaine, 115–35. Sheffield: Sheffield Academic, 1997.

Westermann, Claus. *Genesis: A Commentary.* Minneapolis, MN: Augsburg, 1984.

Wilson, Stephen. "Biblical Masculinities Studies and Multiple Masculinities Theory: Past, Present and Future." In *Hebrew Masculinities Anew*, edited by Ovidiu Creangă, 19–40. Sheffield: Sheffield Phoenix, 2019.

Chapter 9

JUSTICE FOR RAHAB AND THE GIBEONITES
IN THE BOOK OF JOSHUA?
THE ELUSIVE COMMUNITIES OF JUSTICE
IN IMPERIAL/COLONIAL CONTEXTS

Dora Rudo Mbuwayesango
Hood Theological Seminary

1. Introduction

In the book of Joshua, the dominant storyline can be described as the fulfilment of the promise of land made in the distant past to the ancestors of Israel. This fulfilment began with Moses leading the people from Egypt through Sinai to the verge of the Promised Land in the plains of Moab (Exodus–Deuteronomy). The book of Joshua presents the movement of the Israelites from the plains of Moab into Canaan, the final destination. There are two major parts to the book. The first part, Joshua 1–12, depicts the Israelite attempt to follow the divine instructions on how to dispossess the Canaanites who were inhabitants of the land. The second part, Joshua 13–24, recounts the division of the land among the Israelites, Joshua's final words, and the rededication of the covenant. Both the dispossession of the Canaanites and the Israelite possession of the land are presented as sanctioned, indeed as achieved, by Israel's God. Thus, the book of Joshua forms part of the imperial narratives designed to justify ancient Israel's claim to an already occupied land. This is evident in the observation right at the onset of the promise that the Canaanites (Gen 12:9; 13:7) were already inhabiting the land (cf. also Gen 13:12; 15:18–21; 17:8 in which Canaanite ownership of the land is acknowledged).

This colonial ideology dramatized in Joshua 6–11 has been used by colonizers throughout history to justify the oppression of the local inhabitants as well as the exploitation of their resources.[1] Eric A. Seibert rightly notes that colonizers have utilized biblical texts "to support their acts of aggression, theft, and oppression."[2] Thus, modern colonizers have appropriated the biblical texts that depict God as giving the Canaanite land to the Israelites, and further sanctioning the slaughter of the Canaanite peoples in order to justify their despicable and atrocious acts of violence against the land they sought to occupy.

The tendency to appropriate texts like Joshua 6–11 in colonial and imperial contexts has been shown to be greatly problematic by various scholars. For instance, John Collins argues that, "one of the most troubling aspects of this biblical story is the way it has been used, analogically, over the centuries as a legitimating paradigm of violent conquest."[3] Similarly, Ester Epp-Tiessen expresses the challenge that these texts pose to Christians:

> The conquest paradigm portrayed in the book of Joshua and related texts has contributed to untold human suffering over the millennia. Much of this suffering has been perpetrated by Christians. People who have understood and appropriated these texts to provide divine sanction for the conquest of others have turned the Bible into an instrument of oppression.[4]

Since the conquest narratives are particularly troubling to the communities that count the book of Joshua as part of their sacred texts, attempts have

---

1. For a further exploration of this claim, cf. my commentary on "Joshua," in *Global Bible Commentary*, ed. Daniel Patte (Nashville, TN: Abingdon, 2004), 64–73. For studies on the relationship between biblical texts and colonialism, see Michael Prior, *The Bible and Colonialism: A Moral Critique* (Sheffield: Sheffield Academic, 1997); David M. Gunn, "Colonialism and the Vagaries of Scripture: Te Kooti in Canaan (A Story of the Bible and Dispossession in Aotearoa/New Zealand)," in *God in the Fray: A Tribute to Walter Brueggemann*, ed. Tod Linafelt and Timothy K. Beal (Minneapolis, MN: Fortress, 1998), 127–42; Laura E. Donaldson, "Postcolonial and Biblical Reading: An Introduction," *Semeia* 75 (1996): 1–14.

2. Eric A. Seibert, *The Violence of Scripture: Overcoming the Old Testament's Troubling Legacy* (Minneapolis, MN: Fortress, 2012), 18.

3. John J. Collins, *The Bible after Babel: Historical Criticism in a Postmodern Age* (Grand Rapids, MI: Eerdmans, 2005), 62–3; idem, "New Israel, New Canaan: The Bible, the People of God, and the American Holocaust," *USQR* 59 (2005): 25–39.

4. Esther Epp-Tiessen, "Conquering the Land," in *Under Vine and Fig Tree: Biblical Theologies of Land and the Palestinian–Israeli Conflict*, ed. Alain Epp Weaver (Telford, PA: Cascadia, 2007), 72.

been made to find positive implications associated with these texts that can be ethically appropriated. Often, the narratives about the sparing of Rahab and her family (Josh 2:1–24; 6:22–27) and of the Gibeonites (Josh 9:1–27) are highlighted in ways that make the overall imperial ideology of the book palatable. For example, Carolyn Sharp sees the value of the narrative about the encounter between Rahab and the spies as a bridge to a more beneficial message to communities of faith:

> So the liminal moment between Rahab's encounter with the spies and the attack on Jericho is excruciating. It is precisely in that fraught dramatic pause that the implied audience is made to reflect on God's deliverance of Israel at the Jordan (and at the other body of water evoked by this story, the Red Sea) and the importance of remembrance of God's salvation (4:20–24) and covenant-keeping embodied in the rituals of circumcision and Passover observance.[5]

I would argue that such attempts leave the major troubling claims of the narrative unchallenged and consequently perpetuate injustices against the victims in the text and in contemporary unjust structures and systems.

For instance, even though Sharp recognizes the disturbing nature of the book of Joshua, she does not go far enough to challenge the imperial agenda of the book. As she writes in the conclusion to an essay that seeks to offer a feminist and postcolonial analysis of Joshua 1–12,

> Joshua remains a disturbing book, and the first step towards ethical appropriation of its truth is to acknowledge that Joshua can never be 'for us' in any easy way. The book retains its strange and abhorrent qualities, resisting simplistic appropriation just as the commander of the army of the Lord resisted being co-opted by Joshua's agenda (5:14).[6]

It does not seem to me that the commander of the army of the Lord really resists being co-opted into Joshua's overall imperial agenda. Despite his seeming resistance, the commander of the army of the Lord ultimately does not stop Joshua from carrying out the impending slaughter of the people of Jericho. Thus, Josh 5:14 cannot be isolated from its larger context of the slaughter of the people of Jericho (5:1–6:27).

---

5. Carolyn J. Sharp, "'Are You for Us, or for Our Adversaries?' A Feminist and Postcolonial Interrogation of Joshua 2–12 for the Contemporary Church," *Int* 66 (2012): 141–52 (152).

6. Ibid., 152.

In order to transform oppressive, marginalizing and exploitative systems, communities committed to justice need to refrain from evading the horrors reflected in sacred imperial texts. Postcolonial analysis is one approach that helps to sustain a perspective that motivates communities to dismantle unjust systems, whether at local, national or international levels. Postcolonial interpretations focus on dismantling rather than transforming structures, because transformation implies that certain things should remain in place. But to dismantle implies to break down or break apart. In other words, the root cause of exploitative, marginalizing and oppressive systems and structures should not be left in place; and this means that the ideologies undergirding such systems should be exposed and challenged.

Consequently, the stories of the encounters of Rahab and the Israelites, and of the Gibeonites and the Israelites, should be read in the context of the imperial ideology of Joshua 1–12. As an anti-conquest narrative, the presentation of the encounters between the Israelites and the Canaanites is designed to underscore the innocence and vulnerability of the colonizers, and not to promote good relations based on mutual respect. In fact, the act of laying claim to other people's land is the root cause of marginalization, exploitation and oppression of the original inhabitants of the land of Canaan. At the root of the problem is lust for land and resources that belong to other nations. Religion is just one of the tools used in the colonial and imperial process.[7]

Since the conquest narratives in the book of Joshua have been used to support colonizers' acts of aggression, theft and oppression, I propose that these narratives should also play a major role when it comes to issues of reparation. Reparation can be described as the outcome of the acknowledgment and recognition that acts of injustice have actual victims. Postcolonial analysis of sacred imperial texts therefore could help us to be mindful also of the multiple victims of modern imperial ideologies and practices. As we will see in the stories of Rahab and of the Gibeonites, the strategies for hiding the victims and the impact of imperial ideologies and practices are utilized in modern imperial ideologies and practices.

---

7. See, for example, the works by Robert Allen Warrior, "Canaanites, Cowboys, and Indians: Deliverance, Conquest and Liberation Theology Today," *Christianity and Crisis* 49 (1989): 261–5.

2. Anti-Conquest Strategies:
The Innocence and Vulnerability of the Invaders

In the book of Numbers, Moses is depicted as sending spies as a result of divine direction (Num 13:1). But in Josh 2:1–24, Joshua is not depicted as acting according to divine direction; he does so in secret and by sending only two spies rather than twelve. One could ask: who benefits from sending only these two spies? In the book of Numbers, the twelve spies are sent for the benefit of the *ha'am* (the religious and military force combined)[8] in order to convince them to march forward to possess the land. But what is going on in the case of Joshua 2?

One characteristic of imperial narratives is anti-conquest ideology. Based on Mary Louise Pratt's theory, which analyzes particular genres of European travel and exploration writing of South America and Africa in the eighteenth and nineteenth centuries, Musa Dube defines anti-conquest ideology in biblical studies as "literary strategies that allow colonizers to claim foreign lands while securing their innocence."[9] The rhetorical strategy for expressing Israel's innocence in the book of Joshua can be found in the characterization of Joshua as a weak and doubtful leader who needs divine encouragement (cf. also later Rahab's words through the spies) to move forward in their quest to possess the land. According to Pratt, the protagonist of anti-conquest narratives is most often surrounded by an aura, not of authority, but of innocence and vulnerability.[10]

The spies in Num 13:1 had been given an extensive task that covers an assessment of the enemy's strength and the fruitfulness of the land. In contrast, Joshua gives a very simple task: "Go, see the land, especially Jericho" (Josh 2:1a). Interestingly, the men are reported to have gone straight and only to Jericho where they enter a house to lodge, the house of Rahab who is identified as a *zonah* (translated as "prostitute"). The Israelite men have no trouble entering the house of Rahab. Because of Rahab's characterization as a prostitute, her house is automatically interpreted as a brothel, which is then used to explain why the spies go to her house. For instance, Danna Fewell argues that:

---

8. For a discussion of the meaning of *ha'am*, see Dora R. Mbuwayesango, "Numbers," in *Postcolonial Commentary and the Old Testament*, ed. Hemchad Gossai (London: T&T Clark, 2019), 78–84.

9. Musa W. Dube, *Postcolonial Feminist Interpretation of the Bible* (St. Louis, MO: Chalice, 2000), 60.

10. Mary Louise Pratt, *Imperial Eyes: Travel Writing and Transculturation*, 2nd ed. (New York: Routledge, 2008), 55.

The spies go directly to a brothel and "they lay there." The verb "lie" is loaded with sexual overtones, and the context suggests that the spies are not above mixing business with pleasure. The common argument that a brothel would have been the best place to secure information about the city only accents the fact that the spies neither ask questions nor eavesdrop on many conversations.[11]

In terms of her position as a prostitute, Rahab, according to Carolyn Sharp occupies "a permanently precarious position at the margins of the androcentric system of Israelite honor-and-shame-based culture."[12] Thus, her identity as a *zonah* is used to indicate that she is powerless and vulnerable because she has no male protection.

Postcolonial analysis is helpful in understanding this particular characterization of Rahab in this narrative. As Musa Dube aptly points out, gender is employed in imperial literature to represent nations targeted for colonization and to articulate relations of domination and subordination.[13] In addition, it is important to consider how she is depicted in the story and how other references in the Bible contribute to an understanding of *zonah* that informs how the character of Rahab is used in the anti-conquest context.

The visit of the two men to Rahab is reported to the king of Jericho who proceeds to order Rahab to bring out the men because he knows that they are not what they seem to be—they are spies (Josh 2:2–3). At first glance, the king of Jericho seems to be acting to protect his land and his people. However, given the tendency in the text to disempower Canaanite men and Israelite women, while empowering Canaanite women,[14] in Joshua 2 the king of Jericho is depicted as powerless to protect his people. Rahab lies to the king and hides the spies. The men of Jericho are thus deceived to chase after imaginary foreigners all the way to the Jordan. A *zonah* is apparently a woman who is so independent and so powerful that she can make her own bargains with men, and deceive her own king whose interest might be in her own protection. As will be shown later, this particular *zonah* can also make decisions on behalf of her male kin.

---

11. Danna Nolan Fewell, "Joshua," in *Women's Bible Commentary with the Apocrypha*, ed. Carol A. Newsom and Sharon H. Ringe, expanded ed. (Louisville, KY: Westminster John Knox, 1998), 69–72 (69).

12. Sharp, "Are You for Us?" 145.

13. Dube, *Postcolonial Feminist Interpretation*, 73.

14. It is interesting that the danger in intermarriage is presumably that Canaanite women will turn Israelite men away from their God to worship Canaanite gods, while Israelite women are not given the same capability with regard to Canaanite men (Deut 7:1–6).

The book of Proverbs provides some insight into the real status of a *zonah* as being more powerful, but less dangerous than another man's wife or strange/foreign woman. According to Prov 6:26, sleeping with a prostitute leads to poverty and sleeping with another man's wife leads to death. This belief is underscored in a dramatized form in Proverbs 7 with the depiction of a married woman who pretends to be a *zonah* (prostitute) and lures a man to his death. It seems a *zonah* was viewed as having more power than wives. The Israelites did not want their women to be *zonot* (prostitutes) because it took away their total control over these women. The protest of Dinah's brothers in Genesis 34, when they considered Shechem as having usurped their authority over their sister, offers further evidence of this view of the *zonah* in Israelite contexts: "…Should our sister be treated like a prostitute [*zonah*]?" (Gen 34:32). When Israelite males made bargains for a *zonah*'s services, they were negotiating with a woman with power, as demonstrated in the case of Judah who mistook his daughter-in-law for a *zonah* (Gen 38:15).

Thus, contrary to the idea that Rahab is at grave risk of sexual violence and death as the Israelite army approaches on its genocidal mission, her status as a *zonah* makes her the likely Canaanite woman to survive the genocidal army because she is not considered a marriage material. She has no capability to turn Israelite men away from their God. *Zonot* were those kinds of women for which Israelite men were not penalized or shamed for having sex with. With a *zonah*, no other man's rights were violated. But more importantly, a Canaanite *zonah* did not have the ability to turn Israelite males away from their God because she was not committed to her religious, cultural and political identity. Of the three women in the Samson narrative in the book of Judges, only the *zonah* is portrayed as not betraying him (Judg 16:1–3). A Canaanite or Philistine *zonah* would not be interested in recreating her people's culture or repopulating her land.[15]

Rahab's importance in the story concerns her confession to the spies that she is protecting. In her confession, she professes knowledge that the Israelite God had given the land inhabited by her people to the Israelites. She furthermore states that great dread has fallen upon her and her people after hearing the acts of the Israelite God on behalf of the Israelites, and how the Israelites have applied the *ḥerem* (obliteration) practice of the Amorites beyond the Jordan. And finally, Rahab professes the superiority of the Israelites and their God: "[YHWH] your God is indeed God in heaven above and on earth below" (Josh 2:11).

---

15. In fact, she can completely support Israelite interest and be totally assimilated into Israelite royalty.

By these words, Rahab is thus legitimizing the invading Israelites' claim to her own land, the land that her people had occupied since time immemorial, as the narratives in the book of Genesis attest (e.g., Gen 12:7; 13:7, etc.). It is this confession that influences the positive interpretation of Rahab's acts of betrayal of her own people in most Western feminist readings. Alice Ogden Bellis represents the prevalent feminist interpretation as follows:

> Rahab is a hero because she protects the Israelite spies. She is also heroic because she is a woman of faith who takes risks based on faith. In addition, she is clever, like the midwives of Exodus. She outwits the king of Jericho, ignores his death-affirming command, and acts in a way that affirms life—for herself and the Israelite people.[16]

It is interesting that the king of Jericho is viewed as death-affirming while the invading genocidal Israelites are life-affirming. But who is worthy of life-affirming ideology?

After her confession, Rahab now demands payment for what she has already done for the Israelite men. She wants them to reciprocate the *ḥesed* (loyalty) she has shown them by granting a token of their pledge that they would "spare her father and mother, her brothers and sister and all who belong to them…" (Josh 2:13). At this point, it is revealed that Rahab is not a lonely vulnerable woman, but she has men and other women who also have others who belong to them.

Rahab may be vulnerable to the invading Israelites, just as all her people are, but she does not present herself as a powerless woman. Just as Judah had to leave a sign of loyalty to his daughter-in-law whom he thought was a prostitute (Gen 38:18), the men pledge loyalty and faithfulness to her. The men are vulnerable because they are under her protection—at this point, their lives are in her hands. Rahab's encounter with the Israelite spies demonstrates their vulnerability—they need her protection to get out of Jericho alive!

The disempowering of indigenous men in relation to the protection of the indigenous women is a significant characteristic of imperial narratives. Thus, the indigenous men are rendered incapable of protecting their women, while the assumption is that the invading male army is able to protect everyone who is part of the invading population. This depiction of Rahab follows the phenomenon of giving indigenous women capabilities denied to Israelite women (cf. Deut 7:3–4).

---

16. Alice Ogden Bellis, *Helpmates, Harlots, and Heroes: Women's Stories in the Hebrew Bible*, 2nd ed. (Louisville, KY: Westminster John Knox, 2007), 100.

Rahab continues to demonstrate her loyalty not only by keeping their secret, but also by assisting the spies to escape—helping them climb through the window using a rope since her house was attached to the city wall. She even advises them on how not to be detected (Josh 2:15–16). In turn, the men advise Rahab on how she and her family would be spared from the utter destruction of the invaders—she is to tie the same crimson cord to the same window they have used to climb down and gather all her family in the room. The success is predicated on each party keeping its part of the bargain.

After their escape, the men follow Rahab's plans; they hide in the hill country for three days, until the pursuers return to Jericho. The pursuers do a thorough search and fail to find the Israelite spies. When it is safe, the spies come down from the hill country and report their adventures to Joshua. The only words given to them by the author are a summary of Rahab's words: "Truly our God has given all the land into our hands, moreover all the inhabitants of the land melt in fear before us" (Josh 2:24). These words seem to address Joshua's apparent lack of courage and strength.

Rahab's character does not only meet the rhetoric of imperial narratives of employing gender to represent the accessibility of targeted nations, but her portrayal functions as a means to express the innocence and vulnerability of the invaders. In the spy narrative in the book of Numbers, it is the people who need encouragement. However, in the book of Joshua, it seems to be Joshua, the leader who needs to be encouraged through Rahab's words. Thus, as an anti-conquest rhetoric, Rahab's words are for the benefit of Joshua. Through Rahab's words transmitted by the spies, Joshua finally finds the courage needed to move forward with the task divinely given to him. Without Rahab's words, Joshua might not have had the confidence to move forward. Joshua's response to these words of assurance is to proceed towards the land of Canaan by commanding Israel to cross the Jordan, in what can be described as a religious observation. Thus, on the forefront of this procession, one finds the Ark of the Covenant and the rituals that underscore the doctrine of Israel's selection and supremacy.

In the subsequent episode, Jericho is destroyed and Rahab and her family and all who belong to her are spared to live a marginal life on the outskirts of Israel (Josh 6:22–27). Rahab and her family thus play a supporting role in enabling the Israelites to conquer successfully the land that had once belonged to the Canaanites. Joshua addresses chilling words to Rahab and her people, especially the male members of Rahab's family, the only people who would have and desired to rebuild Jericho: "Cursed before the Lord [YHWH] be anyone who tries to build this city—this

Jericho! At the cost of his firstborn he shall lay its foundation, and at the cost of his youngest he shall set up its gate!" (Josh 6:26). The focus on Rahab concludes with the endorsement that the Israelite God was with Joshua (Josh 6:27).

For communities of justice to celebrate the fact that Israel kept the promise of the spies is to perpetuate systems of injustice. It is to ignore the root cause of Rahab's marginalization, and ignoring the root of injustice only perpetuates unjust systems and structures. We cannot dismantle what we admire and endorse. We need to read these narratives from a Canaanite perspective and ask: What is justice for the Canaanites? What would restorative justice look like for Rahab? For Israel to hold on to its unjust claim on Rahab's land and only give her a piece as a consolation prize is not restorative justice.

The theme of the vulnerability and innocence of the Israelites continues in Joshua 7. Suddenly, all is not well regarding God's relationship with Israel because one of the Israelite males puts Israel's possession of the land of the Canaanites in jeopardy. Achan's disobedience puts the fulfilment of the promise that Israel would possess Canaanite land at risk. It is only after Achan's total destruction that Israel is able to defeat Ai through some divinely guided strategy that results in the burning down of the city and the slaughter of all its inhabitants, including men, women and children. Unlike in the case of the city of Jericho, livestock and precious objects are taken as booty by the Israelites (Josh 8:27). The king of Ai is subjected to a gross act of brutality when Joshua is said to "hang the king of Ai on a tree until evening" (Josh 8:29). This act of brutality is furthermore memorialized because "at sunset Joshua commanded, and they took his body down from the tree, threw it down at the entrance of the gate of the city, and raised over it a great heap of stones, which stands there to this day" (Josh 8:29). Moreover, the violence executed by Joshua seems to be divinely sanctioned, as it is followed immediately by a report of Joshua building an altar to the Israelite God, and writing down and reading all the words of the Torah of Moses (Josh 8:30–35).[17] This notice possibly reflects the vulnerability of Joshua since he had just reversed the *ḥerem* demand (Josh 8:2), while the narrator seems to imply that there were no witnesses to the Israelite God issuing that revision (cf. Josh 8:27). According to Josh 6:18, the adherence to the *ḥerem* command is the guarantee that Israel will completely possess the land of the Canaanites.

---

17. Reflection on the erection of monuments might guide communities of faith on how to regard the confederate monuments in America and all colonial monuments in formerly colonized countries.

3. Sanitizing Genocidal Ideology:
The Enslavement of the Gibeonites

While Rahab earns the salvation of her family from the *ḥerem* by lying to her king, and by hiding and aiding the Israelite spies in their escape, the Gibeonites earn their deliverance by lying to Joshua. Sparing the Gibeonites is used much more significantly in the attempt to counter the ethical and theological issues inherent in the desire to annihilate other peoples. As William Ford concludes, "Therefore, in the modern discussion about the ethical and theological problems raised by the conquest, one *partial* response to the question 'What about the Canaanites?' is the counter question 'What about the Gibeonites?'"[18]

But should the sparing of the Gibeonites be used to gloss over the injustices against the Canaanites that are clearly depicted in the conquest narratives? Readers are lured into ignoring the plight of the Canaanites, including the Gibeonites. As in the case of Rahab, the theme of the vulnerability and innocence of the Israelites is at play in the presentation of the encounter between the Israelites and the Gibeonites.

The theme of the vulnerability and innocence of the Israelites is highlighted in how the rest of the Canaanites respond. Instead of melting in fear before the invading Israelites, the majority of the Canaanites "gathered with one accord to fight Joshua and Israel" (Josh 9:2). Then the focus shifts to the depiction of the reaction of one particular group, the Gibeonites who do not gather with the other Canaanite kings but devise a way to survive the Israelite invasion (Josh 9:3–6).

The Gibeonites trick Joshua into believing that they were outside the targeted areas for dispossession and hence persuade Joshua to make a covenant with them instead of applying the *ḥerem* to them (Josh 9:7–15). The Gibeonites thus are depicted as having knowledge of the Deuteronomic instructions on how the Israelites were supposed to deal with the nations outside the land targeted for Israelite occupation, where the *ḥerem* did not apply, namely, entering into treaties if these nations pledged subordination to Israel (Deut 20:10–18).

But more importantly, the Gibeonites accept the Israelite divinely sanctioned claim to their land: "Because it was told to your servants for a certainty that the Lord [YHWH] your God had commanded his servant Moses to give you all the land, and to destroy all the inhabitants of the land before you; so we were in great fear for our lives because of you, and did this thing" (Josh 9:24). This response by the Gibeonites is

---

18. William Ford, "What about the Gibeonites?" *TynBul* 66 (2015): 216.

interpreted as their conversion into Israelite religion although there is no mention of them actually doing so. Ford states that, "This suggests that by responding positively to YHWH, the Gibeonites and Rahab become exempted in some way from the *ḥerem* that is due to the Canaanites."[19] The question about the legitimacy of Israel's claim to the land of the Gibeonites is muted because the Gibeonites are presented as accepting the Israelite ideology of supremacy that is validated by the acknowledgment of the sovereignty of the Israelite God, YHWH. It should be noted that responding positively to YHWH meant accepting the Israelite agenda to displace the Canaanites from their land. Hence, smart Canaanites like the Gibeonites would find ways to mitigate the effects of Israelite invasion—servitude is better than obliteration!

The gullibility of Joshua puts the success of Israelite occupation of the land at risk of being fulfilled. When Joshua realizes that he has been tricked into making a covenant with the Gibeonites, he does not revoke the agreement. Joshua claims to be constrained by the oath that he swore in the name of YHWH (cf. Josh 9:18–19). Rather than praising Israel and in particular Joshua as a people committed to covenants (even ones initiated deceitfully), this narrative is designed to show Israel's vulnerability and innocence in desiring other people's land. It is made clear that Israel did not desire the land of Canaan—the Israelite God just happened to promise it to Israel's ancestors.[20] Left to their own devices, the Israelites were so incompetent that they would never have succeeded in taking possession of the land on their own. The Israelite God had to fight for them and intervene just to ascertain that the promise is fulfilled. This narrative underscores the vulnerability of Joshua, and by extension, of the people of Israel. The Israelites are thus presented as the underdogs with whom the reader automatically sides. Consequently, the anti-conquest strategy of hiding the true victims of unjust claims and acts is successful—Israel is the victim of the Gibeonites and not vice versa.

The nature of the covenant between Joshua and the Gibeonites requires further scrutiny. According to Roland Boer, the Gibeonites can be described actually as "Israelites uncertain about their identity."[21]

---

19. Ibid., 213.

20. The same theme of the Israelites putting the fulfilment of the promise of land in jeopardy is depicted in the narratives about murmuring in the books of Exodus and Numbers and is accentuated in the spy narrative in which the Israelites refuse to move forward but desire to return to Egypt (Num 13:1–14:12).

21. Roland Boer, "Green Ants and Gibeonites: B. Wongar, Joshua 9, and Some Problems of Postcolonialism," *Semeia* 75 (1996): 148.

Nevertheless, such an interpretation functions to erase the victims and the nature of injustice reflected in the texts. The full incorporation of the Gibeonites is ruled out in 2 Sam 21:2:

> Now the Gibeonites were not of the people of Israel, but of the remnant of the Amorites; although the people of Israel had sworn to spare them, Saul had tried to wipe them out in his zeal for the people of Israel and Judah.

Clearly, Gibeonites are not Israelites but victims of dispossession and exploitation. Joshua is so afraid of the consequences of breaching the *ḥerem* that he turns the Gibeonites into divine slaves rather than slaves of Joshua or of the Israelites. By making the Gibeonites hewers of wood and drawers of water for the sanctuary of YHWH (cf. Josh 9:27), he is making a deliberate distinction between Achan and himself. The Gibeonites are not spared to serve Joshua or the Israelite population but the Israelite God; they are in fact living *ḥerem*. The Gibeonites have a covenant with the Israelites not to become integrated into Israelite identity; however, they can become targets of abuse in the politics of Israel (cf. 2 Sam 21:1–14). Their purpose of existence is to serve the Israelite God, but not as willing worshipers. More importantly, instead of serving their own gods, the Gibeonites are made to serve the Israelite God in a way that paralyzes them from negatively influencing the Israelites.[22] As slaves of the Israelite God, they cannot now serve their own gods in a meaningful way. The Gibeonites are not targeted for conversion to Israelite religion—they simply can no longer be Canaanite in a way that sustains them as a people. They are cut off from the land that should give them their identity. They are now hewers of wood and drawers of water for an alien religion. The success of their subjugation is demonstrated in that Gibeon is described as "the mountain of YHWH" (2 Sam 21:6) and the largest of the Israelite sanctuaries (1 Kgs 3:4).

In contrast to the Gibeonites, the king of Jerusalem responds to the fear of the invading Israelites by forming a coalition of five kings against not the Israelites but the Gibeonites (Josh 10:1–5). The Gibeonites in turn seek protection from Joshua, who is able to destroy the coalition of Canaanite kings. The destruction of these cities is not because the Israelites want to dispossess them. In the annihilation of the Canaanite kings and their people, Joshua keeps the covenant with the Gibeonites while the Israelites

---

22. It is interesting that the reason for *ḥerem* is a religious one, namely that the Canaanites would not influence Israel to abandon YHWH. But Canaanite religions do not at all factor in the encounters between the invading Israelites and the indigenous Canaanite peoples.

also defend themselves against the warring Canaanites. It is ironic that the invading Israelites, whose only purpose for advancing into Canaanite land is to kill and pillage, are not characterized as the aggressors.[23] This characterization also shifts the focus from revealing the unjust and exploitative relationship between the Israelites and the Gibeonites. The Israelites are now viewed as keeping covenant with the Gibeonites instead of simply protecting their own interests and advancing their agenda of dispossessing the Canaanites.

Furthermore, the subjective position of the Gibeonites vis-à-vis the Israelites is sanctioned by YHWH. YHWH is depicted as fighting on behalf of those Israelites as they are defending the Gibeonites from the other Canaanite kings: "…[YHWH] threw down huge stones from heaven on them as far as Azekah, and they died; there were more who died because of hailstones than the Israelites killed with the sword" (Josh 10:11). YHWH is more interested in the obliteration of the Canaanites than the Israelites who are the beneficiaries. Thus, the exoneration of the Israelites in the injustices against the Canaanites is underscored by placing "the blame" on the divine realm. The Israelites are not to blame for the genocide of the Canaanites as the conclusion to the narrative about the Gibeonites and the five kings emphasizes, "So Joshua defeated the whole land…he left no one remaining, but utterly destroyed all that breathed, *as [YHWH] the God of Israel had commanded*. Joshua took all these kings and their lands at one time, *because [YHWH] the God of Israel fought for Israel*" (Josh 10:41–42, italics added). The hand of God is greater than that of Joshua (and of the Israelites) in the utter destruction of the Canaanites. The corollary to the innocence of the Israelites in the perpetration of the injustices against the Canaanites is the idea that the Israelites are not required or expected to practice restorative justice vis-à-vis the Canaanites.[24]

---

23. Like Rahab, the Gibeonites are constructed to justify an imperial ideology, and this is the same concept found in the literature that justifies European colonization of Africa. Not only were Africans characterized as warring barbarians, but their dispossession from their lands by the Europeans was to save them from killing each other. This sentiment is well expressed by Albert Schweitzer, who wrote in 1939, "When long-resident natives of the district express to me their discontent at being ruled by the whites, I answer that without the white man they would either have slaughtered each other or ended in the Pahouin cooking pots." Albert Schweitzer, *African Notebook*, trans. C. E. B. Russell (Syracuse, NY: University of Syracuse, 2002), 18.

24. This thinking is clearly reflected in the resistance to the idea of reparations for formerly colonized and enslaved peoples who are victims of modern imperial injustices. Cf. Stephen Kershnar, *Justice for the Past* (Albany, NY: State University

4. Conclusion: Dismantling Unjust Structures

Rahab and the Gibeonites can be said to be different sides of the same coin. They are pawns in imperial narratives that are designed to promote an unjust system with marginalizing, exploitative and oppressive structures. Focusing on themes such as commitment to covenant and ritual does not lead to the dismantling and transformation of unjust structures. In fact, it ends up asking more from the marginalized, oppressed and exploited in societies and communities. Inclusion is not the issue for Rahab, the Gibeonites and the rest of the Canaanites. Justice for them is restoring what was taken from them, namely land and life. Until one truly focuses on the root cause and victims of oppressive, marginalizing and oppressive systems and structures, justice will continue to be elusive. Admiration for biblical Israel's commitment to covenant needs to be balanced by a critique of the nature of the covenant—otherwise, that admiration is misplaced because it only serves to maintain unjust, oppressive and exploitative structures.

The book of Joshua should not be thrown out by faith communities. However, it also should not be sanitized so as to make its ideology acceptable by blurring the root cause of the injustices reflected in the book. Admitting the nature and function of these narratives go a long way towards engaging in the conversations about and the difficult work of dismantling unjust structures and systems. The church, faith communities, and communities of justices need to ask, "What would justice look like for Rahab, the Gibeonites and the rest of the Canaanites who were dispossessed, marginalized, and exploited?"

The quest for justice should involve direct questions about the causes of the marginalization of Rahab and her family, of the exploitation and oppression of the Gibeonites, and of the annihilation of the rest of the Canaanites. Can the beneficiaries of the imperial/colonial ideologies read the book of Joshua from the perspectives of the victims of these same ideologies? How will unjust structures and systems be dismantled when the revelations from such critical analysis are acknowledged and then set aside for views that ultimately maintain the status quo? Are the beneficiaries of imperial and colonial ideologies willing to risk their advantaged positions and benefits in the unjust systems? Or are they willing to go just so far as to maintain their privileged position?

of New York Press, 2004); David Horowitz, *Uncivil Wars: The Controversy over Reparations for Slavery* (San Francisco, CA: Encounter, 2002); John Torpey, *Making Whole What Has Been Smashed: On Reparations Politics* (Cambridge, MA: Harvard University Press, 2006).

If exploitative, marginalizing, and oppressive systems and structures are to be dismantled successfully, then, the focus needs to be on the root cause, and engaging in postcolonial analysis of sacred imperial texts is one good way to do that. Regressing to reading such imperial narratives as the book of Joshua for the sake of maintaining them as sacred text should be avoided. Their value as sacred text is in forcing people to see the contemporary unjust systems and structures in ways that motivate tangible actions to bring about justice. Reconciliation cannot be achieved without establishing justice, and justice should not be confused with inclusion.

The ethical and theological problems raised by the conquest cannot be swept aside by the narratives of the sparing of a few Canaanites like Rahab's family and the Gibeonites. Now that the modern discussion has turned to the task of dismantling marginalizing, oppressive and exploitative systems and structures that the biblical texts have been co-opted to sanction, the questions should be "What should justice look like for the victims?"

Bibliography

Bellis, Alice Ogden. *Helpmates, Harlots, and Heroes: Women's Stories in the Hebrew Bible.* 2nd ed. Louisville, KY: Westminster John Knox, 2007.

Boer Roland. "Green Ants and Gibeonites: B. Wongar, Joshua 9, and Some Problems of Postcolonialism." *Semeia* 75 (1996): 129–52.

Collins John J. *The Bible after Babel: Historical Criticism in a Postmodern Age.* Grand Rapids, MI: Eerdmans, 2005.

Collins John J. "New Israel, New Canaan: The Bible, the People of God, and the American Holocaust." *USQR* 59 (2005): 25–39.

Donaldson, Laura E. "Postcolonial and Biblical Reading: An Introduction." *Semeia* 75 (1996): 1–14.

Dube, Musa W. *Postcolonial Feminist Interpretation of the Bible.* St. Louis, MO: Chalice, 2000.

Epp-Tiessen, Esther. "Conquering the Land." In *Under Vine and Fig Tree: Biblical Theology and the Palestinian–Israeli Conflict*, edited by Alain Epp Weaver, 62–74. Telford, PA: Cascadia, 2007.

Fewell, Danna Nolan. "Joshua." In *Women's Bible Commentary with the Apocrypha*, edited by Carol A. Newsom and Sharon H. Ringe, 69–72. Expanded ed. Louisville, KY: Westminster John Knox, 1998.

Ford, William. "What about the Gibeonites?" *TynBul* 66 (2015): 197–216.

Gunn, David M. "Colonialism and the Vagaries of Scripture: Te Kooti in Canaan (A Story of the Bible and Dispossession in Aotearoa/New Zealand)." In *God in the Fray: A Tribute to Walter Brueggemann*, edited by Tod Linafelt and Timothy K. Beal, 127–42. Minneapolis, MN: Fortress, 1998.

Horowitz, David. *Uncivil Wars: The Controversy over Reparation for Slavery.* San Francisco, CA: Encounter, 2002.

Kershnar, Stephen. *Justice for the Past*. Albany, NY: State University of New York Press, 2004.
Mbuwayesango, Dora R. "Joshua." In *Global Bible Commentary*, edited by Daniel Patte, 64–73. Nashville, TN: Abingdon, 2004.
Mbuwayesango, Dora R. "Numbers." In *Postcolonial Commentary and the Old Testament*, edited by Hemchad Gossai, 70–87. London: T&T Clark, 2019.
Pratt, Mary Louise. *Imperial Eyes: Travel Writing and Transculturation*. 2nd ed. New York: Routledge, 2008.
Prior, Michael. *The Bible and Colonialism: A Moral Critique*. Sheffield: Sheffield Academic, 1997.
Schweitzer, Albert. *African Notebook*. Translated by C. E. B. Russell. New York: Syracuse University Press, 2002.
Seibert, Eric A. *The Violence of Scripture: Overcoming the Old Testament's Troubling Legacy*. Minneapolis, MN: Fortress, 2012.
Sharp, Carolyn J. "'Are You for Us, or for Our Adversaries?' A Feminist and Postcolonial Interrogation of Joshua 2–12 for the Contemporary Church." *Int* 66 (2012): 141–52.
Torpey, John. *Making Whole What Has Been Smashed: On Reparations Politics*. Cambridge, MA: Harvard University Press, 2006.
Warrior, Robert Allen. "Canaanites, Cowboys, and Indians: Deliverance, Conquest and Liberation Theology Today." *Christianity and Crisis* 49 (1989): 261–5.

Chapter 10

COME ON, COME OUT, COME HERE, COME HERE...
QUEER EXPRESSIONS OF DESIRE IN GENESIS 28–31

Charlene van der Walt

University of KwaZulu-Natal

1. Introduction

When navigating the complexity of a life together with the beloved amidst profound distance or absence due to time, space or circumstance, the discovery of a kindred spirit does much to ease the painful sense of isolation. The lyrics of "New York" on the *Fallen Empires* album by Snow Patrol[1] gives beautiful resonant expression to the all-encompassing immediacy of longing for the one loved, yet the one absent:

> If you were here beside me, instead of in New York. If the curve of you was curved on me, I'd tell you that I loved you, before I even knew you, 'cause I loved the simple thought of you...and there's distance and there's silence, your words have never left me, they're the prayer that I say every day. Come on, come out, come here, come here.[2]

The raw poetry and the musical arch of the Snow Patrol song cited above expresses something of the absence of the beloved, the having found you and recognized you, but not being able to be with you to have an everyday life with you. The knowing you, knowing of you, and yet lacking you

---

1. Gary Lightbody and Johnny McDaid, "New York," track 9 on Snow Patrol's album *Fallen Empires* (Polydor, 2011). Hereafter cited as Snow Patrol, "New York."
2. Snow Patrol, "New York."

in the simple fiber of every day informs the haunting refrain so tangibly familiar to those who have ever longed for the beloved into being by simply and honestly willing their presence in the words *come on, come out, come here, come here*. The absence, the distance, the elusiveness of the beloved of life intertwined with the beloved is what silently exists in the heart of this essay. Existence at times overwhelmed by the cruel trick of time and circumstance, existence sometimes drowning in sadness and lament, existence occasionally partaking in cunning deceit and sly tricks to enable closeness, but mostly existence in waiting.

Doing life together, yet profoundly separate is the peculiar fate of those who for various reasons find themselves living in long distance relationships. To quote Roland Barthes:

> [I]t is I who remain. The other is in a condition of perpetual departure, of journeying; the other is, by vocation, migrant, fugitive; I—I who love, by converse vocation, am sedentary, motionless, at hand, in expectation, nailed to the spot, in suspense—like a package in some forgotten corner of a railway station.[3]

This reflection by Barthes speaks of the joy of journeying to the other, of arriving, of coming home, and simultaneously, the nagging knowledge of departure. In the embrace of welcome, either here or there, always undeniably present is the shadow of saying goodbye.

In the ever shrinking and simultaneously expanding Global Village, the possibility of doing life together yet deeply separate is becoming a growing trend. Video calling and real-time messaging contribute to a hyper-reality in which presence is no longer necessarily equated to an embodied nearness or closeness. Ever-evolving career demands—often dehumanizing socio-economic realities, and the consequential possibility of working in one time zone and staying in another, crisscrossing by the injection of jet fuel—lead to many a late-night telephone call, so beautifully articulated by Snow Patrol songwriters, Gary Lightbody and Johnny McDaid, "*I miss it all, from the love to the lightning and the lack of it snaps me in two.*"[4]

Beyond the privilege of choice, doing life in different places has long been the necessity of many South Africans, especially considering the limited availability of sustainable employment, particularly in rural areas, and the enduring reality of socio-economic demands. Necessity driving

---

3. Roland Barthes, *A Lover's Discourse: Fragments* (London: Macmillan, 1978), 13.
4. Snow Patrol, "New York."

the fate of many men and women who have had to silently bear the vulnerability of this life situation looms in the silences between the words that this essay will be contemplating when it considers concepts such as absence, unattainability, longing and desire.

Having to personally grapple with the absence of the beloved and the numerous ways that the complexity of this reality is written on the body, I went in search of a kindred spirit. Propelled by the fragile navigation of the quiet chaos of desire, I longed to find a narrative or literary depiction that would resonate with my own experiences of the ebb and flow of togetherness and absence; a reflective surface that would enable the ongoing and ever-evolving process of sense-making and meaning-making. Beyond the contemporary meditation on the often all-encompassing reality of longing and desire that finds expression in the Snow Patrol lyrics that functions as a kind of soundtrack to the present study, and that I weave throughout the essay as a reminder that some realities require poetry to exist, the essay was initially sparked by the iconic recollection or remembrance of Jacob's desire for Rachel in the narrative cycle contained in Genesis 28–31 and the possible imaginings about what the seven years of present absence might have been like. Although not exactly a relationship marked by physical absence, Rachel's unattainability in her present state of absence with Jacob sparked a sense of recognition. Although the initial starting point of the essay was indeed the desire to reflect on Jacob's arch of desire that can be traced though the narrative development, that is, through the process of reading and reflection, it became a mere departure point for traveling through an intersecting landscape of desire that we encounter beyond the single expression of desire when Jacob identifies Rachel as the object of his affection. A central question that functions as a hermeneutical key to this exploration follows from the Slovenian philosopher Slavoj Žižek's unmasking of the dynamo of desire when he poignantly asks: "What is it that you want?"[5]

2. *Queering Desire*

Before embarking on a critical rereading of the narrative captured in Genesis 28–31 by employing Žižek's provocative question as a hermeneutical tool, first, I would like to problematize and contextualize my personal recollection of the Jacob story, and then, slow down the argument by reflecting on the nature and theoretical underpinnings of the notion of desire.

---

5. Slavoj Žižek, *The Sublime Object of Ideology* (London: Verso, 1989), 111.

When initially recalling the story from memory, my main point of departure was in line with the hetero-patriarchal thrust of the narrative. I remembered the story from Jacob's vantage point, as he has arguably dominantly been understood and portrayed as the central character of the narrative. I remembered the expression of his desire for the beautiful Rachel. I remembered his hard work aimed at facilitating a union with Rachel, and the drama that resulted from Laban's trickery when Jacob receives Leah as a wife, rather than the desired Rachel.

My discovery of other strands of desire resulted from a deliberate adjustment of the hermeneutical focus in the engagement with the text. The matter of fact nature of my remembered recollection of this story is, to my mind, but one example of the pervasiveness and the unquestionable dominance of heteropatriarchy. The pervasive construction of patriarchal heteronormativity is the result of a systematic normalization of heterosexuality and it is dominantly present in the contemporary societal landscape, and in African contexts, in particular.[6] According to Andrew Martin et al., "this is the idea, dominant in most societies, that heterosexuality is the only 'normal' sexual orientation, only sexual or marital relations between women and men are acceptable and each sex has certain natural roles in life, so-called gender roles."[7] Patriarchy and subsequent heteronormativity thus equate being human to being a man, and a man is understood to be above a woman, and in ideal union with a woman. This system then further informs dominant ideas of masculinity, family, marriage and citizenship.

Drawing from these theoretical insights, it follows that desire, who is the object of desire and who is desired, will undoubtedly strongly be influenced by notions of patriarchy, heteronormativity and rigid binary gender constructions. Making space for more bodies to matter, and for a rich diversity of expressions of desire to emerge, necessitates a deliberate commitment to transgressing and destabilizing the dominant and often entrenched understandings and expressions of being gendered in the

---

6. Gust Yep describes this process as follows: "The process of normalization of heterosexuality in our social system actively and methodically subordinates, disempowers, denies and rejects individuals who do not conform to the heterosexual mandate by criminalizing them, denying them protection against discrimination, refusing them basic rights and recognition, or all of the above." Gust A. Yep, "The Violence of Heteronormativity in Communication Studies," *Journal of Homosexuality* 45, no. 2–4 (2003): 11–59 (24–5).

7. Martin Andrew, Annie Kelly, Laura Turquet, and Stephanie Ross, "Hate Crimes: The Rise of Corrective Rape in South Africa," *Action Aid* 2009, https://www.actionaid.org.uk/sites/default/files/doc_lib/correctiveraperep_final.pdf.

world as well as a commitment to interrogating the power implications of these constructions. It is with this aim that I employ insights form Queer Theory to trouble singular heteropatriarchal understandings of desire in the selected segment of the Jacob narrative cycle. According to Schneider, Queer Theory "is a critical theory concerned principally with cultural deployments of power through social constructions of sexuality and gender."[8] Derived from the idea of denaturalizing and de-essentializing stable identities, queer theory is derived from a tradition that is interested in developing new language and critical theory to interrogate heterosexual supremacy and the resulting systemic implications of heteronormativity. Queer as a radical deconstructivist project has as its aim the troubling and destabilization of normative and stable social categories and identity constructions. In the development of the argument, I will employ insights form Queer Theory to illuminate and amplify the divergent strands of desire that can be traced though the narrative construction.

Consequently, I deem it important to draw attention to the often systemic and institutionalized expression of the affinity between heteropatriarchy and dominant socio-economic systems. In order to highlight and articulate something of the systemic implications when dominant ideologies such as patriarchy, heteronormativity and capitalism align, the term heteropatriarchy has recently been reframed as "econo-heteropatriarchy."[9] This fresh expression of heteropatriarchy affirms the analysis that patriarchy and heteronormativity are the structural result when culture and religion align to inform dominant constructions of gender, and this has very real systemic and pragmatic implications. This system is not a mere conceptual construction or an idea, but it has very real consequences for bodies, and finds expression in the intersection of socio-economic realities, class, race, gender, and sexuality construction.

Although much of the discussion of Genesis 28–31 below will probe personal, private, or intimate expressions of desire, it is important to pay attention to the socio-economic frame of the narrative. Much of the

---

8. Laurel Schneider, "Queer Theory," in *Handbook of Postmodern Biblical Interpretation*, ed. A. K. M. Adam (St. Louis, MO: Chalice, 2000), 206.

9. Gerald West theoretically explores the notion of econo-heteropatriarchy, and for more in this regard, see Gerald O. West, "A Trans-textual and Trans-sectoral Gender-economic Reading of the Rape of Tamar (2 Sam 13) and the Expropriation of Naboth's Land (1 Kgs 21)," in *Faith, Class, and Labor: Intersectional Approaches in a Global Context*, ed. Jin Young Choi and Joerg Rieger (Eugene, OR: Wipf & Stock, 2020), 105–21. Furthermore, for more on the relationship between religion, culture, and gender, cf. Tinyiko Sam Maluleke and Sarojini Nadar, "Breaking the Covenant of Violence against Women," *JThSA* 114 (2002): 5.

personal and intimate expressions of desire in the narrative is imbedded in a complex frame determined by the pursuit of socio-economic gain and consequential power hegemony between the men in the narrative. Therefore, even when exploring the contours of Rachel's or Leah's desire (not even to mention the predominantly glossed over existence of the handmaids, Zilpah and Bilhah), as they are apparent in the narrative, such contours of desire always remain within the systemic container of econo-heteropatriarchy. The way in which Rachel and Leah are objectified—treated as mere objects or disposable possessions by Laban when he plays his cruel trick on Jacob on his wedding night—is but one expression of the pervasive dehumanizing systemic reality of their world.

I highlight this systemic dimension upfront in my narrative analysis as I sense that much of the contemporary theorizing being done about identity politics often lacks a robust engagement with the systemic realities informing othering, stigma, and dehumanization. To engage with life-denying contextual and embodied realities informed by econo-heteropatriarchy comprehensively, the perceived inescapabilty and pervasiveness of the systemic issues that inform these realties warrant interrogation, destabilizing, and re-imagining. In the development of the argument of the essay, I hope to highlight some strategies of resistance which become visible in the character development, as the plot of their narrative evolves.

3. *Dynamics of Desire*

Following from this brief theoretical reflection on the imperative of the Queer project in the process of destabilizing pervasive systemic realities such as econo-heteropatriarchy, I now turn my attention to the dynamics of desire. It has often been noted that distance or absence does wonders to kindle desire in a relationship but simultaneously poses great challenges to the nurturing of a sense of stable intimacy and dependable proximity. Feelings of understandable vulnerability and disconnection easily equate to the erosion of intimacy when distance remains and stretches out over time. Absence and unattainability, however, spark desire and are fundamental to desire. Desire is excited through prohibition, through the moment of censorship that seeks to banish it, yet this is a restriction that rubs desire to renewed energy.[10] Kathryn Harding writes in this regard that, "Sexual desire in particular cannot be sustained when the state of

---

10. Roland Boer, "The Second Coming: Repetition and Insatiable Desire in the Song of Songs," *BibInt* 8 (2000): 279.

union with the loved being is an uninterrupted, perpetual possibility; it is precipitated by separations, deferrals, absences, all of which further incite desire, make the heart grow fonder."[11] Desire is a powerful dynamo for existence, for mobility, for being. For the French psychoanalyst Jacques Lucan, desire functions so centrally that it can be substituted for being. Our desire for the other propels us, brings us in motion and determines our course.[12]

When tracing the mechanics of desire in Lacan's triad of need–demand–desire, Žižek identifies the raw kernel of desire in the question, "You demand something of me, but what do you really want, what are you aiming at with this demand?"[13] Desire is then the subtraction of need from demand, the casting off of demand from its connection with need, whereby it attains the status of the want that is not what one demands.[14]

As stated at the outset of the essay, wanting life together, desiring union and yet being hampered somehow by reality and circumstance propelled the search for a kindred spirit. Being prone to prose rather than poetry led one, as already alluded to, past the elusive lovers expressing desire for union in the Song of Songs to Jacob and his iconic laboring for love's fulfilment as he spends seven years in the present absence of Rachel.

By reading this well-known tale of love, desire and deceit from a position of Queering econo-heteropatriarchal elements of the text, I aim to illustrate that the narrative becomes an important reflective surface for contemporary readers like myself, and a space for the development of moral imagination.[15] By tracing the contours of desire in the narrative beyond the main heteropatriarchal thrust of Jacob's desire to the silent and painfully complex longings and desires of Rachel and Leah, the narrative cracks open space for reflections on non-binary or queer expressions of desire. Merely by making visible small counter voices in the text and allowing for divergent expressions of desire, space is created for more honest and embodied contemporary reflections that can be described as a Queer expression of desire in Genesis 28–31.

---

11. Kathryn Harding, "'I Sought Him but I Did not Find Him': The Elusive Lover in the Song of Songs," *BibInt* 16 (2008): 43–59, 48.
12. Jacques-Alain Miller, and Dennis Porter, *The Seminar of Jacques Lacan. Book 7. The Ethics of Psychoanalysis: 1959–1960* (London: Routledge, 1992), 321.
13. Žižek, *The Sublime Object*, 111.
14. Cf. also Boer, "The Second Coming."
15. Cf. Martha C. Nussbaum, *Sex and Social Justice* (New York: Oxford University Press, 1999), 183.

Truly engaging our own experiences of desire and reflecting on the raw energy it unleashes may seem such a daunting task that we rather choose to continue to live in superficial understandings of what propels us, unable to name the longings of our heart. I would like to propose that the world of the narrative and the dramatic unfolding of the destiny of characters imbedded in these narratives become a safe space for readers to confront complex and often difficult to understand life realities. In the encounter with those who desire within the narrative, interpreters may find a space where they dare to reflect on their own experience of longing and desire—even if these longings and desires are considered strange, counter, or outside the expected norm. The messy, complex, and painful world depicted in narratives through the act of reading and interpretation, becomes a dynamic space for ethical reflection and contemplation by contemporary readers. As argued elsewhere, I believe that our sense-making capacity is deeply influenced and nurtured by our engagement with narrative.[16]

4. *Jacob's Desire*

As already highlighted above, the thrust of the initial narrative contained in Genesis 29 is strongly propelled by the dynamics of Jacob's desire for Rachel. A desire sparked as so beautifully articulated by Snow Patrol in "New York": "The lone neon lights and the ache of the ocean and the fire that was starting to spark."[17] At the outset of the chapter, Jacob's trajectory is, however, not so much informed by moving towards something as it is by running away from something, as we encounter Jacob fleeing the consequences of his deceiving collaboration with his mother, Rebecca, after disguising his way into the blessing intended for his older brother. It is his mother who sends him in the direction of Laban (cf. Gen 27:43–44), and Jacob's tears of joy at arrival at his kinfolk's place (29:11) can be read as relief for finding that his journey has come to an end. The type scene introduced to the reader at the communal well hints at the fact that Jacob's journey might have come to an end in more ways than is apparent at face value. To be sure, the mere sight of Rachel propels Jacob, who until this point comes across as rather lackluster, into action as he rolls away

---

16. Charlene van der Walt, "Is There a Man Here? The Iron Fist in the Velvet Glove in Judges 4," in *Feminist Frameworks: Power, Ambiguity, Intersectionality*, ed. L. Juliana Claassens and Caroline Sharp (London: Bloomsbury T&T Clark, 2017), 117–32.
17. Snow Patrol, "New York."

singlehandedly (a job that usually requires a couple of strong men) the stone blocking the opening of the well (29:10). Bruce Vawter comments on the "ironic contrast with the earlier picture of Jacob the recluse, whose will and initiative were at the passive disposal of a domineering mother now no longer with him. Jacob's gaze meets Rachel; it is more than mere sight; gaze transcends sight."[18] It constitutes an "act of grounding" that opens a space for the unknown, as Luce Irigaray puts it.[19]

Jacob is introduced to Laban, and beyond the formal recognition as 'my bone and my flesh' (29:14) the tricking or deceiving Jacob is shown to have met his match. After a month's stay, terms and conditions are negotiated and the desire of Jacob's heart finds expression as he declares his intention to marry Rachel (29:18). Although the reader has already made acquaintance with Rachel, both of Laban's daughters are now introduced formally—Leah the one with the lowly eyes and Rachel the beautiful (29:17). It is Rachel for whom he will labor in love. As also explored by Meyers, Jacob's quick expression of love warrants a question mark informed by contemporary philosopher's uneasiness with the seemingly innocent declaration—I love you—as it threatens to re-inscribe the other as the object of my experience.[20] Luce Irigaray offers an alternative when she writes: "I love you risks reducing the other to the object of my love. This way of speaking should be used with caution. It would be better to say... I love to you, or in you I love which both is and becomes, that which is foreign to me. I recognize you goes hand in hand with: you are irreducible to me, just as I am to you," or, as she puts it in *The Way of Love*, "I love to who you are, to what you do, without reducing you to the object of my love."[21] Consequently, it is never stated whether the love felt by Jacob is reciprocated, but in line with the powerbrokers in a patriarchal system, the deal is struck regardless and he labors for seven years like it is a couple of days, undoubtedly fueled by the intensity of his love's desire.

After the completion of the allotted time follows the imperative of demand, a feast is made, wine is shared, and in the darkness, a switch takes place. Rachel, the object of Jacob's desire, is replaced with Leah,

---

18. Bruce Vawter, *On Genesis: A New Reading* (London: Chapman, 1977), 318.

19. Luce Irigaray, *The Way of Love*, trans. Heidi Bostic and Stephen Pluháček (London: Continuum, 2002), 72.

20. Jacob D. Myers, "Before the Gaze Ineffable: Intersubjective Poiesis and the Song of Songs," *Theology & Sexuality* 17, no. 2 (2011): 148.

21. Luce Irigaray, *Love to You: Sketch for a Felicity within History*, trans. Alison Martin (New York: Routledge, 1996), 138. Cf. also p. 60.

as Laban treats his daughters as property to be bargained with. On the mechanics involved in the deception, Melissa Jackson remarks, "Leah's wedding attire must have provided the temporary cover required for this deception, but the deception was indeed brief, lasting only until morning, when 'Behold!' It was Leah."[22] Hamilton also comments on the irony:

> Jacob, once the subject of deceit, now becomes the object of deceit. The perpetrator of subterfuge becomes the victim. The nemesis is made all the more pungent by the fact that Jacob is caught in the same device he himself has once used. He pretended to be Esau in front of Isaac. Leah pretends to be Rachel next to Jacob. While Jacob's ruse was pretending to be his older brother, Leah's ruse is pretending to be her younger sister. Jacob is deceived as he deceived his father.[23]

Laban, in response to Jacob's outrage, employs a patriarchal playbook strategy by drawing on tradition when he quotes custom (29:26) that is filled with illuminating vocabulary, as he states that the "firstborn" will not be slighted by "the younger" (terms earlier employed to describe Jacob and Esau, cf. Gen 25:23; 27:19). After the obligatory week of feasting, Jacob finally gets what he wants in this strange love story with a twist when Rachel becomes his wife alongside her older sister Leah. With Jacob's desire fulfilled, he exits the desired landscape on this level and focuses his attention on other socio-economic conquests, affirming Žižek's observation that, "One has to maintain desire in its dissatisfaction."[24]

The episode, however, ends on an ominous note when it is simply stated that Jacob loved Rachel more that Leah (29:30). Joan Ross-Burstall elaborates:

> The dynamic of Jacob's partiality to Rachel has as its counterpart his willful neglect of Leah. Leah's is the face of Laban's mastery and deception; her image is the broken image of the promised Rachel. The elder and the younger sister are unequally yoked in competition for their jointly owned husband.[25]

---

22. Melissa Jackson, *Comedy and Feminist Interpretation of the Hebrew Bible: A Subversive Collaboration* (Oxford: Oxford University Press, 2012), 52.

23. Victor P. Hamilton, *The Book of Genesis: Chapters 18–50*, NICOT (Grand Rapids, MI: Eerdmans, 1995), 262; see also Megan Boler, *Feeling Power: Emotions and Education* (London: Psychology Press, 1999).

24. Slavoj Žižek, *The Indivisible Remainder: An Essay on Schelling and Related Matters* (London: Verso, 1996), 96.

25. Joan Ross-Burstall, "Leah and Rachel: A Tale of Two Sisters," *Word & World* 14 (1994): 165.

Jacob's yearning deferred and obstructed by Laban's interference offers one narrative portrait engaging the dynamics of desire. However traumatic, we find Jacob negotiating the obstacles placed in the path to love's fulfilment, and it is worth speculating that beyond getting what he wants, he also gets what he needs. As noted earlier, my initial interest was on the iconic idea of Jacob's desire for Rachel as well as the sacrifice of seven years' labor for the fulfilment of that desire, and the interpretative richness it offers modern interpreters negotiating similar, yet profoundly different life realities. By following the thread of Jacob's unfolding desire I, however, stumbled upon the dynamics of desire for two others, set into motion by Jacob's pursuit of his destiny and brought about by Laban's sly interference.

5. *Extending Desire*

The lone neon lights and the warmth of the ocean and the fire that was starting to go out. (Snow Patrol, "New York")

Genesis 30 has often been glossed over by interpreters as merely an account of the children born to Jacob, and as an etiological narrative describing the birth of the twelve tribes of Israel. On closer inspection, however, the narrative does not primarily concern Jacob or the birth of the nation of Israel; rather, it is a tale of two women, Rachel and Leah. By allowing Žižek's earlier question directed to Jacob to extend also to the characters of Rachel and Leah—namely, "What do you want?"—as a means of unmasking the dynamics of desire, important alternative and counter portraits emerge from the narrative.

Leah, the first unwanted and subsequently demoted wife of Jacob and the older daughter of Laban, has not always been treated kindly by scholars and has often found herself undeserving of mention. She has been blamed for deceiving Jacob, although Jacob clearly blames Laban for the infringement and addresses him as the one who stood in the way of true love (Gen 29:25).

To be sure, Leah describes herself as being unloved or even hated, and it is God who sees this, and who in an act of liberating compassion takes note of her distress and opens her womb (29:31). In the naming of the sons she bears for Jacob, we discover the painfully fragile longing of Leah's heart. Both Ross-Burstall and Wilma Ann Bailey, in varying degrees, pick up on the language of lament and expressions of longing articulated by Leah in the naming of her children and it becomes apparent that Leah simply desires the love of Jacob. We find expressions of Leah's lament in the process of name-giving, a means of revealing the inner meanings of the significance of the births, the longing for a husband who does not love her although she is his first wife.[26]

The devastating isolation experienced in the loveless union with Jacob finds expression in the heart-wrenching names given to the sons Leah bears (29:32–34):

> Reuben: Because the Lord has looked on my affliction; surely now my husband will love me.
>
> Simeon: Because the Lord has heard that I am hated, has given me this son also.
>
> Levi: Now this time my husband will be joined to me, because I have borne him three sons.

Considering the focus of this exploration, the dynamics of the desires of Leah's heart, I find Bailey's argument regarding the development that takes place in Leah, and that can be deduced from the naming of her children, both insightful and convincing. She states that:

> After the birth of her first son, Leah expressed the hope that her husband would change his attitude toward her, that he would love her. After the birth of her third son, she simply states that her husband is now joined to her. But with this last son, Leah has changed her expectation. She is now no longer hoping for something but demanding something. When Zebulun is born, she says "Now my husband will raise me up" (Gen 30:20)…(or) "Now my husband will honour me" (Gen 30:20). Leah cannot make her husband love her but he is tied to her and she can demand that he honour her."[27]

Leah develops through the unfolding of the narrative from one who could easily have remained the victim of her father's deceit and her husband's disregard to a model of liberation and empowerment for many contemporary readers who are trapped within the confines of patriarchal structures as she discovers a changed sense of self. Baily further shows that, by the end of the narrative, Leah has grown. She controls her husband by bargaining with patriarchy rather than allowing him to control her emotionally. She uses the social conventions of her own society to get the recognition that she craves. Leah is not simply content to accept her

---

26. Ibid., 164–70; Wilma Ann Bailey, "Intimate Moments: A Study of Genesis 29:31–30:21," *Proceedings* 29 (2009): 1–14.

27. Ibid., 10.

fate; she demands the respect she has earned.[28] In Leah, we thus encounter a portrait of desire transformed or redirected, and a liberating kindred spirit for all who have to lay down the torch of love's desire.

6. *The Quiet Chaos of Desire*

Just give me a sign, there's an end with a beginning to the quiet chaos driving me back. (Snow Patrol, "New York")

If in the encounter with Leah, we find desire transformed, in the case of Rachel, we find the fulfilling of desire delayed. From the inception of the narrative, Rachel possesses the love of Jacob that Leah so desperately craves. In contrast to the fruitfulness of Leah, however, Rachel is barren; and the principal longing of Rachel's heart is for a child of her own. The intensity of Rachel's desire for a child finds poignant expression when she utters in blaming despair, "Give me children or I shall die" (30:1). Rachel jealously longs for the gift of fruitfulness, which the narrative states God bestows on Leah due to Jacob's disregard of her.

We find Rachel, as other barren matriarchs before her, expressing her dismay about her situation (even going as far as blaming Jacob). We find her plotting, scheming, and negotiating (by offering her maidservant as surrogate to Jacob, and by negotiating conjugal visits with Leah in return for the mandrakes that her son Reuben found in the field) in order to will into being that which is not naturally forthcoming. Moreover, as we see in the cited examples above when engaging the landscape of Leah's desire, Rachel's dismay also is painfully expressed in terms of the naming of the sons born to her through surrogacy. After much time has passed, God remembers her also, and a son is born to Rachel. Joseph's name suggests something of the trauma that Rachel experienced as one who bears no children in a society that equates women's value with the fruitfulness of their womb when she states, "God has taken away my reproach" (30:23).

An interesting twist in the unfolding of the narrative cycle deserves our attention, especially when considering the broader econo-heteropatriarchal frame of the narrative as discussed at the outset of the essay, and the way in which both Rachel and Leah are bartered with as mere objects in the initial negotiation by Laban. Scholars have long deliberated and indeed reached no consensus on the interpretation of the significance of the motives behind Rachel's stealing of her father's *teraphim*. Jaqueline Lapsley, to my mind, makes a compelling argument in linking Rachel's

---

28. Ibid., 6–10.

angry act of thieving to the communal grievance of neglect and exploitation that she voices in collaboration with her sister regarding their treatment by Laban.[29] I also read Rachel's theft as an act of protest, symbolically, rebelling against the patriarchal structures that aim at keeping her in her place. But I furthermore find in her actions a reclaiming of agency. Funlọla Ọlọjẹde remarks that Rachel at the beginning of the narrative cycle is identified by her professional title as a shepherdess, indicating a strong sense of personhood and agency.[30]

Due to her father's scheme of deceit and the complex dynamic within the family that results from it, however, Rachel personally experiences the trauma of dehumanization. In stealing what is of worth to Laban and tricking him by employing, in Mikhail Bakhtin's terms, a "double voiced" response when stating, "I cannot rise before you for I have the way of women" (Gen 31:35), Rachel remains seated, thereby, hiding the stolen goods. In this regard, Lapsley argues, Rachel reclaims her agency and balls a fist of resistance against the culture that does not allow her to voice her grievances in outright speech.[31] To my mind, the tempering period of desire delayed becomes the incubator for the nurturing of Rachel's sense of self and the consequential reclaiming of her agency.

7. Conclusion

This essay represents an attempt to reach beneath the surface of the text or maybe to read against the traditional grain of interpretation in order to hear something of what the *Word Whispers*, as Lapsley has suggested.[32] It has sought to allow Žižek's unmasking question about desire to shed new light on the motivations or passions that propel the characters imbedded in the narrative landscape. Rather than resolving the complicated, often intersecting, dynamic brought about by our own painful experiences of absence, the dynamo of desire and the vulnerability of longing as the reflective surface constituted by the trials and tribulations of Jacob, Rachel, Leah, and Laban, mimic the ebb and flow of our own existence, as we each negotiate the unresolvedness of the journey of love's fulfilment.

---

29. Jacqueline E. Lapsley, *Whispering the Word: Hearing Women's Stories in the Old Testament* (Louisville, KY: Westminster John Knox, 2005), 21–34.

30. Funlọla Ọlọjẹde, "Rachel: The Shepherdess among Shepherds," in *Men in the Bible and Related Literature: In the Grip of Specific Males*, ed. John T. Green (Newcastle: Cambridge Scholars, 2015), 1–16.

31. Lapsley, *Whispering the Word*, 27.

32. Ibid., 10.

Countering the dominant thrust of the narrative trajectory presupposed by the heteropatriarchal ideology informing the construction and dominant interpretation of the narrative, the essay sought to create space for alternative strands of desire to be traced. By closely listening to the longings and desires expressed by both Rachel and Leah as they navigate the landscape of life, love, and future, it is hoped that those contemporary kin, who find their desires deemed unimportant, inexpressible, or impossible, will find courage, solace, and guidance in the life-affirming strategies employed in the narrative.

We find in the story three unique examples of grappling with the dynamics of desire imbedded within pervasive life-denying systemic realities. The aim of these reflections is clearly not to be a final conclusion or to be used as a "how-to" guide for Bible engagement when it comes to navigating the desires of our heart. Rather, it is another attempt aimed at destabilizing and troubling what is considered normal or unquestionable when it comes to the ethical engagement of the Bible, as well as the navigation of issues and bodies situated at the intersection of gender, sexuality, and religion.

Thus, instead of negating, hiding, or denying the longings of our heart because they do not fit the heteropatriarchal idea of what is to be desired or who is allowed to desire, it is my hope that the complexity and the messiness of the narrative landscape, depicting the intersecting and contradicting strands of human desire, would offer those of us who are trying to find our way a place of hope, guidance, insight, or fresh perspective. Or perhaps just a simple *sign that there is an end with a beginning to the quiet chaos driving me back.*[33]

Bibliography

Andrew, Martin, Annie Kelly, Laura Turquet, and Stephanie Ross. "Hate Crimes: The Rise of Corrective Rape in South Africa." *Action Aid 2009*, https://www.actionaid.org.uk/sites/default/files/doc_lib/correctiveraperep_final.pdf.

Bailey, Wilma Ann. "Intimate Moments: A Study of Genesis 29:31–30:21." *Proceedings* 29 (2009): 1–14.

Barthes, Roland. *A Lover's Discourse: Fragments.* London: Macmillan, 1978.

Boer, Roland. "The Second Coming: Repetition and Insatiable Desire in the Song of Songs." *BibInt* 8 (2000): 276–301.

Boler, Megan. *Feeling Power: Emotions and Education.* London: Psychology Press, 1999.

Hamilton, Victor P. *The Book of Genesis: Chapters 18–50.* NICOT. Grand Rapids, MI: Eerdmans, 1995.

---

33. Snow Patrol, "New York."

Harding, Kathryn "'I Sought Him but I Did not Find Him': The Elusive Lover in the Song of Songs." *BibInt* 16 (2008): 43–59.

Irigaray, Luce. *Love to You: Sketch for a Felicity within History.* Translated by Alison Martin. New York: Routledge, 1996.

Irigaray, Luce. *The Way of Love.* Translated by Heidi Bostic and Stephen Pluháček. London: Continuum, 2002.

Jackson, Melissa. *Comedy and Feminist Interpretation of the Hebrew Bible: A Subversive Collaboration.* Oxford: Oxford University Press, 2012.

Lapsley, Jacqueline E. *Whispering the Word: Hearing Women's Stories in the Old Testament.* Louisville, KY: Westminster John Knox, 2005.

Lightbody, Gary, and Johnny McDaid. "New York." Track 9 on Snow Patrol's album *Fallen Empires*. Polydor, 2011.

Maluleke, Tinyiko Sam, and Sarojini Nadar. "Breaking the Covenant of Violence against Women." *JThSA* 114 (2002): 5–18.

Miller, Jacques-Alain, and Dennis Porter. *The Seminar of Jacques Lacan. Book 7, The Ethics of Psychoanalysis: 1959–1960.* London: Routledge, 1992.

Myers, Jacob D. "Before the Gaze Ineffable: Intersubjective Poiesis and the Song of Songs." *Theology & Sexuality* 17 (2011): 139–60.

Nussbaum, Martha C. *Sex and Social Justice.* New York: Oxford University Press, 1999.

Ọlọjẹde, Funlọla. "Rachel: The Shepherdess among Shepherds." In *Men in the Bible and Related Literature: In the Grip of Specific Males*, edited by John T. Green, 1–16. Newcastle: Cambridge Scholars, 2015.

Ross-Burstall, Joan. "Leah and Rachel: A Tale of Two Sisters." *Word & World* 14 (1994): 165.

Schneider, Laurel. "Queer Theory." In *Handbook of Postmodern Biblical Interpretation*, edited by A. K. M. Adam, 206–12. St. Louis, MO: Chalice, 2000.

Van der Walt, Charlene. "Is There a Man Here? The Iron Fist in the Velvet Glove in Judges 4." In *Feminist Frameworks: Power, Ambiguity, Intersectionality*, edited by L. Juliana Claassens and Caroline Sharp, 117–32. London: Bloomsbury T&T Clark, 2017.

Vawter, Bruce. *On Genesis: A New Reading.* London: Chapman, 1977.

West, Gerald O. "A Trans-textual and Trans-sectoral Gender-economic Reading of the Rape of Tamar (2 Sam 13) and the Expropriation of Naboth's Land (1 Kgs 21)." In *Faith, Class, and Labor: Intersectional Approaches in a Global Context*, edited by Jin Young Choi and Joerg Rieger. Eugene, OR: Wipf & Stock, 105–21.

Yep, Gust A. "The Violence of Heteronormativity in Communication Studies." *Journal of Homosexuality* 45, no. 2–4 (2003): 11–59.

Žižek, Slavoj. *The Indivisible Remainder: An Essay on Schelling and Related Matters.* London: Verso, 1996.

Žižek, Slavoj. *The Sublime Object of Ideology.* London: Verso, 1989.

Chapter 11

Postcolonial Botho/Ubuntu: Transformative Readings of Ruth in the Botswana Urban Space*

Musa W. Dube

University of Botswana

1. *Postcoloniality, Gender, and Spatiality*

According to Vincent Mudimbe, at the heart of colonization is the drive to manage and to organize, which he describes as "the procedures of acquiring, distributing and exploiting lands in colonies; the policies of domesticating natives; and the manner of managing ancient organizations and implementing new modes of production."[1] Mudimbe identifies three complimentary actions in this process—"the domination of physical space, the reformation of natives' minds and the integration of local economic histories into the Western perspective."[2] Furthermore, he argues that "[t]hese complimentary projects constitute what might be called the

---

* The author acknowledges the following members of the Circle of Concerned African Women Theologians, Botswana Chapter, who were part of the research project Botho and Community Building in the Urban Space, sponsored by the John Templeton Foundation: Malebogo Kgalemang, Tirelo Modie, Rose Gabaitse, Senzokhuhle D. Setume, Mmapula Kebaneilwe, Elisabeth Motswapong and Tshenolo Madigele.

1. Vincent Y. Mudimbe, *The Invention of Africa: Gnosis, Philosophy and the Order of Knowledge* (London: James Curry, 1988), 2.
2. Ibid.

colonizing structure, which completely embraces the physical, human, and spiritual aspects of the colonizing experience."[3] Similarly, in his book, *Culture and Imperialism*, Edward Said points out that,

> Imperialism after all is an act of geographical violence through which virtually every space in the world is explored, charted, and finally brought under control. For the native, the history of colonial servitude is inaugurated by loss of locality to the outside; its geographical identity must thereafter be searched for and somehow restored.[4]

Most Southern African cities and towns have colonial roots. They were founded as colonial trading posts and ports, or as administrative or mining towns. Gaborone City, the capital city of Botswana, was founded in 1965 after the redrawing of colonial boundaries seceded the Bechuanaland administrative town, Mafikeng, to South Africa. The colonial history discussed in this essay as well as its gendered impact on communities and the geography is regional to Southern Africa since the area was primarily colonized by the British Empire with continual competition with Dutch settler-colonizers of South Africa, and with the exception of Mozambique, which was colonized by Portugal, and South West Africa, colonized by Germany. The discovery of minerals in Kimberly in South Africa (1863) led to the recruiting of labor immigrants from the whole of Southern Africa, which impacted families and reconstituted gender roles. As Ifi Amadiume has argued (from the context of Nigeria), colonial history sub-ordinated African women and created dualistic gendered relations, by creating jobs that excluded women and by promoting educational curricula that trained African women, who were farmers and controllers of the market, to be housekeepers—basically, training them for the domestic roles as wives and servants.[5]

In this essay, we demonstrate how the colonial reorganization of space in Southern Africa created a gendered space that tended to marginalize women, and distanced them from towns and cities. Second, we introduce the concept of *Botho/Ubuntu* and show how women in Botswana read the book of Ruth to rebuild community in Gaborone City through a recently created ritual called the Naomi Shower. The Naomi Shower, named after the biblical character in the book of Ruth, was designed for parents

---

3. Ibid.
4. Edward Said, *Culture and Imperialism* (New York: Kopf, 1993), 77.
5. Ifi Amadiume, *Male Daughters, Female Husbands: Gender and Sex in an African Society* (New York: Zed, 1988); eadem, *Reinventing Africa: Matriarchy, Religion and Culture* (New York: Zed, 1997).

whose children are getting married, particularly, those who are receiving a daughter or son-in-law.

2. Gendered Colonial Integration and Reconstitution of Space

Postcolonial studies indicate that the colonial re-arrangement of space, for the purposes of acquiring the resources (material and human) of the colonized, was not only legitimized according to claims of racial superiority, but was also arranged according to sexuality and gender. In the earliest days of the modern empire, white women were largely discouraged from going to the colonies, as colonies were held to be unsuitable spaces for women. The empire was thus a male space, where empire boys had sexual freedom that would not be easily entertained at home.[6] They kept native mistresses, and some of them married indigenous women. As the modern empire was moving towards its peak, the ideology of racial superiority necessitated stricter sexual practices and associations. Liaisons with indigenous women were discouraged and children from such associations were denied citizenship in colonial mother countries. Exploring the case of the German colonies, Daniel Walther writes that "sex in this context became racialized and a defining feature of civilization. In sexual relations it meant that the partner had not only to be opposite sex, but also white."[7] Those who preferred same-sex relations, whether with natives or fellow Europeans, were tried, banned from the colonies, and returned home for undermining imperial power, normally accompanied by reports drawing from scientific, moral, religious and legal perspectives.

With this turn of events, white women began to be actively recruited to the colonies as servants, prostitutes, missionaries and marriageable women. In her book, *European Women and the Second British Empire*, Margret Strobel writes, "from the dominant ideology, they [European women] were inferior sex within the superior race… For most European women, the empire presented opportunities not found in Europe,"[8] and they soon became important indicators of racial superiority. As pointed out by Colonial Service Recruitment document, "a woman should go

---

6. Margret Strobel, *European Women and the Second British Empire* (Indianapolis, IN: Indiana University Press, 1991); and regarding the German colonial history, see Daniel Walther, "Sex, Race and Empire: White Sexuality and the 'Other' in Germany's Colonies 1894–1914," *German Studies Review* 33, no. 1 (2010): 45–71.

7. Daniel Walther, "Racializing Sex: Same Sex Relations, German Colonial Authority, and *Deutschtum*," *Journal for the History of Sexuality* 17, no. 1 (2016): 1–14.

8. Strobel, *European Women*, xi.

out feeling that she has great responsibility and worthy object in giving to the native women of the country, the best of our civilization."[9] This role was best taken up by missionary women, whose curricula sought to train indigenous women as housekeepers. Unfortunately, as Jacklyn Cock notes,

> Missionaries and settlers in Southern Africa ignored the contrasting gender role definitions prevalent in precolonial African society. These did not stress dependence and passivity in women. African women's role in economic production demanded high levels of competence. Qualities of energy, self-reliance, stoicism, courage and endurance are demanded in peasant women everywhere. But in the mission education to which African girls were given accesses, Western gender role definitions predominated while female responsibilities were ignored… Their education was aimed largely at socialising the girls into domestic roles both in the girls' own home and, as servants, in those of other people. This education fitted in with the ideology of subordination which the colonists saw as appropriate for all blacks, males as well as females.[10]

In Southern Africa, indigenous gendered roles presented the colonial state with a challenge in its attempt to reorganize space and gender, and to recruit wage labor for their projects, such as domestic work, farming and mining. Women in the Southern African region were the farmers and the major suppliers of labor to their households. Although men's work was cattle farming, younger boys tended cattle in the cattle post, and men seemed to be sitting down doing nothing, a factor that was not acceptable to the westerners, as attested by various colonial records.[11] Southern African women were thus seen as beasts of burden, slaves to their men and responsible for hindering men from undertaking wage labor in colonial farms and mines. With the discovery of minerals, towns and

9. See Strobel, *European Women*; and Cherryl Walker (ed.), *Women and Gender in Southern Africa to 1945* (Cape Town: David Phillip, 1990).
10. Jacklyn Cock, "Domestic Service and Education for Domesticity: The Incorporation of Xhosa Women into Colonial Society," in Walker (ed.), *Women and Gender*, 88, 89.
11. Jean Comaroff and John Comaroff, *Of Revelation and Revolution: The Dialectics of Modernity in a South African Frontier*, vol. 2 (Chicago, IL: Chicago University Press, 1997), 119–64, discuss the missionary Robert Moffat's concern that farming was a woman's role among Batswana-speaking groups. He called the Batswana men lazy. Thereafter, he introduced the plough and cattle into the farm, a woman's space, but, in so doing, he introduced a more male-dominated economy. Robert Moffat, *Missionary Labours and Scenes in Southern Africa* (London: Snow, 1842), cited in Comaroff and Comaroff, *Of Revelation and Revolution*.

cities began to emerge and more labor was needed. Recruiting permanent male laborers was imperative. But only a few indigenous people were interested in undertaking wage labor, unless just temporarily, to buy some coveted Europeans goods such as guns. Once such a goal was achieved, black African laborers sought to return to their native homes. Indigenous women were blamed for working for these men, which was the reason they were disinterested in taking up full-time paid work. In addition, economic and social values were not measured in monetary terms—another reason why these women were unwilling to be integrated in the colonial wage labor economic system.

Consequently, several strategies were adopted. For example, by the end of nineteenth century, hut tax was introduced in Southern Africa as a whole to pressurize black men to take up wage labor in newly introduced colonial cities in South Africa such as Kimberly and Johannesburg. With hut tax, every household needed to generate money to pay its annual taxes. Although the picture is much more complex, more men were recruited from all Southern African countries to work in South African mines, leaving women as heads of households. If women were already providers for their households, the picture became more complex, for in settler colonies such as Rhodesia and South Africa, black populations were removed from their lands into reserves—which were crowded, arid places.[12] Other factors that caused men to take up wage labor included natural disasters, such as rinderpest, droughts and the killing of cattle among the Xhosas. Overall,

> "Civilizing the native" meant forcing the men into labour—not, however, for themselves, nor to unburden African women, but to labour for whites. At first, the thrust of colonial policy was to procure male labour, not to prevent female migration as such. Since, however, the availability of such labour depended on the continued viability of homestead production, it became politic for colonial policy-makers to intervene on the side of chiefs and homestead heads, against female migration.[13]

If wage labor in towns was a new option for making a living in the colonial economy, indigenous women were unwelcome in the new urban spaces. First, white women feared that black women could attract their husbands. Except for the Eastern Cape in South Africa, where several factors had impoverished the Xhosas, forcing both men and women into

---

12. Musa W. Dube, "Boundaries and Bridges: Journeys of a Postcolonial Feminist Scholar," *Journal of European Society Women in Theological Research* 22 (2014): 139–56.

13. Walker (ed.), *Women and Gender*, 181.

wage labor at a much earlier period, domestic work in white households was dominated by black men. As black men took to the cities, both by coercion and by choice, black African women were somewhat debarred from towns. Many reasons were advanced from both white settlers and African men. Ironically, once black African men were forced to bow to wage labor, both white men and black men cooperated to keep black women away from the cities. Patriarchy and imperialism cooperated to exclude women from cities in Southern Africa. White settlers needed women to remain in the homestead economies, handling agriculture and raising children, while black men worked for the white masters. Similarly, black men were eager to keep their women away from towns and cities to maintain their families. Consequently,

> Some strategies used to prevent female migration involved direct prohibition on the mobility of women through pass laws and restricted access to transport. Thus in Zululand women had to be identified by a man known to the pass officer before they would be given permission to leave the colony; after 1899 no woman was to be issued with a pass unless accompanied by her male guardian... In 1915 the Basutoland administration approved the legally dubious Native Women Restriction (Basutoland) Proclamation on the grounds that it is expedient to prohibit native women residing in the territory from leaving the Territory against the will of their husbands, fathers, or natural guardians.[14]

While the above description covers exclusionary laws applied to women in South Africa and Lesotho, Walker refers to Isaac Schapera, the anthropologist who worked the longest among the Batswana, to highlight that the same exclusionary practice was applied among Batswana women. She points out that,

> ...Schapera (1947) has described similar efforts by the chiefs, with the support of colonial administration, to control the mobility of women in Bechaunaland (modern day Botswana). Such controls began a long time ago, when the Ngwato chief introduced a law that no woman could leave the reserve by rail without the permission of the chief, who posted special representatives at the railway to enforce it... In 1930 the Kgatla chiefdom only agreed to South African Railways extending its road motor service into the reserve on condition that its own men be employed as conductors, to ensure that women did not make use of the new service as a way of escaping from home.[15]

14. Ibid.
15. Ibid.

Indeed, the Tati-siding sub-chiefs, acting on the rule of their Ngwato paramount chief, "issued a declaration that any woman who had left home without permission, in this case to go to Rhodesia, would not be allowed to return, so as to prevent her from enticing other women to follow suit."[16] In 1924, the Urban Areas act was passed, requiring "single female work seekers entering town to stay in labor depots; if they failed to find work they could be endorsed out."[17] In so doing, there was cooperation between colonial powers and their colonized authorities to debar indigenous women from entering the towns and cities. Be that as it may, women pressed by the changed circumstances of their lives, including crowdedness in infertile reserves, some driven by adventure, others by rebellion from cultural expectations, always found a way to explore other opportunities to make a living in the colonial urban space. Arrival in a hostile, gendered and colonial urban space forced many African women to resort to beer-brewing and prostitution, since black men were providing domestic service.[18]

Those who secured domestic work often faced sexual violence from the white master and expulsion by the white mistress, as well as disapproval from their mother-in-laws, as aptly described by Lorretta Ngcobo in her book, *And They Did Not Die*. Jezile, the main character in the book, is a black married woman who goes to work as a housekeeper in the house of a white mistress.[19] Her white master sexually abuses her and Jezile gets pregnant and gives birth to a child of mixed race. The white mistress fires her for the "colored child," her mother-in-law throws her out of the home for being unfaithful to her husband, and the church does not welcome her either. Jezile is now jobless, without a home, without community, and with a child. Ngcobo's novel captures the violence meted by the colonial and patriarchal structures against black women. In her article, "Rape, Race and Colonial Culture: The Sexual Politics of Identity in the 19th Century Cape Colony," Pamela Scully highlights how sexuality, woven with race, gender and class became central for the construction of identities in colonial contexts and how women's body became indicators of colonial ideologies. In such contexts, the characterization of the colonized as people with hypersexual appetites often justified the rape of black women, while women from the colonial side were constructed as in need of protection from the untamed sexual appetites of native men, which is well attested in Margaret Strobel's book on *European Women*

16. Ibid.
17. Ibid., 186.
18. Ibid., 187.
19. Loretta Ngcobo, *And They Did Not Die* (London: Books, 1990).

and Second British Empire.[20] Black women in the colonial urban space were vulnerable to dehumanizing experiences and were even unprotected by the law.[21] Although it is far removed from the colonial times, the modern Southern African urban space was founded on hostility towards black African women. Not only did it alienate them from the homestead economy, it alienated them from the supportive community and extended families, and denied them the right to paid public work. How then do the Showers of Gaborone City, a transformative movement of Batswana women, seek to make the urban space a woman-friendly space?

3. Botho/Ubuntu *Movements in the Urban Space of Botswana*

This essay forms part of a larger project of the Circle of Concerned African Women Theologians, Botswana chapter. The project entitled, "*Botho/Ubuntu* and Community Building in the Urban Space: An Exploration of Naomi, Laban, Baby and Bridal Showers in Gaborone City," was fully sponsored by the John Templeton Foundation through the Nagel Institute in Calvin College. We decided to undertake this project after we noticed an escalating proliferation of showers in Gaborone City. Apart from the well-known bridal and baby shower, new showers were created, namely Naomi and Laban showers, which focus on parents of couples that are preparing to get married. Although our research focused on showers, women-centered networks and empowerment activities in Gaborone include organizing *metshelo*,[22] grocery top-up, garden top-up, house-warming ceremonies, among others. Recently, while one of us was speaking to a friend in a parking lot, the subject of women's showers in Gaborone came up in conversation. In that discussion an interesting comment was made: "They say even if you have a construction project, create a shower for it!" Although it was a joke, this comment captures the strong spirit of women networking and empowering one-another.

---

20. Strobel, *European Women*.

21. See Pamela Scully, "Rape, Race and the Colonial Culture: The Sexual Politics of Identity in the 19th Century Cape Colony in South Africa," *The American Review* 100, no. 2 (1995): 335–59; and Pumla Dineo Gqola, *Rape: A South African Nightmare* (Johannesburg: MF Books, 2015), 31–49, who link the current rape epidemic in South Africa to colonial histories.

22. *Metshelo* are women or even communal money schemes in which each member contributes an agreed amount of money every month, which members may decide to loan out, invest or give to one member on a rotational schedule. This is a commonly practiced scheme in South Africa. *Metshelo* means, literally, "pouring," referring to the contributions that are pooled.

Through these showers, Gaborone City women create support communities for themselves in the urban space. Yet the showers also capture the indigenous practice of giving free labor to one another, drawing from the non-wage labor economies of precolonial times.[23] The cultural practice was that whenever one had a project that needed many hands, a *letsema//molaletsa* would be organized. Neighbors and the community at large are invited to spend the day assisting the organizer, while s/he provides the participants with food for the day. *Molaletsa* literary means "an invitation [to give a hand]." The multiplication of these movements in Gaborone City got us thinking, and we sought to investigate whether the proliferation of showers is an expression of *Botho/Ubuntu* in the urban space where community cannot always be taken for granted, such as in the rural areas. We also wanted to find out how the shower movement constructs and reconstructs gender. With the latter, we were exploring the transformative and transgressive aspects of the showers. The postcolonial framework of this chapter seeks to analyze how the Gaborone women shower movement is also a decolonizing movement, transgressing the exclusive patriarchal and colonial boundaries.

Botho/Ubuntu is a philosophical concept of the Bantu people, a linguistic group that stretches from Southern to East, Central and some parts of West Africa.[24] The *Botho/Ubuntu* philosophy stresses that one's own humanity can be measured only by one's capacity to welcome, respect, care and empower the Other.[25] That is, "one's identity or social status, goes hand in hand with one's responsibility or sense of duty towards, or in relation to others."[26] How do we know that one is not human? It is when one is unable to recognize the humanity of the Other and to uphold their dignity. According to Mluleki Munyaka and Mokgethi Motlhabi, one who does not demonstrate the spirit of *Ubuntu* is often described as *akangumntu* and *akanabuntu* (being without humanity or not human), and this,

---

23. See Musa Dube et al., "*Botho/Ubuntu*: Community-building and Gender Constructions in Botswana," *Journal of ITC* 1 (2016): 1–22, which discusses several indigenous networks for empowering one another.

24. Dumi O. Mmualefe, "Towards Authentic Tswana Christianity: Revisiting *Botho*" (MA thesis, Eden Theological Seminary, 2004).

25. Botswana Government, *Vison 2016: Towards Prosperity for All* (Gaborone: Botswana Government, 1996), 4–5, offers one of the most beautiful definitions of *Botho/Ubuntu*.

26. Felix Murove, "African Ethics: Beyond the Ethic of the Savage Evidence," in *African Ethics: An Anthology of Comparative and Applied Ethics*, ed. Munyaradzi Felix Murove (Scottsville: UKZN, 2009), 17.

does not mean that he or she is not still a member of community. Furthermore, it does not mean that he or she no longer possesses human nature or human dignity, as a person's intrinsic value remains and cannot be taken away. The only problem with such a person is his or her conduct, manifested in the lack of, or refusal to make use of, an inner state of being human and able to do good deeds for the wellbeing of others in society.[27]

Were the *Botho/Ubuntu* concept 100 percent honored, then Bantu people would have zero tolerance for any form of discrimination, such as sexism, HIV and AIDS stigma, patriarchy, tribalism, homophobia, environmental degradation and other social ills. Although *Botho/Ubuntu* has not been upheld religiously within the community of practitioners, the concept remains a critical philosophy that reminds the community members that to dehumanize the Other, to fail to uphold their dignity, is to dehumanize oneself and to fail to live in community.

Botho/Ubuntu, therefore, underlines relationality and community. This relational perspective is best captured by the popular saying, "*Motho ke motho ka batho*," in Sotho-Tswana languages or "*Umuntu ngu muntu nga bantu*" in Nguni languages. The saying holds that a human being is only human through other human beings or that "a person is only human through living in community." Similarly, the community is only a community when it recognizes the dignity of all its members. Explicating the meaning of this proverb, Mogobe B. Ramose says:

> It means that to be human is to affirm one's humanity by recognizing the humanity of others and, on that basis, to establish humane relations with them... The concept of *Botho* or *Ubuntu*, as it is referred in indigenous African languages, is not readily translatable to humanism, especially if humanism is understood as a specific trend in the evolution of western philosophy. Humanness is a better rendition of the concept. Humanness suggests both a condition and a state of becoming.[28]

The *Botho/Ubuntu* concept extends beyond human relations, for it includes environmental, economic and divine relationships, showing that they should be affirming relationships. Puleng LenkaBula thus explains that *Botho/Ubuntu* is "a concept which attempts to describe a person as being-with-others" and that "its core message is about being human

---

27. Mluleki Munyaka and Mokgethi Motlhabi, "Ubuntu and Its Socio-Moral Significance," in Murove (ed.), *African Ethics*, 73.
28. See Mogobe B. Ramose, "Ecology through Ubuntu," in Murove (ed.), *African Ethics*, 308–14.

in relation to other people and creation" as a whole.[29] Underlining this inclusive perspective, Ramose explains that:

> Humanness (Botho/Ubuntu) regards being, or the universe, as a complex wholeness involving the multi-layered and incessant interaction of all entities... The principle of wholeness applies also to the relation between human beings and physical or objective nature. To care for another, *implies caring for physical nature as well*. Without such care, the interdependence between human beings and nature would be undermined.[30]

The spiritual aspect of the *Botho/Ubuntu* is manifested in the extension of community to include the living dead (ancestors) whose primary duty is to enforce moral obligation from one to another.[31]

4. *Postcoloniality Meets* Botho/Ubuntu *and the Urban Space*

Are the Gaborone women networks, expressed in organizing showers for another woman who is either getting married, expecting a child, receiving a daughter-in-law or son-in-law, an expression of *Botho/Ubuntu* in the Botswana urban space? How are the self-initiated networks of women empowerment in the urban space a postcolonial movement, counteracting the historical and structural exclusion and violence? We attended 34 showers (twelve of which were Naomi Showers) in Gaborone, involving 451 participants, and collected data from the field, using qualitative methods, such as participant observation where we attended the event and recorded the proceedings. We also carried out a survey, given to all participants. Thereafter, we used a semi-structured interview guide to carry out some interviews on key participants, such as organizers, relatives, neighbors, church members and recipients of the shower. We identified people who were likely to receive a shower by gathering information on all the forthcoming marriages posted on the magistrate and church notice boards, through gift shops and invitations. The aim of the project was to investigate the expression of *Botho/Ubuntu* in Gaborone by focusing on how women build community in the urban space, as well as to investigate how gender is constructed and reconstructed in such spaces.

---

29. Puleng LenkaBula, "Beyond Anthropocentricity: *Botho/Ubuntu* and the Quest for Economic and Ecological Justice in African," *Religion and Theology* 15 (2008): 379.

30. Ramose, "Ecology," 309.

31. T. Metz and Joseph Gaie, "The African Ethic of Ubuntu/Botho: Implications for Research on Morality," *Journal of Moral Education* 39, no. 3 (2010): 273–90.

In the latter, our quest was to establish whether the shower movement was transformative by transgressing the boundaries of class, gender, age and postcoloniality.

In this essay, we analyze some aspects of this fieldwork research, focusing on the Naomi Shower.[32] This is one of the newly created showers, organized for a woman who is about to receive a daughter-in-law. When the news of a forthcoming wedding becomes known and the preparations become advanced, friends, relatives, colleagues, fellow church members, neighbors and various other associates will organize a shower for the woman who is receiving the daughter-in-law (or son-in-law). Finally, the day of the shower arrives, which is a celebratory moment of openly sharing food, dance and advice on challenges of the mother-in-law and daughter-in-law relationship and an exploration of how to be a good mother-in-law, one who welcomes, cares for, empowers and loves her daughter-in-law. There are gifts to the new mother-in-law, which serve either to assist her with the forthcoming wedding or to provide her with petty cash for groceries for the forthcoming months, just in case she was dependent on her son, the soon-to-be husband.

5. *Biblical Naomi and Ruth*

The Naomi Shower is actually modelled after the biblical book of Ruth, which features Naomi as Ruth's mother-in-law. The book of Ruth is known for its woman-centered characters—Naomi, Ruth, Orpah and the women of Bethlehem who came out to welcome Naomi back to home from Moab. Naomi, who felt so harshly treated by life, insisted that she should be called Mara (that is, "bitter") for having lost a husband and two sons (Ruth 1:20). She was bitter due to her loss. Naomi was supposedly a self-declared old widow who was no longer capable of giving birth to more sons who would remarry her widowed daughters-in-law (Ruth and Orpah). She freed her daughters-in-law to return, not to their fathers' houses, but rather to their mothers' houses (Ruth 1:8–13). Ruth, the widowed daughter-in-law, chose to cling to Naomi, insisting that she

---

32. Analysis of the findings of the research project focusing on baby showers and bridal showers has already appeared in published articles such as Elisabeth Motswapong et al., "A Little Baby Is On the Way: *Botho/Ubuntu* and Community-Building in Gaborone Showers," *Gender Studies: A Journal of West University of Timisoara* 16, no. 1 (2018): 3–13, and Senzokhuhe Doreen Setume et al., "Exploring the Concept of *Botho/Ubuntu* through Bridal Showers in the Urban Space of Gaborone, Botswana," *Managing Development in Africa* 2, no. 3 (2017): 173–91.

would go where Naomi went, to die and be buried where Naomi would be buried, and that Naomi's people would be her people and Naomi's God would be her God (Ruth 1:16). Given their tough resettlement in Bethlehem, Naomi and Ruth watched each other's back. Ruth went out to work to bring food home, while Naomi used her kinship connections to organize Ruth's remarriage to a man of means, Boaz. When Ruth gave birth to a son, the women of Bethlehem surrounded Naomi and declared that Ruth's son was born to Naomi and that Ruth herself was more to her than seven sons (Ruth 4:15). And Naomi took the child and laid him on her bosom.

How has the book of Ruth inspired postcolonial gender-inclusive *Botho/ Ubuntu* ethics in the Botswana urban space amongst Batswana women? As noted, *Botho/Ubuntu* can be seen as the ethic of defining one's identity through the capacity to care for, welcome, affirm and respect the Other. Batswana women's reading of the book of Ruth occurs in the popular activity of the Naomi Shower, an event organized by women for another woman who is receiving a new daughter-in-law (or son-in-law).

A number of African women in the academy have offered critical readings of the book of Ruth. For example, Musimbi Kanyoro points out that Ruth's commitment to her mother-in-law is consistent with African culture, in which one marries the family and not just the individual. Hence, though her husband was dead, Ruth could not simply return to her biological family—she remained committed to her husband's family.[33] Sarojini Nadar has read the book from the point of view of an Indian widow, who was expected to sacrifice herself upon the death of her husband. She commends Ruth for her decision to work and become a provider for her mother-in-law and herself.[34] Elsewhere, I have re-read the story of Ruth from the perspective of Orpah who returned to her mother's house,[35] and from the perspective of divination,[36] whereas Madipoane Masenya has interpreted the book from a womanist perspective based on

---

33. Musimbi Kanyoro, "Cultural Hermeneutics: An African Contribution," in *Other Ways of Reading: African Women and the Bible*, ed. Musa W. Dube (Atlanta, GA: Society of Biblical Literature, 2001), 101–13.

34. Sarojini Nadar, "South African Indian Womanist Reading of the Character of Ruth," in Dube (ed.), *Other Ways*, 159–78.

35. Musa W. Dube, "The Unpublished Letters of Orpah to Ruth," in *A Companion to the Book of Ruth and Esther*, ed. Athalya Brenner (Sheffield: Sheffield University Press, 1999), 145–50.

36. Musa W. Dube, "Divining Ruth for International Relations," in *Postmodern Interpretations of the Bible*, ed. A. K. M. Adam (St. Louis, MO: Chalice, 2001), 67–80.

the Sotho-Pedi culture.[37] Furthermore, Athalya Brenner's edited volume, *Ruth and Esther: A Feminist Companion to the Bible*, offers a collection of various feminist interpretations of Ruth from other contexts and perspectives. The following are non-academic interpretations of Ruth that occurred in the context of the Naomi Showers, which are made within the larger gendered colonial history of marginalizing women in the urban space.

6. Reading Ruth in the Context of Naomi Shower in Gaborone City and Semi-urban Areas

Consistent with our research project, the data were collected from the Naomi Showers organized for prospective mothers-in-law in Gaborone and its environs. The Naomi Shower was founded by a group of women who noticed that one of their friends, who had a son, was very controlling and possessive. They were concerned that she would interfere with her son's forthcoming marriage. These women therefore organized what they called a Naomi Shower for her, where they discussed the challenges of being a mother-in-law and all that could complicate the relationship between a woman and her daughter-in-law. In the book of Ruth, Naomi was identified as a woman who had a good relationship with her daughter-in-law. Naomi must have been a good mother-in-law since she gave Ruth, her young widowed daughter-in-law, the choice to return to her mother's house, where she would have an opportunity to remarry, but Ruth chose to remain with her. Not only did Ruth choose to stay with Naomi, she chose to cling to her, notably taking a lifetime vow, by saying to her mother-in-law: "Do not press me to leave you or turn from following you! Where you go, I will go; where you lodge, I will lodge; your people will be my people. And your God my God, where you die I will die, there I will be buried" (Ruth 1:16–17).

Ruth's vow to cling to her mother-in-law was a testimony to Naomi's successful role as a mother-in-law. Following the first session organized for their friend, the women were sought after to hold two showers a month in and around Gaborone. Some sessions are now initiated by other church women, who are not linked to the founding group. In other words, the Naomi Shower has become a networking movement that creates a space for women to discuss their issues and to give themselves the space to preach amongst themselves.

---

37. Madipoane Masenya, "*Ngwetsi* (Bride): The Naomi–Ruth Story from an African-South African Woman's Perspective," *Journal of Feminist Studies in Religion* 14, no. 2 (1998): 81–90.

At the end of our field research, we had attended twelve Naomi Showers in Gaborone and surrounding villages. We listened to the women's interpretation of Ruth and observed that *Botho/Ubuntu* had become a motivating factor in their project of building community in the urban space. In this essay, we also place their interpretation within the larger historical context that excluded women from the urban spaces of Southern Africa. The founders and popular facilitators of Naomi Shower work as a team of four and sometimes six. One of the members serves as the director of the ceremony, while another serves as the opening speaker, laying down the goals of the Naomi Shower. The other members specialize in the interpretation of the book of Ruth, exploring the relationship between mother-in-law and daughter-in-law as well as rituals of uniting the families, while the last participant prays extensively for the new marriage and the newly united families to relate in harmony.

7. *Introducing the Shower*

Since the Naomi Shower is a relatively new shower, compared to bridal and baby showers that have been around for a while, the facilitators often introduce the Naomi Shower, explaining its goal and objectives. The first thing they underline is that God created marriage, hence, marriage should be preserved. Anyone who attacks marriage attacks God, and calls a curse upon him/herself, as in the case of Aaron and Miriam in Exodus who complained about Moses' wife, and consequently Miriam was cursed with leprosy (Num 12). Pointing out that marriage in Botswana is also under attack, the speaker cites the very high divorce rate, and the high percentage of single-headed households, gender-based violence, and HIV and AIDS, among other social ills (SADC Gender Barometer 2018). Given these concerns, the speaker says they are therefore holding a Naomi Shower in order to talk about giving away a daughter in marriage and receiving a daughter-in-law. The goal is that marriage be strengthened.

Citing the biblical example of Sarah and Hagar (Gen 16; 21) and the two wives of Jacob (Gen 30:1–22), the introductory speaker stresses that women sometimes abuse other women and exploit them. Sarah asked Abraham a favor to grant her a child through Hagar (Gen 16:2), but later it seemed she forgot it was her own initiative when she asked Abraham to throw out Hagar and her child (Gen 21:8–20). In the story of Jacob, we again see women abusing other women and making their lives difficult in the family. The wives of Jacob, like Sarah, gave their maids to their husbands without seeking the consent of these women. Part of their behavior, explains the speaker, was motivated by rivalry. Sarah saw Hagar and Ishmael as competitors with her and Isaac. She did not want Isaac her son to share inheritance with Ishmael. Competition for material resources among women is thus named as a major vice, hindering harmonious relationships between women, which also characterizes the relationship of a mother-in-law and her new daughter-in-law. In one such session, the introductory speaker was one of the Naomi Shower's founding members, Mrs Mokgoniemang, who summarized it as follows:

> We are therefore here to explore how to receive daughters-in-law in our families and to build affirming relationships. We are holding this shower so that we can honor God the creator of marriage, so that we can avoid the curse of Miriam. We realize that while there are numerous bridal showers held for the soon to be brides, to prepare them for the marriage institution, no one, on the other hand, prepares the parents of the couple who are about to marry. There is an assumption, rather, that these parents know how to receive a daughter-in-law or a son-in-law. Evidence on the ground, however, indicates otherwise, since mothers-in-law are known to oppress their daughters-in-law, leading to the collapse of the marriage. Reading the book of Ruth gives us a good example on building a healthy relationship with our daughters-in-law.

8. *Postcolonial* Botho/Ubuntu *Reading of Ruth for Community Building*

The Naomi Shower, particularly among its founding members, focuses on three texts in the book of Ruth 1:6–7; 3:1–3 and 4:16. Before the speaker begins to interpret the book of Ruth, she introduces the bride-to-be and her parents and asks them to sit together before the guests. She then introduces the future bridegroom and his parents and asks them to sit beside their in-laws. She asks for their family names and the names of the new couple so that she can address them properly. Once all this is done, she turns to the mother of the groom and asks,

> Do you know that amidst all these people you are the most likely *moloi* (that is, a witch)? You are the woman who will receive your new daughter-in-law in your home and village. If you do not receive her; if you see her as your competitor; if you undermine her as the wife of your son; if you do not teach her the culture of your people and introduce her to your relatives, you will be a *moloi*, a witch. A witch is the evil one who destroys good relationships. We are holding this shower for you so that you will learn how to be Naomi—the woman who cultivated a healthy relationship with her daughter-in-law, Ruth.

Throughout the session, the speaker addresses all the six members individually, but primarily focuses on the mother-in-law of the bride, who is seen as the counterpart of Naomi in the book of Ruth.

(a) *Ruth 1:6–7: She Journeyed with Her Daughter-in-law All the Way*

Turning to the text, the Naomi Shower facilitator reads Ruth 1:6, which states, "Then Naomi started to return with her daughters-in-law from the country of Moab… So she set out from the place where she had been living she and her two daughters-in-law, and they went on their way to go back to the land of Judah." The journey of Naomi's return to her native country with her daughters-in-law is read as a metaphor for accompanying a daughter-in-law, who by virtue of a patriarchal culture, often leaves her native land and home to join her husband in his native land, village, or city. Naomi, like the Batswana-in-laws who go out to seek a new daughter-in-law, must walk with her all the way to her new home. She should introduce her to her people as Naomi brought Ruth to the women of Bethlehem; she should be the one who integrates her daughter-in-law into her new family as Naomi introduced Ruth to Boaz, a kinsman.

This reading, clearly, is an intercultural interpretation of the passage through a Setswana cultural lens. It is informed by the procedures and processes of a Setswana marriage in which the in-laws go to seek the hand of the bride-to-be in marriage and bring her with them to the home of her husband. Beyond the cultural, however, it is also a transgressive reading, since "walking" with the daughter-in-law calls for a supportive networking between women rather than the often conflicting and patriarchally informed relationship between the daughter-in-law and the mother-daughter-in-law.

(b) *Ruth 3:1–3: "Wash and Anoint Yourself, and Put on Your Best Clothes"*

The speaker begins an explication of this verse with reference to a cultural perspective, which holds that "a new daughter-in-law" is just a child, who needs to be taught her duties and the proper duties of being a wife as well as her role in the wider community. Then, she reads from Ruth 3:3, explaining that Naomi taught and trained her daughter-in-law, saying, "Wash, and anoint yourself, and put on your best clothes." This instruction is hardly used in reference to Boaz, nor in regard to capturing a man or her own husband, but rather in relation to her new community and their cultural expectations. Consequently, a mother-in-law should be responsible for ensuring that her new daughter-in-law is properly dressed for various communal occasions before taking her out to introduce her to relatives and the community at large. The speaker notes that a daughter-in-law who is a professional and lives in the city dresses according to the fashions of Gaborone City, but when she arrives home in the village, the mother-in-law should be responsible for training her to appear in the public in appropriate outfits, particularly, for communal gatherings such as funerals, weddings and other *merero* (communal discussion meetings). A daughter-in-law whose dress is improper in the village points to the lapses of the mother-in-law. Naomi played her role well by advising Ruth to wash and perfume herself, and to put on her best clothes.

A critical thing happens at this stage of the interpretation of the book of Ruth. Referring to the Setswana cultural understanding of a new daughter-in-law as "a child," the interpreter begins to draw heavily on the metaphor of birthing and blood ties to seal the new relationship with cords that cannot be broken. Pointing to the bride-to-be, the speaker says,

> This girl should become your daughter. She must be a daughter. I bid you today that you should consider yourself pregnant with her, expecting her. Next week, the day before the wedding occurs, you should enter into birth pains to deliver her as your own blood daughter. There is and should be no difference between her and your other children.

(c) *Ruth 4:16: "Naomi Took the Child and Became a Nurse"*

Turning to Ruth 4:16, the speaker then spells out the role of the mother-in-law in raising the children with her new daughter. The verse reads, "Then Naomi took the child and laid him on her bosom, and became his nurse." The speaker emphasizes that at no point should her new daughter fail to go to work or to go on a work-related trip because there is no nanny to care for the children. The new mother should be there for her grandchildren, taking care of them while her new daughter attends to the demands of her job. Moreover, the children of the new daughter should be given priority and care. They should not, at any time, be discriminated against to favor the children of the supposedly "real blood daughter." This part is accompanied by a demonstration of how the child should be securely tied on the back of the mother-in-law, so that if the latter were to trip and fall on her face, the child would remain uninjured. The Naomi Shower imagines and constructs the daughter-in-law as a professional woman in the city, one who must be fully supported by her new mother in her career growth. The relationship of the mother-in-law and daughter-in-law is thus re-imagined through the metaphor of blood ties to seal it with cords that cannot be broken. These two women from different generations thus form a strong supportive network; that is, a supposedly mature woman welcomes a younger woman as her own daughter and mentors her to succeed as a wife and a mother, as well as a community member and professional woman.

9. *Rituals of Birthing* Ubuntu *Relationships in the Urban Space*

Maintaining the metaphor of blood ties, participants close the session by performing two rituals of uniting the new couple with their new parents. First, the parents of the couple are all asked to rise, one couple on the right and another on the left, facing each other. The mothers come out first, and face each other; the fathers follow immediately behind their wives. The bride-to-be takes her place behind her parents. Similarly, the future groom takes his place behind his parents. The new couple is asked to stretch their hands and hold each other, thereby, folding their parents in between. At this point, the bride-to-be is looking at the face of her new mother and her fiancée is looking at the face of his new mother. Something new happens. Both of them have been born anew into each other's family. From that point, their new positions allow them to see, hear and know the needs of their new parents more than the biological child of the parents do. They are, therefore, responsible for answering to this new family into which they have just been born. The groom is charged to care for the family of his wife, while the wife is charged to care for his family.

This ritual seals the new social birth that the Naomi Shower seeks to promote through the tying of strong *Botho/Ubuntu* cords of welcoming, caring and respecting the other. After emerging from this new birth experience, each of the mothers is asked to hug her new child for an extended time and to welcome her/him. The speaker asks the new daughter and new mother to hug each other and deliver an open message to one another. It is a proper Ruth-moment, one that transgresses the age and patriarchal boundaries. In other words, whereas the text presents Ruth as making a vow to Naomi, her mother-in-law says nothing back to her. In the Naomi Shower space, however, this is reconstructed into a reciprocal act—both the daughter and mother-in-law declare their vows and love towards each other. They speak openly, in the presence of people, that they would welcome, support, and love one another.

This is often a moving moment that leaves the audience, the new mothers and their new daughter crying—the cry of a new-born baby, being born again into a new family. Even we the researchers could not refrain from weeping. However, this weeping also signifies the breaking of ancient oppressive bonds that often characterize family relationships between mothers and daughters-in-law. The chains are broken in the Naomi Shower space. In patriarchal cultures, where women are economically dependent on men, the mother-in-law often sees the daughter-in-law as a foreign intruder and competitor, one who comes to dispossess her of her son. In many cases, she would do all in her power to prove that she is the mother and has better control or power over her son. Sometimes, such relationships are resolved amicably with time, but sometimes the tension between the two women is a permanent wound, or the relationship remains characterized by tension and conflict throughout their lives.[38] The pain that the mother-in-law inflicts on the daughter-in-law has puzzled many women and their children for ages. Therefore, the Naomi Shower targets this patriarchal tension and rivalry between the two women and seeks to lay a new foundation for a harmonious beginning and future for them.

The second ritual involves ushering the new mothers into their new status. First, a traditional mat is rolled out for them to sit on with their legs outstretched. This sitting position is in itself, for the mother-in-law, the mark of a wise woman, a relaxed and confident woman who is not threatened by the arrival of a younger woman, her daughter-in-law. Her sitting position indicates that she is now ready to allow her new daughter to run the show in the house, and to advise her only when necessary. After assuming this sitting position, the program facilitator continues to talk to them as she garbs them. The emphasis is that the new woman must be received into the family and treated like a blood daughter. The two mothers are garbed with white shawls and pronounced happy and capable

---

38. Indeed, contemporary African creative writers admit that the mother–daughter-in-law relationship remains a space of pain. In Imbolo Mbue's *Behold the Dreamers*, featuring Neni the main character who has just moved from Cameroon to New York, Neni states that now that she has moved to the USA, she does not, among other things, have to "meet with her friends and listen to them bash their mothers-in-law"; Imbolo Mbue's *Behold the Dreamers* (London: 4th Estate, 2016), 14. The comment suggests that bashing mothers-in-law was quite common. Chimamanda N. Adichie's *Half of a Yellow Sun* explores more explicitly the competition or tension between mothers and daughters-in-law. Odenigbo and Olanna, an academic couple, seem to be content living together without formal marriage and a child, to the annoyance of Olanna's mother-in-law. The older woman decides that Olanna is not good enough for her son. She finds a girl from the village and regularly brings her to the campus, to the house where Odenigbo and Olanna live, washes and massages her, and tells her to go into her son's bedroom whenever Olanna is not at home. The young girl becomes pregnant, gives birth, but refuses to keep the baby.

mothers, ones who would welcome their new children, walk with them, pray for them, mentor them and support them in their marital, parental, communal and professional roles.

10. Conclusion—Decolonizing and Depatriachalizing the Urban Spaces

The Naomi Shower uses *Botho/Ubuntu* concepts as well as the biblical text to build bridges and spaces for young women in the urban space, which, as noted in the introduction to this essay, was colonially constructed as a male space. The young women counter the challenges that often hamper their professional and marital success. Building on the tradition of the African woman as an important productive member of the homestead, the Naomi Shower takes for granted that the new daughter is also a professional woman who takes on her new duties as a wife, mother and community member with the full support of her new mother. In carrying out the rituals of creating a welcoming space for young women in the urban space and home, the Naomi Shower also decolonizes the patriarchal colonial construction of the urban space as an unwelcoming space for African women in Southern Africa. The African woman remained in the village. Moreover, as Cock's statement above attests, the patriarchal colonial economy constructed colonized women as homemakers even though they were already farmers. In the Naomi Shower's transgressive reconstruction, the young woman traverses the boundaries between urban and rural or professional and private space, and between the older and younger—being trained to wear the proper clothes for each place and time.

The Naomi Shower and the rest of the Showers in the Gaborone context thus claim the urban space as a place where women will live and thrive together along with all that matters to them. They deconstruct patriarchy that pits one woman against the other in competition for a man—mostly because they are supposedly dependent on that particular man. The Naomi Shower encourages young women to be professionals and the older women to support them to ensure that their professional lives are successful. The Naomi Shower thus constructs a younger woman who is mentored, connected, successful and self-sufficient, and who moves freely and capably between the rural and urban areas. Their teaching is notable for its silence on the submissiveness of a wife to her husband or the headship of a man. Rather, their teaching is notable for creating a savvy young woman who is trained to succeed both in the private and public space, one who crosses the boundaries of age, class, gender and coloniality. Through their own networks, the founding women of the Naomi Shower create women-centered agency, as women empower and support each other instead of competing with each other. In that way, the Naomi Shower decolonizes the historically masculine urban space, making it a space for females to thrive.

Bibliography

Adichie, Chimamanda. *Half of a Yellow Sun: A Novel*. London: 4th Estate, 2017.
Amadiume, Ifi. *Male Daughters, Female Husbands: Gender and Sex in an African Society*. London: Zed, 1987.
Botswana Government. *Vison 2016: Towards Prosperity for All*. Gaborone: Botswana Government, 1996.
Cock, Jacklyn. "Domestic Service and Education for Domesticity: The Incorporation of Xhosa Women into Colonial Society." In *Women and Gender in Southern Africa to 1945*, edited by Cherryl Walker, 76–96. Cape Town: David Phillip, 1990.
Comaroff, Jean, and John Comaroff. *Of Revelation and Revolution: The Dialectics of Modernity in a South African Frontier, Vol. 2*. Chicago, IL: The University of Chicago Press, 1997.
Dube, Musa W. "Boundaries and Bridges: Journeys of a Postcolonial Feminist Biblical Scholar." *Journal of the European Society of Women in Theological Research* 22 (2014): 139–56.
Dube, Musa W. "Divining Ruth for International Relations." In *Postmodern Interpretations of the Bible*, edited by A. K. M. Adam, 67–80. St Louis, MO: Chalice, 2001.
Dube, Musa W. "The Unpublished Letters of Orpah to Ruth." In *Ruth and Esther: A Feminist Companion to the Bible*, edited by Athalya Brenner, 145–50. Sheffield: Sheffield Academic, 1999.
Dube, Musa W., et al. "*Botho/Ubuntu*: Community-building and Gender Constructions in Botswana." *Journal of ITC* 4 (2016): 1–22.
Gqola, Pumla Dineo. *Rape: A South African Nightmare*. Johannesburg: MF Books, 2015.
LenkaBula, Puleng. "Beyond Anthropocentricity: Botho/Ubuntu and the Quest for Economic and Ecological Justice in Africa." *Religion and Theology* 15 (2008): 375–94.
Kanyoro, Musimbi. "Cultural Hermeneutics: An African Contribution." In *Other Ways of Reading: African Women and the Bible*, edited by Musa W. Dube, 101–13. Atlanta, GA: Society of Biblical Literature, 2001.
Masenya, Madipoane. "Ngwetsi (Bride): The Naomi–Ruth Story from an African-South African Woman's Perspective." *Journal of Feminist Studies in Religion* 14, no. 2 1998: 81–90.
Mbue, Imbolo. *Behold the Dreamers: A Novel*. London: 4th Estate, 2016.
Metz, T., and Joseph B. R. Gaie. "The African Ethic of *Ubuntu/Botho*: Implications for Research on Morality." *Journal of Moral Education* 39, no. 3 (2010): 273–90.
Mmualefe, Dumi O. *Towards Authentic Tswana Christianity: Revisiting Botho*. Master's thesis, Eden Theological Seminary Missouri, 2004.
Moffat, Robert. *Missionary Labours and Scenes in Southern Africa*. London: Snow, 1842.
Motswapong, Elisabeth et al. "A Little Baby Is on the Way: *Botho/Ubuntu* and Community-Building in Gaborone Showers." *Gender Studies: A Journal of West University of Timisoara* 16, no. 1 (2018): 3–13.

Mudimbe, Vincent Y. *The Invention of Africa: Gnosis, Philosophy and the Order of Knowledge.* London: James Curry, 1988.

Munyaka, Mluleki, and Mokgethi Motlhabi. "Ubuntu and Its Socio-Moral Significance." In *African Ethics: An Anthology of Comparative and Applied Ethics*, edited by Munyaradzi Felix Murove, 63–84. Pietermaritzburg: UKZN, 2009.

Murove F. Munyaradzi. "African Ethics: Beyond the Ethic of the Savage Evidence." In *African Ethics: An Anthology of Comparative and Applied Ethics*, edited by Munyaradzi Felix Moruve, 14–32. Scottsville: UKZN, 2009.

Nadar, Sarojini. "A South African Indian Womanist Reading of the Character of Ruth." In *Other Ways of Reading: African Women and the Bible*, edited by Musa W. Dube, 159–78. Atlanta, GA: Society of Biblical Literature, 2001.

Ngcobo, Loretta. *And They Did Not Die.* London: Books, 1990.

Ramose, Mogobe, B. "Ecology through Ubuntu." Pages 308–14 in *African Ethics: An Anthology of Comparative and Applied Ethics*. Edited by Munyaradzi Felix Murove. Pietermaritzburg: UKZN Press, 2009.

SADC. *SADC Gender Protocol Barometer 2018.* Gaborone: SADC, 2018.

Scully, Pamela. "Rape, Race and Colonial Culture: The Sexual Politics of Identity in the 19th Century Cape Colony, South Africa." *The American Review* 100, no. 2 (1995): 335–59.

Setume, Senzokhuhe Doreen, et al. "Exploring the Concept of Botho/Ubuntu through Bridal Showers in the Urban Space of Gaborone, Botswana." *Managing Development in Africa* 2, no. 3 (2017): 173–91.

Strobel, Margaret. *European Women and the Second British Empire.* Indianapolis, IN: Indiana University Press 1991.

Walker, Cherryl (ed.), *Women and Gender in Southern Africa to 1945*. Cape Town: David Phillip, 1990.

Walther, Daniel. "Sex, Race and Empire: White Male Sexuality and the 'Other' in Germany's Colonies, 1894–1914." *German Studies Review* 33, no. 1 (2010): 45–71.

Walther, Daniel. "Racializing Sex, Same Sex Relations and German Colonial Authority, and Deutschtum." *Journal for the History of Sexuality* 17, no. 1 (2016): 1–14.

Chapter 12

Tamar Summons Jesus: A Trans-Textual (2 Samuel 13:1–22; Mark 5:22–43; Matthew 20:17–34) Search for Sectorial Solidarity with Respect to Gender and Masculinity

Gerald O. West

*School of Religion, Philosophy, and Classics & Ujamaa Centre,
University of KwaZulu-Natal*

1. Introduction

This essay documents and analyzes how Tamar summoned Jesus, how an organic community-driven process in which the realities of violence against women summoned Contextual Bible Study (CBS) work on (more) redemptive forms of African masculinity, and how community-based CBS work summoned university-based biblical studies pedagogy.

The first section of the essay documents how the Ujamaa Centre for Community Development and Research at the University of KwaZulu-Natal in South Africa has worked with the Bible with particular local communities of the poor and marginalized trans-contextually. African context summons the biblical text, from context to context. The second section of the essay then reflects on how community-based CBS work contributes to university-based biblical studies pedagogy. Biblical studies pedagogy is shaped by and contributes to community-based biblical hermeneutics. These two sections then converge in the final section of the essay in which trans-contextual interpretation generates trans-textual interpretation in which the Bible is conceptualized as a site of struggle.

Trans-textual interpretation participates in both a radical hermeneutic of reception in which readers' contextual agendas drive the interpretive process, and a radical hermeneutic of production that recognizes the final canonical form of the Bible as a site of struggle and that enables redactional co-opted source texts to speak from within their particular sectoral struggles. Interpreted trans-textually, 2 Sam 13:1–22, Mark 5:22–43, and Matt 20:17–34 provide the biblical shape to this essay. The passages are understood as the remnants of redacted sources that reflect sectoral concerns about gender and masculinity. Transgressive trans-textual interpretation, it is argued, nurtures interpretive and social trans-formation.

2. *Context Summoning Text*

The context of the struggle against apartheid summoned the formation of the Institute for the Study of the Bible (ISB) in the late 1980s,[1] what would later become the Ujamaa Centre for Community Development and Research (in the mid–1990s). Soon, however, the ISB was summoned by women to work with them in the struggle against patriarchy. One of our earliest community-based partnerships was with the Umtata Women's Group in Umtata, a large rural town, in the early 1990s. One of the first biblical texts we began working together with was Mark's account of the healing of two women in Mark 5:22–43. Guided by Mark's geographical shifts in setting in 5:21 from "the country of the Gerasenes" (5:1) to "his home town" (6:1), we recognized the literary unit from 5:22–43 as a single story.[2] Our early work on this text with the Umtata Women's Group focused quite specifically on the two women.[3]

As other organized groups of women invited us to work with them, this emerging CBS became a focal resource. In 1995, as part of the

---

1. Gerald O. West, *Biblical Hermeneutics of Liberation: Modes of Reading the Bible in the South African Context*, 2nd ed. (Maryknoll, NY: Orbis; Pietermaritzburg: Cluster, 1995), 216–38.

2. Gerald O. West, "Constructing Critical and Contextual Readings with Ordinary Readers: Mark 5:21–6:1," *JThSA* 92 (1995): 61.

3. West, "Constructing Critical and Contextual Readings"; Gerald O. West, "The Dumb Do Speak: Articulating Incipient Readings of the Bible in Marginalized Communities," in *The Bible and Ethics*, ed. John W. Rogerson, Margaret Davies, and M. Daniel Carroll R. (Sheffield: Sheffield Academic, 1995), 174–92.

ISB's partnership with women's groups in Amawoti,[4] a peri-urban shack-settlement within the city of Durban-eThekwini, Malika Sibeko and Beverley Haddad facilitated a similar version of the Mark 5 CBS.[5] And when the ISB held its major Biannual Workshop in 1996, bringing together women's groups from around South Africa, this CBS was used as the first of the CBS series under the theme "Women and the Bible in South and Southern Africa." The first day of the Workshop was devoted to reflections on women's realities and experiences (as part of the "See" moment in the See–Judge–Act process), and the Mark 5 CBS was facilitated on the second day of the Workshop (as part of the "Judge" moment in the See–Judge–Act process) under the sub-theme "Women and Culture."

At that same Biannual Workshop, we were invited by the women to facilitate a CBS on the third day under the sub-theme, "Women and Violence." Gloria Plaatjie and I facilitated the first version of the CBS work we have done on the Tamar story (2 Sam 13:1–22).[6] The context of violence against women, including violence against women from within the church, summoned Tamar. Drawing on the pioneering literary-critical narrative work of Phyllis Trible in the early 1980s on the story of rape of Tamar within the household of King David,[7] we constructed our first version of a CBS on gender-based violence. This CBS has gone on to be used in countless contexts of gender-based violence around the world,[8] but part of its power then (in 1996) was that this biblical story was an unknown text. There was amazement when the story was first read aloud in English and various African languages. Participants paged back and forth in their Bibles to confirm that this story was indeed included, for none of them had ever heard of this biblical story. Amazed, they said, "If this story is in the Bible, then we will not be silent/silenced."

What had summoned us to this story was, firstly, the capacity of CBS work to facilitate the action–reflection cycle of praxis within a See–Judge–Act process. As a methodology, CBS was beginning to take

---

4. Graham Philpott, *Jesus Is Tricky and God Is Undemocratic: The Kin-Dom of God in Amawoti* (Pietermaritzburg: Cluster, 1993).

5. Malika Sibeko and Beverley G. Haddad, "Reading the Bible 'with' Women in Poor and Marginalized Communities in South Africa (Mark 5:21–6:1)," *Semeia* 78 (1997): 83–92.

6. Gerald O. West and Phumzile Zondi-Mabizela, "The Bible Story that Became a Campaign: The Tamar Campaign in South Africa (and Beyond)," *Ministerial Formation* 103 (2004): 4–12.

7. Phyllis Trible, *Texts of Terror: Literary-Feminist Readings of Biblical Narratives* (Philadelphia, PA: Fortress, 1984), 37–63.

8. West and Zondi-Mabizela, "The Bible Story."

a potentially emancipatory shape.[9] Secondly, what summoned us to this particular biblical story was the contours of a text in which Tamar was an articulate agent, speaking for herself, amidst and against the male voices of destruction and death (including the voices of the narrator, David, Jonadab, Amnon, and Absalom) that surround her story. The women we worked with were astounded that such an eloquent women's voice should have been ignored by their churches. Though raped by her brother Amnon and silenced by her brother Absalom, Tamar was not silent. Her resilient and resisting voice remained, despite her desolation in the house of her brother (2 Sam 13:20), and despite the desolation of her contemporary African sisters in the house of the church.

From within this particular CBS came another summons. In almost every Tamar CBS (as this CBS has come to be known), the concern was raised by women about how we might work with men. Among the summons to a contextual urgency to engage with men was an escalating HIV epidemic. "What would have happened," one woman asked after a Tamar CBS, "if Amnon had also infected Tamar with HIV?"[10] By the mid-2000s, the Ujamaa Centre was doing extensive intersectional work, constructing CBS that would engage with the intersecting realities of unemployment, gender, HIV, and masculinity. Within this work, summoned by Tamar and a growing body of African women, we began work on constructing a series of CBS on forms of "redemptive masculinity."[11]

In 2005, some initial work was done to adapt the Tamar Bible study to work with men, but we had yet to find a form of the Tamar CBS that offered emancipatory capacities for men. While we reflected on how we might use the remarkable impact of the Tamar CBS to engage men more directly—for the focus of our Tamar CBS was on women as survivors of gender-based violence—we returned to Mark 5:22–43. When invited by groups in local churches in Pietermaritzburg and by regional faith-based non-governmental agencies in KwaZulu-Natal to work with them

---

9. Gerald O. West, "Reading the Bible with the Marginalised: The Value/s of Contextual Bible Reading," *Stellenbosch Theological Journal* 1, no. 2 (2015): 235–61.

10. West and Zondi-Mabizela, "The Bible Story."

11. Ezra Chitando and Sophie Chirongoma (eds.), *Redemptive Masculinities: Men, HIV, and Religion* (Geneva: World Council of Churches, 2012); Gerald O. West, "Deploying the Literary Detail of a Biblical Text (2 Samuel 13:1–22) in Search of Redemptive Masculinities," in *Interested Readers: Essays on the Hebrew Bible in Honor of David J. A. Clines*, ed. James K. Aitken, Jeremy M. S. Clines, and Christl M. Maier (Atlanta, GA: Society of Biblical Literature, 2013), 297–312.

on issues of masculinity, we returned to this text, but shifted the focus to include Jesus as "a man."

In 2006, the Ujamaa Centre was invited by the Pietermaritzburg Agency for Christian Social Awareness/Action (PACSA) and the KwaZulu-Natal Christian Council (KZNCC) to facilitate a workshop on "Jesus the Man," as part of their "Men, Gender, and HIV/AIDS Project." I facilitated a CBS on Mark 5:22–43 and Bob Ekblad, who was visiting from a sister project in the USA, facilitated a dialogical form of Bible Study on Matt 20:17–34. In re-using the Mark 5:22–43 story of the two women, we included a CBS question on the kind of masculinity Jesus embodied in his encounters and engagements with the two unnamed women.[12] Overall, the workshop provided safe and sacred space to talk about masculinities, particularly among men, but as one woman said, as she left the workshop, "The trouble is that our men are not like Jesus." Our workshop report in the 2006 Annual Report notes that, "While questions were raised about whether Jesus represents God rather than men/males, we agreed that the Bible studies did challenge dominant forms of masculinity."[13] We would return later to this CBS in order to include Jairus' masculinity alongside the masculinity of Jesus.

During this same workshop, in his dialogical Bible Study,[14] Ekblad facilitated a participatory and interactive Bible Study in which he contrasted two sets of men/masculinities in Matt 20:17–34. Ekblad's unusual delimitation of the text enabled a dialogue to be established between the request of the two "sons of Zebedee" (20:20)—made on their behalf by their mother—and the request of the "two blind men sitting by the roadside" on the outskirts of Jericho (20:29). I was amazed at the capacity of this Bible Study to generate conversation about different masculinities. In response, and with Ekblad's affirmation, I constructed a CBS version of his dialogical Bible Study.[15]

---

12. Ujamaa, "Redemptive Masculinity: A Series of Ujamaa Centre Contextual Bible Studies that Proclaim Life for Men and Women," Ujamaa Centre, 2009, http://ujamaa.ukzn.ac.za/Libraries/manuals/Redemptive_masculinities_series_1.sflb.ashx.

13. Ujamaa, "Annual Report," Ujamaa Centre, 2006, http://ujamaa.ukzn.ac.za/RESOURCES_OF_UJAMAA/AnnualReports_Evaluation.aspx.

14. For examples and an analysis of Ekblad's dialogical process, see respectively, Bob Ekblad, *Reading the Bible with the Damned* (Louisville, KY: Westminster John Knox, 2005); Gerald O. West, "Artful Facilitation and Creating a Safe Interpretive Site: An Analysis of Aspects of a Bible Study," in *Through the Eyes of Another: Intercultural Reading of the Bible*, ed. H. de Wit et al. (Amsterdam: Institute of Mennonite Studies & Vrije Universiteit, 2004), 211–37.

15. Ujamaa, "Redemptive Masculinity."

CBS work is praxis, and so participates in the constant cycle of action–reflection within the See–Judge–Act process. As we engaged with our various partners in intersectional work which included a focus on redemptive masculinities, these two CBS were adapted. Each has been done many times in many different contexts as part of the Ujamaa Centre's "Redemptive Masculinities" campaign.[16] Among the CBS that make up this series is a "masculinity" version of the Tamar CBS that we had been trying to discern for more than ten years. Summoned by the "4th Pan African Conference of the Circle of Concerned African Women Theologians: The Girl Child, Women, Religion and HIV and AIDS in Africa," in Yaoundé, Cameroon in 2007, we produced a version of the Tamar CBS that focuses on the kind of man Amnon is/becomes and the kind of man Tamar summons.[17]

Each of these CBS and each of the changes we have made to them have been summoned by actual local communities. Contextual realities have not only forged CBS methodology, they have forged particular CBS. But as is clear from almost any CBS, each CBS makes use of the critical methods and critical detail of biblical studies. In my early work, I characterized CBS as located in the nexus between "accountability" to actual local communities of the poor and marginalized and "responsibility" to the discipline of biblical studies.[18] This remains an accurate and useful account of how I understand the work of CBS in my vocation of activism, scholarship, and pedagogy.[19]

3. Community Summoning Pedagogy

Much of the pedagogy of what is now the School of Religion, Philosophy, and Classics at the University of KwaZulu-Natal has been formulated through careful and rigorous intentionally "contextual" directed debate

---

16. Ibid.

17. Gerald O. West, "The Contribution of Tamar's Story to the Construction of Alternative African Masculinities," in *Bodies, Embodiment, and Theology of the Hebrew Bible*, ed. Tamar Kamionkowski and Wonil Kim (London: T&T Clark, 2010), 190–2; West, "Deploying the Literary Detail of a Biblical Text," 309–11.

18. West, *Biblical Hermeneutics of Liberation*, 84, 129.

19. Gerald O. West, "The Vocation of an African Biblical Scholar on the Margins of Biblical Scholarship," in *Voyages in Uncharted Waters: Essays on the Theory and Practice of Biblical Interpretation in Honor of David Jobling*, ed. Wesley J. Bergen and Armin Siedlecki (Sheffield: Sheffield Phoenix, 2006), 152–64, and "Accountable African Biblical Scholarship: Post-colonial and Tri-Polar," *Canon & Culture* 20 (2016): 56–7.

within the School.[20] My own contribution to this debate, drawing on collegial strands of already present reflection and the specific contributions from feminist pedagogy,[21] was to envisage "contextual" pedagogy as a threefold cord/chord. Contextual pedagogy braided (1) the embodied "engagement" with the Bible that students bring to the discipline in their biblical studies modules, (2) with the "critical distance" that methods of biblical studies construct in the reading of the biblical text, (3) through forms of "contextuality" like context-led community-based CBS.[22] "Contextuality," I argued, enabled students to recognize the capacity of biblical studies' critical detail (generated by biblical studies' critical methods) as a resource for community-based (systemic) social change. Contextuality enabled biblical engagement and biblical critical distance to forge emancipatory alliances.

The biblical studies curriculum reflects this pedagogical orientation. Instead of beginning the first year of biblical studies with an introduction to the Old Testament (and Hebrew), we begin with an introduction to the New Testament (and Greek), because we recognize that the vast majority of our students come from a New Testament oriented Christian experience. Already in the first module of the second year of biblical studies ("Text, Interpretation, and Culture"), we demonstrate that each of the major biblical studies cluster of methods, literary-critical narrative and socio-historical, offer critical detail that may be useful for CBS-type work in local churches and communities. The second-semester module in the second year ("Critical Tools for Biblical Study") deepens the students' critical capacities with a careful focus on literary-critical narrative methods and socio-historical critical methods. These capacities

---

20. James R. Cochrane and Jonathan A. Draper, "The Parting of the Ways: Reply to John Suggit," *JThSA* 59 (1987): 66–72; Jonathan A. Draper, "Old Scores and New Notes: Where and What Is Contextual Exegesis in the New South Africa?" in *Towards an Agenda for Contextual Theology: Essays in Honour of Albert Nolan*, ed. McGlory T. Speckman and Larry T. Kaufmann (Pietermaritzburg: Cluster, 2001), 148–68; Gerald O. West, "The School of Religion, Philosophy, and Classics: Doing Contextual Theology in Africa in the University of Kwazulu-Natal," in *Handbook of Theological Education in Africa*, ed. Isabel Apawo Phiri and Dietrich Werner (Pietermaritzburg: Cluster, 2013), 919–26.

21. Kathleen Weiler, "Freire and a Feminist Pedagogy of Difference," *Harvard Educational Review* 61 (1991): 449–74.

22. Gerald O. West, "Power and Pedagogy in a South African Context: A Case Study in Biblical Studies," *Academic Development* 2, no. 1 (1996): 47–65; idem, "Beyond the 'Critical' Curtain: Community-Based Service Learning in an African Context," *Teaching Theology and Religion* 7, no. 2 (2004): 71–82.

are then appropriated in the capstone exit module in the third year ("Biblical Theology") in which we foreground contextual realities, using these realities to summon particular critical detail from particular biblical texts through both literary-critical narrative and socio-historical methods. Literary-critical narrative methods almost always precede the use of socio-historical methods, precisely because literary-critical narrative methods are closer to (though different from) the students' "ordinary" ecclesial and devotional interpretive "methods." Embodied engagement with the Bible is our starting point, taking seriously the "cultural capital" students bring with them to academic biblical studies.

In the compulsory third-year module ("Biblical Theology") and our postgraduate core module ("Biblical Interpretation"), we work overtly with the notion of the Bible as "a site of struggle." Shaped by, but going beyond the biblical hermeneutics of *The Kairos Document*,[23] we appropriate Itumeleng Mosala's notion of the Bible as "a site of struggle."[24] Mosala reminds us that biblical studies has always been aware of "the tendency in biblical literature for older traditions to be reused to address the needs of new situations."[25] What Mosala adds to this understanding is the ideological nature of such reuse. Redactional activity is not ideologically innocent.[26]

Among the contextual realities that constitute the third-year Biblical Theology module, the postgraduate Biblical Interpretation core module, and the elective biblical studies module "Issues of Gender and Masculinity" (in the second semester of our postgraduate program), is an emphasis on gender and masculinity. Disciplined by accountability to context, pedagogy always begins with the reality of violence against women before moving to matters of masculinity. Trible's literary-critical narrative work enabled us to construct the Tamar CBS, and so we return in our biblical studies classrooms to 2 Samuel 13 and the many critical (and contextual) literary-critical narrative readings of this text within biblical scholarship.[27] We demonstrate to our students how

---

23. Gerald O. West, "The Co-optation of the Bible by 'Church Theology' in Post-Liberation South Africa: Returning to the Bible as a 'Site of Struggle'," *JThSA* 156 (2017): 191–2.

24. Itumeleng J. Mosala, *Biblical Hermeneutics and Black Theology in South Africa* (Grand Rapids, MI: Eerdmans, 1989), 185.

25. Ibid., 101.

26. Gerald O. West, "Redaction Criticism as a Resource for the Bible as 'A Site of Struggle'," *OTE* 30, no. 2 (2017): 529.

27. See, for example, Hans de Wit and Janet Dyk (eds.), *Bible and Transformation: The Promise of Intercultural Bible Reading*, Semeia Studies 81 (Atlanta,

Trible's literary-critical narrative detail enabled us to construct the Tamar CBS, then how, summoned by another contextual reality, literary-critical narrative methods enabled us to generate a version of the Tamar CBS in which the focus shifts to contending masculinities, including indications of a "redemptive" masculinity.[28] Furthermore, by redactionally delimiting the Tamar source-narrative from within the larger "court narrative" or "succession narrative," we enable our students to recognize ideological contestation within the final canonical form concerning masculinity. Tamar's story, though constrained by patriarchy, contends with the dominant forms of masculinity that characterize the story/ies of David and other aspiring "hegemonic" males.[29]

4. Trans-textuality Summoning Sectoral Solidarity

The Tamar story offers a productive entry point for working with students on Mosala's notion that the Bible is "a site of struggle." We introduce students to the notion of internal and intrinsic contestation within biblical texts using Walter Brueggemann's argument for two contending theological trajectories running behind (socio-historically) and within (narratively) all biblical texts (including both the Old Testament/Hebrew Bible and the New Testament).[30] Brueggemann offers

---

GA: Society of Biblical Literature, 2015); L. Juliana M. Claassens, "Trauma and Recovery: A New Hermeneutical Framework for the Rape of Tamar (2 Samuel 13)," in *Bible through the Lens of Trauma*, ed. Elizabeth Boase and Christopher G. Frechette (Atlanta, GA: Society of Biblical Literature, 2016), 177–92.

28. West, "Deploying the Literary Detail of a Biblical Text," 309–11.

29. David J. A. Clines, "David the Man: The Construction of Masculinity in the Hebrew Bible," in *Interested Parties: The Ideology of Writers and Readers of the Hebrew Bible*, ed. David J. A. Clines (Sheffield: Sheffield Academic, 1995), 212–43; Ovidiu Creangă, *Men and Masculinity in the Hebrew Bible and Beyond* (Sheffield: Sheffield Phoenix, 2010); Jon-Michael Carman, "Abimelech the Manly Man? Judges 9.1–57 and the Performance of Hegemonic Masculinity," *JSOT* 43 (2019): 301–16; R. W. Connell and James W. Messerschmidt, "Hegemonic Masculinity: Rethinking the Concept," *Gender & Society* 19, no. 6 (2005): 829–59.

30. Walter Brueggemann, "A Shape for Old Testament Theology, I: Structure Legitimation," in *Walter Brueggemann, Old Testament Theology: Essays on Structure, Theme, and Text*, ed. Patrick D. Miller (Minneapolis, MN: Fortress, 1992), 1–22; idem, "A Shape for Old Testament Theology II: Embrace of Pain," in idem, *Old Testament Theology*, 22–44; idem, "Trajectories in Old Testament Literature and the Sociology of Ancient Israel," in *The Bible and Liberation: Political and Social Hermeneutics*, ed. Norman K. Gottwald and Richard A. Horsley (Maryknoll, NY: Orbis, 1993), 201–26.

a manageable two-trajectory way into the notion of the Bible as a site of struggle in which a prophetic theology of inclusion contends with a monarchic trajectory of consolidation. We then use David Jobling's narratively based postulate of an early pre-canonical form of the book of Judges in which the cycles of Judges ends with Samuel (1 Sam 12), and his argument that canonical redactions have divided this "Deuteronomic Extended Book of Judges" (Judg 2:11–1 Sam 12) for governmental and economic ideological purposes.[31] The first stage of canonization, which produced the Masoretic Jewish canon, separates the book of Judges from the book of Samuel (1 and 2 Samuel). The second stage of canonization, which produced the Greek and eventually the Christian canons, separates the book of Samuel into two books and inserts Ruth between Judges and 1 Samuel. The ideological effect of these separations and insertions is clear—kingship and its tributary mode of production are preferable to judgeship and its agricultural-communitarian mode of production.[32]

These introductory notions of the Bible as a site of struggle prepare the way for Mosala's more complex and more adversarial notion of "struggle." According to Mosala's persuasive argument, the enduring problem is that the final canonical form of the Bible (and any biblical book within it) is a form shaped by the dominant sectors of particular historical periods in the Bible's production-formation. Dominant sectors have through the redactional processes of the Bible's composition co-opted the ideological perspectives of other marginalized social sectors for their own ideological purposes. For example, we reflect on how the male redactors of the story of David may well have co-opted a story of Tamar's rape (probably originally told and circulated among women) because it provides a motive for the animosity between Absalom and Amnon, two of the principal contenders for the dynastic throne of David.

Because particular biblical texts or particular redactional editions have an ideological orientation deriving from the socio-historical struggles of the sites in which they were produced, the appropriation of any biblical text "is always a contradictory process embodying in some form a 'struggle'."[33] The contemporary interpretive struggle consists, Mosala argues, in depending on the sectoral forces involved, "either to harmonize

---

31. David Jobling, *1 Samuel*, ed. David W. Cotter, Berit Olam Studies in Hebrew Narrative and Poetry (Collegeville, MN: Michael Glazier/Liturgical, 1998), 43–76.

32. Gerald O. West, "Scripture as a Site of Struggle: Literary and Socio-Historical Resources for Prophetic Theology in Post-Colonial, Post-Apartheid (Neo-Colonial?) South Africa," in *Scripture and Resistance*, ed. Jione Havea (New York: Lexington/Fortress Academic, 2019), 157–8.

33. Mosala, *Biblical Hermeneutics*, 32.

the contradictions inherent in the works and events" (as dominant sectors tend to do), "or to highlight them with a view to allowing social… [sectoral] choices in their appropriation" (as poor and marginalized sectors must now do).[34] It is the organized poor and marginalized, working with socially engaged biblical scholars, in their struggles for justice who have the capacity to discern the ideological identity and agenda of particular biblical source texts. If (and only if) through their contemporary struggle-trained interpretive eyes they discern "kin struggles in biblical communities" within and behind the canonical biblical text, then there is the potential that "[t]hese biblical struggles…serve as a source of inspiration for contemporary struggles, and as a warning against their co-optation."[35]

Mosala offers us a notion of struggle in which ancient poor and marginalized sectors are always socio-historically present but only partially represented in the final canonical form of the text. If we as socially engaged biblical scholars read with similar poor and marginalized sectors today, together we may discern kin struggles in their fragmentary forms within the final canonical form. Mosala's notion of the Bible as a site of struggle requires the embodied presence of poor and marginalized sectors "reading with" socially engaged biblical scholars in collaborative processes like CBS, and requires processes like CBS to be constitutive of biblical studies pedagogy. Furthermore, I will now argue, Mosala's notion of the Bible as a site of struggle requires that we read trans-textually for trans-formation.

I must explain precisely what I mean by "trans-textual," for it derives its force from both a radical hermeneutics of reception and a radical hermeneutics of production. I use "trans-textual" (with the hyphen) in a deliberate manner. Gérard Genette, for example, uses the term "transtextuality" as a superordinate term, including within its domain other relational forms such as "intertextuality."[36] I use the term differently, following the prompting of Jione Havea, where "trans" is understood as "to cross over" and "to transgress." I include a third component, potentially constructed by these two components, "to trans-form" or "to trans-act." My usage emphasizes actual readers as interpretive agents in constructing trans-actions across biblical texts. However, reader-driven trans-textual resonances may lead to "intertextual" identifications, discerning kin

---

34. Ibid.
35. Ibid., 196, cf. also 88.
36. Gérard Genette, *The Architext: An Introduction* (Berkeley, CA: University of California Press, 1992), 83–4.

sectoral connections across socio-historical sites of struggle, where we might claim trajectories of socio-historical sectoral solidarity.

As indicated, the construction of any CBS draws on both accountability to particular local community-based sectoral groups and their emancipatory projects and responsibility to the critical detail of biblical texts. CBS embraces what Sharon Welch refers to as "a feminist ethic of risk,"[37] whereby text and context are brought into a tripolar conversation that is mediated by an ideological commitment to interpreting the Bible for systemic social (including religious and theological) change.[38] CBS accepts the risk of partiality, both in terms of recognizing the partial-incomplete reality of any interpretive choice and in terms of embracing the partial-ideological nature of such interpretive choices. Again, CBS interprets for particular forms of systemic change, constructing partial tripolar relationships between kin struggles in contemporary contexts and kin struggles in and behind biblical texts. While the primary purpose of CBS is to serve particular community-based systemic struggles outside the university biblical studies program, the university-based biblical studies program is also a site of struggle. As I have indicated, community-based CBS work summons particular forms of pedagogy.

Among the forms of biblical studies pedagogy we have forged, alongside the more familiar biblical studies approaches, is the search for sectoral solidarity across biblical texts. Within this understanding of trans-textual interpretation, community-based summons have led us to the women of Mark 5:22–43, who have led us to Tamar (2 Sam 13:1–22), who has led us to Jesus and Jairus (Mark 5:22–43), who have led us to the masculinities of Matt 20:17–34, which have led us to the masculinities of Amnon (2 Sam 13:1–22), which have led us to the masculinities of Jesus, Jairus, and the three male disciples (Mark 5:22–43). In each case, CBS community-based work and academic classroom-based work have collaborated.

Our early work on Mark 5:22–43 was shaped by socially engaged scholarly work which recognized that Mark had a particular commitment to demonstrating a Jesus who contended with dominant understandings

---

37. Sharon D. Welch, *A Feminist Ethic of Risk* (Minneapolis, MN: Fortress, 1990).

38. For a fuller discussion of the "tripolar" African biblical studies approach, see Jonathan A. Draper, "African Contextual Hermeneutics: Readers, Reading Communities, and Their Options between Text and Context," *Religion & Theology* 22 (2015): 9–12; West, "Accountable African Biblical Scholarship," 42–5.

of both scripture and economic systems.[39] If Mark was about systemic contestation, might not Mark offer resources for engaging with gender systems, we reasoned. This was how our work on Mark 5:22–43 as a text about women began, moving from academic scholarship to community-based CBS work, and then into university-based pedagogy.

Working with women through CBS work that foregrounded women led, as I have indicated, to being summoned to offer CBS resources for engaging with violence against women. Again, academic biblical scholarship on 2 Sam 13:1–22 offered potential resources for CBS work with women.[40] CBS work on this text (2 Sam 13:1–22) then made a significant contribution to how we worked with the "court history" or "succession narrative" (2 Sam 6/7–1 Kgs 2). Tamar's story radiated resonances with texts on either side, including 2 Sam 11:1–5 (the rape of Bathsheba) and the rape of David's *pilaegeshim* (2 Sam 16:21–22), reconstituting the shape of the dominant narrative about manly dynastic matters. Biblical studies began to re-read these intertexts trans-textually, engaging with scholarly squabbles about whether Bathsheba was raped,[41] but recognizing the disruptive and contending voices that these kindred texts inserted into the dominant narrative.[42]

Work with women on both Mark 5:22–43 and 2 Sam 13:1–22 summoned CBS work on masculinity, in particular, redemptive forms of masculinity. This led to a return to Mark 5:22–43, initially, with an emphasis on the masculinity of Jesus, but then an engagement with the masculinity of Jairus. The CBS was shaped by an overt pairing of the

39. See, for example, Ched Myers, *Binding the Strong Man: A Political Reading of Mark's Story of Jesus* (Maryknoll, NY: Orbis, 1988); Herman C. Waetjen, *A Reordering of Power: A Socio-Political Reading of Mark's Gospel* (Minneapolis, MN: Fortress, 1989); Richard A. Horsley, *Hearing the Whole Story: The Politics of Plot in Mark's Gospel* (Louisville, KY: Westminster John Knox, 2001).

40. Of particular importance for our work has been Trible, *Texts of Terror*.

41. See, for example, George G. Nicol, "The Alleged Rape of Bathsheba: Some Observations on Ambiguity in Biblical Narrative," *JSOT* 22 (1997): 43–54; Hyun Chul Paul Kim and M. Fulgence Nyengele, "Murder S/He Wrote? A Cultural and Psychological Reading of 2 Samuel 11–12 by Hyun Chul Paul Kim and M. Fulgence Nyengele," in *Pregnant Passion: Gender, Sex, and Violence in the Bible*, ed. Cheryl A. Kirk-Duggan (Atlanta, GA: Society of Biblical Literature), 95–116; Alexander Izuchukwu Abasili, "Was It Rape? The David and Bathsheba Pericope Re-Examined," *VT* 61 (2011): 1–15.

42. Gerald O. West, "Interrogating Ahithophel: Intersecting Gender and Class in Biblical Text and South African Context," in *Texts of Terror Extended*, ed. Monica Jyotsna Melanchthon and Robyn Whitaker (Atlanta, GA: Society of Biblical Literature, forthcoming).

two women and two men. The key text-oriented questions in the CBS are Questions 4, 5, and 6:

4. Mark connects these two women, seeing similarities in their encounters with Jesus. By re-reading the story carefully we can identify a number of similarities between these two women. What do these two women characters have in common in the text and their world?
5. Mark connects the two men, Jesus and Jairus, seeing similarities in the ways in the kind of men they are and how they relate to women. What kind of men are Jesus and Jairus?
6. More specifically, both Jesus and Jairus are disrupting the gender systems of their time. What gender systems are being disrupted and reconceptualized? What changes for these two women because two men contest dominant gender systems?

The use of both literary-critical narrative and socio-historical resources is clear in the framing of these questions, offering critical biblical studies resources in question form. The use of these biblical studies methods enabled this CBS to become a resource for biblical studies pedagogy, inviting students to read backwards from the CBS to discern how the CBS draws on methods of biblical studies and the literary-critical narrative and socio-historical detail such methods generate. This exercise also drew attention to the details not selected for the CBS, prompting an exercise in which we both acknowledged the ideo-theological dimensions of interpretation and delved more deeply into the contours of the text.

A similar classroom-based exercise with the Matt 20:17–34 text, reading backwards from the CBS, prompted a return to the Mark 5:22–43 text with further exegetical possibilities. In the Matt 20:17–34 CBS, the key text-oriented questions are:

3. What does the mother of Zebedee want for her sons? How does Jesus respond to this request?
4. What do the two blind men want from Jesus? How does Jesus respond to this request?
5. What kind of masculinities are reflected by each of these two pairs of men, the two disciples and the two blind men?

The two pairs, of women and of men, in Mark 5:22–43 summoned the two pairs of men in Matt 20:17–34. The pedagogical intent of Jesus mentoring his male disciples to be different kinds of men in Matthew was clear to both the third year and postgraduate class, as they followed the text's shift in focus from twelve disciples (v. 17) to two disciples (vv. 20–21) to ten disciples (v. 24) to twelve disciples (v. 25), as Jesus offers a contending understanding of masculine power and leadership. Jesus offered, we agreed, a contending form of masculine authority, which prepared the disciples not to respond as the crowd did (v. 31), but instead to observe how Jesus practiced an alternative form of masculinity in making time to see and hear and heal and include marginalized disabled men (vv. 32–34).

As we read relevant biblical scholarship on Matthew and masculinity,[43] we came to see Matt 20:17–34 as a good example of how Janice Capel Anderson and Stephen Moore characterize Matthew's narrative construction of "multiple, contradictory assumptions regarding masculinity."[44] Though Matthew regularly refers to socio-historical "hegemonic masculine roles," including male-to-male relationships, Anderson and Moore argue that literal socio-cultural kinship "regularly gives way to spiritual or fictive kinship."[45] As they go on to argue, "Literal kinship ties are portrayed as problematic, involving discord and rejection," but in contrast, the "spiritual kinship categories" of "father," "brother," and "son," as well as the relational categories of "master/slave," "master/disciple," and "king/subject," "define each other through their interrelationships—and redefine "masculinity" in the process."[46] "The narrative identity narratively constructed for male disciples [and male readers] in Matthew," they continue, "amounts to an *anomalous* masculinity, when measured by traditional Greco-Roman standards."[47]

The pedagogical intent of Jesus' construction of anomalous masculinities in Matt 20:17–34 then led us back to Mark 5:22–43 to re-examine a detail of that text that we had not fully understood. Why, we had wondered, did Jesus allow only the dominant three disciples (v. 37) to join him in entering the house of Jairus? Perhaps, we now argue, having engaged in trans-textual exegesis, there was a similar pedagogical intent. Perhaps Jesus was intent on modelling to the dominant males among his male disciples an alternative masculinity.

---

43. Stephen D. Moore and Janice Capel Anderson (eds.), *New Testament Masculinities*, Semeia Studies 45 (Atlanta, GA: Society of Biblical Literature, 2003).

44. Janice Capel Anderson and Stephen D. Moore, "Matthew and Masculinity," in *New Testament Masculinities*, ed. Stephen D. Moore and Janice Capel Anderson, Semeia Studies 45 (Atlanta, GA: Society of Biblical Literature, 2003), 71.

45. Ibid., 75.

46. Ibid., 75–6.

47. Ibid., 76.

Adding its trans-textual voice to such contestations about masculinity was 2 Sam 13:1–22. In our redemptive masculinity version of the Tamar CBS, the key text-oriented questions are:

4. How would you characterize Amnon's masculinity? What kind of man is Amnon?

    Consider:
    What prevents Amnon initially from acting on his "love" for Tamar (v. 2)?
    Why does Amnon's "love" (v. 1) change to "sickness" (v. 2)?
    What enables Amnon to act on his sickness/lust (vv. 4–6)?
    How does he react to Tamar's attempts to reason/argue with him (vv. 12–14)?
    How does he behave after he has raped Tamar (vv. 15–17)?

5. What kind of man does Tamar expect or hope Amnon to be? What kind of man could Amnon be according to Tamar?

    Consider:
    What does she say (vv. 12–13, 16), and what do each of the things she says tell us about her understanding of what it means to be "a man"? Pay attention to each thing she says.
    What does she do (v. 19), and what do each of the things she does tell us about her understanding of what it means to be "a man"?

The format of our CBS questions here encourages a "slow" re-reading of the text.[48] Question 4 constructs the kind of man Amnon is; question 5 imagines the kind of man Amnon might be. Contending masculinities are clear. Tamar's voice imagines another kind of man. Is such a "man" possible? Of course! Is Jesus such a "man"? Trans-textual reading offers hermeneutical opportunities for an exegesis of this question.

Tamar's voice summons Jesus, trans-textually, to account for the kind of man he will be and the kind of men he will mentor. Community-based eyes trained in the struggle against systemic gender injustice have directed our gaze to see, with them, trans-sectoral resonances across biblical texts, transgressing traditional biblical studies trajectories.

---

48. John Riches et al., *What Is Contextual Bible Study? A Practical Guide with Group Studies for Advent and Lent* (London: SPCK, 2010), 41.

Tamar summons biblical scholars to become both socially engaged and exegetically transgressive in order to serve others like her with trans-textual trans-sectoral interpretive resources. The trans-formation of systemic injustice is led by organized sectors of women survivors, served by forms of contextual biblical interpretation like CBS.

5. Conclusion

This essay demonstrates both the exegetical and emancipatory potential of trans-contextual and trans-textual interpretation. Drawing on a radical hermeneutics of production in which redacted sources retain some of their gendered sectoral markers, community-based projects for gender justice summon socially engaged biblical scholars and ordinary readers with struggle-trained eyes to collaborate in a radical hermeneutic of reception through CBS processes. Such reading practices are trans-gressive—transgressing the boundaries between academy and community, and transgressing the boundaries between historically distinct biblical texts. Yet systemic gender trans-formation in contexts in which the Bible remains a significant religio-cultural reality requires such trans-gressive reading practices. Reading together trans-textually discerns kindred sectoral struggles across biblical time and space, enabling Tamar to summon Jesus to join her in contesting and trans-forming dominant forms of masculinity, contending for redemptive, anomalous, forms of masculinity.

Bibliography

Abasili, Alexander Izuchukwu. "Was It Rape? The David and Bathsheba Pericope Re-Examined." *VT* 61 (2011): 1–15.

Anderson, Janice Capel, and Stephen D. Moore. "Matthew and Masculinity." In *New Testament Masculinities*, edited by Stephen D. Moore and Janice Capel Anderson, 1–15. Semeia Studies 45. Atlanta, GA: Society of Biblical Literature, 2003.

Brueggemann, Walter. "A Shape for Old Testament Theology, I: Structure Legitimation." In *Walter Brueggemann Old Testament Theology: Essays on Structure, Theme, and Text*, edited by Patrick D. Miller, 1–21 Minneapolis, MN: Fortress, 1992.

Brueggemann, Walter. "A Shape for Old Testament Theology, II: Embrace of Pain." In *Walter Brueggemann, Old Testament Theology: Essays on Structure, Theme, and Text*, edited by Patrick D. Miller, 22–44. Minneapolis, MN: Fortress, 1992.

Brueggemann, Walter. "Trajectories in Old Testament Literature and the Sociology of Ancient Israel." In *The Bible and Liberation: Political and Social Hermeneutics*, edited by Norman K. Gottwald and Richard A. Horsley, 201–26. Maryknoll, NY: Orbis, 1993.

Carman, Jon-Michael. "Abimelech the Manly Man? Judges 9.1–57 and the Performance of Hegemonic Masculinity." *JSOT* 43 (2019): 301–16.

Chitando, Ezra, and Sophie Chirongoma (eds.). *Redemptive Masculinities: Men, HIV, and Religion*. Geneva: World Council of Churches, 2012.

Claassens, L. Juliana M. "Trauma and Recovery: A New Hermeneutical Framework for the Rape of Tamar (2 Samuel 13)." In *Bible through the Lens of Trauma*, edited by Elizabeth Boase and Christopher G. Frechette, 177–92. Semeia Studies 86. Atlanta, GA: Society of Biblical Literature, 2016.

Clines, David J. A. "David the Man: The Construction of Masculinity in the Hebrew Bible." In *Interested Parties: The Ideology of Writers and Readers of the Hebrew Bible*, edited by David J. A. Clines, 212–43. Sheffield: Sheffield Academic, 1995.

Cochrane, James R., and Jonathan A. Draper. "The Parting of the Ways: Reply to John Suggit." *JThSA* 59 (1987): 66–72.

Connell, R. W., and James W. Messerschmidt. "Hegemonic Masculinity: Rethinking the Concept." *Gender & Society* 19, no. 6 (2005): 829–59.

Creangă, Ovidiu. *Men and Masculinity in the Hebrew Bible and Beyond*. Sheffield: Sheffield Phoenix, 2010.

De Wit, Hans, and Janet Dyk (eds.). *Bible and Transformation: The Promise of Intercultural Bible Reading*. Semeia Studies 81. Atlanta, GA: Society of Biblical Literature, 2015.

Draper, Jonathan A. "African Contextual Hermeneutics: Readers, Reading Communities, and Their Options between Text and Context." *Religion & Theology* 22 (2015): 3–22.

Draper, Jonathan A. "Old Scores and New Notes: Where and What Is Contextual Exegesis in the New South Africa?" In *Towards an Agenda for Contextual Theology: Essays in Honour of Albert Nolan*, edited by McGlory T. Speckman and Larry T. Kaufmann, 148–68. Pietermaritzburg: Cluster, 2001.

Ekblad, Bob. *Reading the Bible with the Damned*. Louisville, KY: Westminster John Knox, 2005.

Genette, Gérard. *The Architext: An Introduction*. Berkeley, CA: University of California Press, 1992.

Horsley, Richard A. *Hearing the Whole Story: The Politics of Plot in Mark's Gospel*. Louisville, KY: Westminster John Knox, 2001.

Jobling, David. *1 Samuel*. Berit Olam Studies in Hebrew Narrative and Poetry. Collegeville, MN: Liturgical, 1998.

Kim, Hyun Chul Paul, and M. Fulgence Nyengele. "Murder S/he Wrote? A Cultural and Psychological Reading of 2 Samuel 11–12 by Hyun Chul Paul Kim and M. Fulgence Nyengele." In *Pregnant Passion: Gender, Sex, and Violence in the Bible*, edited by Cheryl A. Kirk-Duggan, 95–116. Semeia Studies 44. Atlanta, GA: Society of Biblical Literature, 2003.

Moore, Stephen D., and Janice Capel Anderson (eds.). *New Testament Masculinities*. Semeia Studies 45. Atlanta, GA: Society of Biblical Literature, 2003.

Mosala, Itumeleng J. *Biblical Hermeneutics and Black Theology in South Africa*. Grand Rapids, MI: Eerdmans, 1989.

Myers, Ched. *Binding the Strong Man: A Political Reading of Mark's Story of Jesus*. Maryknoll, NY: Orbis, 1988.

Nicol, George G. "The Alleged Rape of Bathsheba: Some Observations on Ambiguity in Biblical Narrative." *JSOT* 22 (1997): 43–54.

Philpott, Graham. *Jesus Is Tricky and God Is Undemocratic: The Kin-Dom of God in Amawoti*. Pietermaritzburg: Cluster, 1993.

Riches, John, Helen Ball, Roy Henderson, Craig Lancaster, Leslie Milton, and Maureen Russell. *What Is Contextual Bible Study? A Practical Guide with Group Studies for Advent and Lent*. London: SPCK, 2010.

Said, Edward. *Culture and Imperialism*. New York: Kopf, 1993.

Sibeko, Malika, and Beverley G. Haddad. "Reading the Bible 'with' Women in Poor and Marginalized Communities in South Africa (Mark 5:21–6:1)." *Semeia* 78 (1997): 83–92.

Trible, Phyllis. *Texts of Terror: Literary-Feminist Readings of Biblical Narratives*. Philadelphia, PA: Fortress, 1984.

Ujamaa. "Annual Report." Ujamaa Centre. 2006. Accessed September 10, 2019, http://ujamaa.ukzn.ac.za/RESOURCES_OF_UJAMAA/AnnualReports_Evaluation.aspx.

Ujamaa. "Redemptive Masculinity: A Series of Ujamaa Centre Contextual Bible Studies that Proclaim Life for Men and Women." Ujamaa Centre. 2009, http://ujamaa.ukzn.ac.za/Libraries/manuals/Redemptive_masculinities_series_1.sflb.ashx.

Waetjen, Herman C. *A Reordering of Power: A Socio-Political Reading of Mark's Gospel*. Minneapolis, MN: Fortress, 1989.

Weiler, Kathleen. "Freire and a Feminist Pedagogy of Difference." *Harvard Educational Review* 61 (1991): 449–74.

Welch, Sharon D. *A Feminist Ethic of Risk*. Minneapolis, MN: Fortress, 1990.

West, Gerald O. "Accountable African Biblical Scholarship: Post-Colonial and Tri-Polar." *Canon & Culture* 20 (2016): 35–67.

West, Gerald O. "Artful Facilitation and Creating a Safe Interpretive Site: An Analysis of Aspects of a Bible Study." In *Through the Eyes of Another: Intercultural Reading of the Bible*, edited by H. De Wit, L. Jonker, M. Kool, and D. Schipani, 211–37. Amsterdam: Institute of Mennonite Studies & Vrije Universiteit, 2004.

West, Gerald O. "Beyond the 'Critical' Curtain: Community-based Service Learning in an African Context." *Teaching Theology and Religion* 7, no. 2 (2004): 71–82.

West, Gerald O. *Biblical Hermeneutics of Liberation: Modes of Reading the Bible in the South African Context*. 2nd ed. Maryknoll, NY: Orbis; Pietermaritzburg: Cluster, 1995 (1991).

West, Gerald O. "Constructing Critical and Contextual Readings with Ordinary Readers: Mark 5:21–6:1." *JThSA* 92 (1995): 60–9.

West, Gerald O. "The Contribution of Tamar's Story to the Construction of Alternative African Masculinities." In *Bodies, Embodiment, and Theology of the Hebrew Bible*, edited by Tamar Kamionkowski and Wonil Kim, 184–200. London: T&T Clark, 2010.

West, Gerald O. "The Co-optation of the Bible by 'Church Theology' in Post-Liberation South Africa: Returning to the Bible as a 'Site of Struggle.'" *JThSA* 156 (2017): 185–98.

West, Gerald O. "Deploying the Literary Detail of a Biblical Text (2 Samuel 13:1–22) in Search of Redemptive Masculinities." In *Interested Readers: Essays on the Hebrew Bible in Honor of David J. A. Clines*, edited by James K. Aitken, Jeremy M. S. Clines, and Christl M. Maier, 297–312. Atlanta, GA: Society of Biblical Literature, 2013.

West, Gerald O. "The Dumb Do Speak: Articulating Incipient Readings of the Bible in Marginalized Communities." In *The Bible and Ethics*. Edited by John W. Rogerson, Margaret Davies, and M. Daniel Carroll R., 174–92. Sheffield: Sheffield Academic Press, 1995.

West, Gerald O. "Interrogating Ahithophel: Intersecting Gender and Class in Biblical Text and South African Context." In *Texts of Terror Extended*, edited by Monica Jyotsna Melanchthon and Robyn Whitaker. International Voices in Biblical Studies. Atlanta, GA: Society of Biblical Literature, forthcoming.

West, Gerald O. "Power and Pedagogy in a South African Context: A Case Study in Biblical Studies." *Academic Development* 2, no. 1 (1996): 47–65.

West, Gerald O. "Reading the Bible with the Marginalised: The Value/s of Contextual Bible Reading." *Stellenbosch Theological Journal* 1, no. 2 (2015): 235–61.

West, Gerald O. "Redaction Criticism as a Resource for the Bible as 'a Site of Struggle'." *OTE* 30, no. 2 (2017): 525–45.

West, Gerald O. "The School of Religion, Philosophy, and Classics: Doing Contextual Theology in Africa in the University of KwaZulu-Natal." In *Handbook of Theological Education in Africa*, edited by Isabel Apawo Phiri and Dietrich Werner, 919–26. Pietermaritzburg: Cluster, 2013.

West, Gerald O. "Scripture as a Site of Struggle: Literary and Socio-Historical Resources for Prophetic Theology in Post-Colonial, Post-Apartheid (Neo-Colonial?) South Africa." In *Scripture and Resistance*, edited by Jione Havea, 149–63. New York: Lexington/Fortress Academic, 2019.

West, Gerald O. "The Vocation of an African Biblical Scholar on the Margins of Biblical Scholarship." In *Voyages in Uncharted Waters: Essays on the Theory and Practice of Biblical Interpretation in Honor of David Jobling*, edited by Wesley J. Bergen and Armin Siedlecki, 142–71. Sheffield: Sheffield Phoenix, 2006.

West, Gerald O., and Phumzile Zondi-Mabizela. "The Bible Story that Became a Campaign: The Tamar Campaign in South Africa (and Beyond)." *Ministerial Formation* 103 (2004): 4–12.

Index of References

Hebrew Bible/Old Testament

Genesis
1:22	124
1:28	124
2–3	86
3:12	21
3:16	85
5:30	11
5:32	11
8:17	124
9:1	124
9:7	124
12:7	135
12:9	128
13:7	128, 135
13:12	128
15:18–21	128
16	175
16:2	175
17	87
17:6	124
17:8	128
17:20	124
19	7, 99, 104, 110, 117
19:16	104
19:18–20	123
19:19	104
19:30–38	105, 115, 117, 121–3, 125
19:30	104
19:32	124
19:34	124
21	175
21:8–20	175
25:23	154
26:22	124
27:19	154
27:43–44	152
28–31	7, 147, 149, 151
28:3	124
29	56, 152
29:10	153
29:11	152
29:14	153
29:17	153
29:18	153
29:25	155
29:26	154
29:30	154
29:31	155
29:32–34	156
30	155
30:1–22	175
30:1	157
30:20	156
30:23	157
31:35	158
34	134
34:1–2	21
34:32	134
35:11	124
38	56
38:15	134
38:18	135
43:16	30

Exodus
1–4	101
12:12	41
21:37	30
34:30–35	14

Leviticus
1–7	86
1	90
4–5	90
10–16	90
11–15	86–88
11	86, 87, 89, 91
11:1–15:33	87
11:1	86
11:46	86
12–15	84, 90
12	6, 80, 82–4, 86–94
12:1–8	85
12:1	86, 87
12:2–4	87, 90
12:2	87, 93
12:3	87
12:4	88
12:5	87, 88, 90, 93
12:6–8	90
12:6–7	87
12:6	89
12:7	86, 89, 90
12:8	87, 89, 90
13–14	86
13	87
13:1	86
13:59	86
14:1	86
14:32	86
14:33	86
14:54	86

Index of References

Leviticus (cont.)		21:14	21	*Judges*	
15	86, 87, 89	22:22–29	56	2:11	193
15:1	86	23:1–2	112	16:1–3	134
15:19–23	87	23:2–3	110	19	21, 43, 101
15:32–33	86	23:2	110		
17–26	82, 86	23:4	112	*Ruth*	
18–20	82	24:1–4	54	1:6–7	176, 177
20:10	56	24:1	56	1:8–13	172
20:22	108	32:18	85	1:16–17	174
20:26	109			1:16	173
24:10–22	14	*Joshua*		1:20	172
		1–12	128, 130,	3:1–3	176, 177
Numbers			131	3:3	177
9:1–14	14	2	56, 132	4:15	173
12	175	2:1–24	130, 132	4:16	176, 178
12:1–15	14	2:1	132		
13:1–14:12	139	2:2–3	133	*1 Samuel*	
13:1	132	2:11	134	12	193
15:32–36	14	2:13	135	25:11	30
16:30–33	14	2:15–16	136		
26:33	13	2:24	136	*2 Samuel*	
26:64–65	12	4:20–24	130	6	196
27	5	5:1–6:27	130	7	196
27:1–11	16	5:14	130	11:1–5	196
27:3–4	13	6–11	129	12	70
27:3	12	6:18	137	13	191
27:5	14	6:22–27	130, 136	13:1–22	8, 184–6,
27:6–7	15	6:26	137		195, 196,
27:8–11	15	6:27	137		199
31	21	7	137	13:1	199
33:4	41	8:27	137	13:2	199
36:1–13	15	8:29	137	13:4–6	199
36:6–7	16	8:30–35	137	13:12–14	199
36:10	16	9:1–27	130	13:12–13	199
		9:2	138	13:15–17	199
Deuteronomy		9:3–6	138	13:17	199
1:6	12	9:7–15	138	13:19	199
2:3	12	9:18–19	139	13:20	187
3:5	17	9:24	138	16:21–22	196
6:8	70	9:27	140	21:1–14	140
6:10–11	17	10:1–5	140	21:2	140
6:13	70	10:11	141	21:6	140
7:1–6	133	10:41–42	141		
7:3–4	135	13–24	128	*1 Kings*	
8:7–9	13	24:2	41	2	196
8:15	11			3	73
20:10–18	138			3:4	140

1 Kings (cont.)
9:16	16
16	37
16:31–33	42
18:18–19	40
21	70
21:19	40
21:20–24	40
21:24–25	40
21:25	42

2 Kings
4	71
4:13	71
4:38–41	71
5	72
6	73
6:20–31	30
6:24	73
6:26	73
8	69–71, 73
8:1–6	6, 67
8:1	72
8:3	72
8:4	72
8:5	72
8:6	73
9–10	6, 42
9	37
9:1–3	40
9:6–10	40
10:18	42
17:29–41	41

Nehemiah
9:25	17

Job
2:9	43, 45
38:29	85
42:13	45

Psalms
68:6	18
127:3	84

Proverbs
6:26	134

Isaiah
21:2–3	85
26:16–21	85
42:5	81
51:17–18	125
66:7–14	85

Jeremiah
2–4	56
2–3	53, 60
2:1–4:4	6, 52, 53, 55–9, 62–4
2:1–3:5	54
2:1–2	53, 59
2:3	53, 59
2:4–13	53, 60
2:4	59
2:6	12
2:8	59
2:13	54
2:14–17	53
2:14–15	59
2:18	54, 59
2:20–25	54
2:23–24	58
2:23	54, 59
2:24	54
2:25	54
2:26	59
2:31	60
2:35	59
3:1–5	54, 60
3:6–11	54, 59
3:6–10	54
3:6	54
3:7	60
3:8	56
3:11–20	54
3:12	54, 60
3:14	54
3:19	54, 60
3:21–4:4	55
3:21	55, 62
3:22–25	54, 55, 61
3:22	55, 61
3:23	61
3:24	61
3:25	61
4:1–4	54, 55
4:1–2	62
4:10	62
4:31	85
7:16	63
11–20	62
11:14	63
13:21	85
14:11	63
15:16	58
15:18	62
16:2	58
20:7	58, 63
20:14–18	63
22:23	85
30:6	85
32	59
32:23	59
32:29–35	59
44:15	60
48:41	92
49:22	92
49:24	85
50:43	85

Lamentations
1	25
1:5	26
1:17	25
2	32
2:2	30
2:4	31
2:5	30, 31
2:8	30
2:16	30
2:18–19	27
2:18	27
2:19	27
2:20–22	27–9, 32, 33
2:20	29, 30

2:21	31	20:24	198	*Luke*	
2:22	31	20:25	198	2:22–24	90
2:23	31	20:29	188		
3	32	20:31	198	*1 Timothy*	
				2:13–15	80
NEW TESTAMENT		*Mark*			
Matthew		5	186	MISHNAH	
20:17–34	8, 184,	5:1	185	*Niddah*	
	185, 188,	5:21	185	3, 7	89
	195, 197,	5:22–43	8, 184,		
	198		185, 187,		
20:17	198		188, 195–8		
20:20–21	198	5:37	198		
20:20	188	6:1	185		

Index of Authors

Abasili, A. 196, 200
Adichie, C. 180, 182
Ahmed, S. 108, 111–13
Alexander, J. C. 22, 34
Amadiume, I. 162, 182
Amit, Y. 71, 78
Anderson, J. C. 198, 200
Andrew, M. 148, 159

Bailey, R. 109, 110, 113
Bailey, W. A. 156, 157, 159
Ball, H. 202
Barbour, A. R. 75, 78
Barthes, R. 146, 159
Baumann, G. 57, 58, 65
Bechtel, L. M. 105, 113
Becker, E.-M. 22, 34
Beckman, G. 85, 94
Bellis, A. O. 135, 143
Bennett, H. V. 82, 94
Bergant, D. 25, 34
Berges, U. 27, 30, 31, 34
Bergmann, C. D. 84, 91, 92, 94
Berlin, A. 25, 34
Bertholet, A. 94
Bier, M. J. 25, 34
Boase, E. 25, 34
Boer, R. 139, 143, 150, 151, 159
Boler, M. 154, 159
Brenner, A. 58, 65, 122, 126, 174
Brown Givens, M. S. 47, 50
Brueggemann, W. 74, 78, 81, 82, 86, 94, 95, 192, 200
Burns, A. 1, 2, 8
Butler, J. 111, 113

Camp, C. 70, 72, 73, 78
Carman, J.-M. 192, 200
Carroll, R. P. 55, 65
Caruth, C. 22, 34

Chirongoma, S. 118, 126, 187, 201
Chitando, E. 118, 126, 187, 201
Claassens, L. J. M. 16, 19, 81, 85, 92, 95, 99, 111, 113, 192, 201
Clines, D. J. A. 122, 126, 192, 201
Coats, G. W. 14, 15, 19, 117, 122, 126
Cochrane, J. R. 190, 201
Cock, J. 164, 182
Collins, J. J. 129, 143
Comaroff, Je. 164, 182
Comaroff, Jo. 164, 182
Connell, R. W. 116, 126, 192, 201
Creangă, O. 192, 201
Crowell, B. L. 39, 50

Dangarembga, T. 50
Davies, E. W. 48, 50
De Wit, H. 191, 192, 201
Diamond, A. R. P. 55–7, 59, 65
Dijk-Hemmes, F. van 58, 65
Dillmann, A. 95
Dobbs-Allsopp, F. W. 24, 25, 34
Dochhorn, J. 22, 34
Donaldson, L. E. 129, 143
Douglas, M. 82, 83, 95
Draper, J. A. 190, 195, 201
Dube, M. W. 17, 19, 38, 50, 132, 133, 143, 165, 169, 173, 182
Dyk, J. 191, 192, 201

Ekblad, B. 188, 201
Epp-Tiessen, E. 129, 143
Erbele-Küster, D. 83, 89, 91, 94, 95
Exum, J. C. 57, 59, 65, 108, 113

Fewell, D. N. 71, 78, 133, 143
Field, S. 22, 34
Finkelstein, A. 23, 34
Fischer, G. 55, 65
Ford, W. 138, 139, 143

Frechette, C. G. 34
Freud, S. 22, 34
Fritz, V. 72, 73, 78
Frymer-Kensky, T. 24, 34
Fuchs, E. 48, 50

Gaie, J. B. R. 171, 182
Garrett, D. A. 25, 34
Genette, G. 194, 201
Gentry, C. E. 36, 48, 50
Gerstenberger, E. S. 87–9, 95
Gilkey, L. B. 75, 76, 78
Gnuse, R. K. 41, 50
Gorman, F. H. 87, 90, 95
Gottwald, N. K. 25, 34
Gqola, P. D. 46, 50, 168, 182
Gravett, E. O. 42, 43, 45, 46, 51
Guest, D. 32, 34, 58, 65
Gunn, D. M. 129, 143
Gwaltney, D. 24, 25, 34

Haddad, B. G. 186, 202
Haddox, S. E. 117, 123, 126
Hamilton, V. P. 124, 126, 154, 159
Harding, K. 151, 160
Hartley, J. E. 88, 95
Häusl, M. 57, 65
Hays, N. 90, 95
Henderson, R. 202
Hens-Piazza, G. 25, 30, 34
Herman, J. 22, 23, 34
Hiebert, P. S. 16, 19
Hieke, T. 82, 89, 90, 93, 95
Hillers, D. R. 25, 34
Holt, E. K. 22, 34
Horowitz, D. 142, 143
Horsley, R. A. 196, 201
House, P. R. 25, 34
Howard, C. 72, 78

Irigiray, L. 153, 160

Jackson, M. 103, 104, 113, 154, 160
Jobling, D. 193, 201

Kadhem, A. 22, 35
Kaiser, W. C., Jr. 87, 95
Kalmanofsky, A. 85, 95
Kamionkowski, S. T. 91, 95
Kanyoro, M. R. A. 93, 95, 173, 182

Kauffman, J. 22, 35
Kelly, A. 148, 159
Kennedy, H. 36
Kershnar, S. 141, 142, 144
Kim, H. C. P. 196, 201
Kitcher, P. 46, 47, 51
Kiuchi, N. 86, 95
Klawans, J. 93, 95
Klopper, F. 47, 48, 51
Knierim, R. P. 14, 15, 19
Knoppers, G. N. 40, 51
Koblinsky, M. 80, 95
Kohn, E. 124–6
Kondemo, M. M. 121, 127
Kornfeld, W. 90, 95
Kristeva, J. 107, 113
Kugler, R. 91, 95

Lancaster, C. 202
Landy, F. 25, 35
Lapsley, J. E. 102, 113, 158, 160
Lee, A. C. C. 31, 35
LenkaBula, P. 171, 182
Leshota, P. 116, 118, 126
Levine, B. E. 92, 95
Leys, R. 22, 35
Lightbody, G. 145, 160
Linafelt, T. 25, 35
Lindhorst, T. P. 37, 51
Lomax, T. 47, 51
Longman III, T. 25, 35
Lovin, R. W. 76, 78
Low, K. B. 101–3, 105, 113

Maarsingh, B. 88, 92, 95
Macwilliam, S. 58, 65
Maddox, M. 100–102, 113
Magdalene, R. F. 43, 51
Maier, C. M. 53, 54, 58, 60, 65
Maluleke, T. S. 149, 160
Masenya, M. 47, 51, 121, 127, 174, 182
Masters, N. T. 37, 51
Mays, J. L. 83, 95
Mbiti, J. S. 121, 126
Mbue, I. 180, 182
Mbuwayesango, D. R. 16, 17, 19, 129, 132, 144
McDaid, J. 145, 160
McFarlane, A. C. 22, 35
McKane, W. 55, 65

McKenzie, S. L. 40, 51
McKinlay, J. E. 106, 113
Messerschmidt, J. W. 192, 201
Mettler, K. 77, 78
Metz, T. 171, 182
Meyer, E. E. 94, 95
Meyers, M. K. 37, 51
Miles, J. 109–11, 113
Milgrom, J. 84, 88, 93, 95
Miller, J.-A. 151, 160
Milton, L. 202
Mmualefe, D. O. 169, 182
Moffat, R. 164, 182
Mokoena, L. 40, 42, 51
Monahan, J. L. 47, 50
Moore, S. D. 198, 200, 201
Morrow, W. S. 81, 83–5, 90–2, 95
Mosala, I. J. 191, 193, 194, 201
Motlhabi, M. 170, 182
Motswapong, E. 172, 182
Mouton, E. 80, 94, 95
Mudimbe, V. Y. 161, 162, 182
Munyaka, M. 170, 182
Murove, M. F. 169, 182
Myers, C. 196, 201
Myers, J. D. 153, 160

Nadar, S. 149, 160, 173, 182
Ngcobo, L. 167, 182
Nicol, G. G. 196, 201
Niditch, S. 124, 127
Niebuhr, R. 75, 78
Njoroge, N. 81, 96
Noth, M. 88, 89, 96
Nussbaum, M. C. 151, 160
Nyengele, M. F. 196, 201

O'Connor, K. 25, 35, 52, 55–7, 59, 61, 64–6
Oduyoye, M. A. 121, 127
Ọlọjẹde, F. O. 56, 66, 158, 160
Otto, E. 82, 96

Parry, R. A. 25, 35
Philpott, G. 186, 201
Pippin, T. 48, 49, 51
Porter, D. 151, 160
Porter, J. R. 84, 88, 96
Pratt, M. L. 132, 144

Prior, M. 129, 144
Provan, I. 25, 35
Pruin, D. 39, 40, 42, 51

Ramose, M. B. 170, 171, 182
Rashkow, I. 102, 103, 113
Renkema, J. 25, 35
Rice, D. F. 74, 78
Riches, J. 199, 202
Römer, T. 41, 51
Roncace, M. 73, 78
Ross, S. 148, 159
Ross-Burstall, J. 154, 160
Russell, M. 202

Sabella, J. L. 75, 78
Said, E. 162, 183, 202
Sailhamer, J. H. 86, 96
Salters, R. B. 25, 35
Sasson, V. 44, 51
Schearing, L. 87, 92, 93, 96
Schipper, M. 116, 127
Schmidt, W. H. 86, 96
Schneider, L. 149, 160
Schüssler Fiorenza, E. 38, 51
Schwartz, R. M. 111, 114
Schweitzer, A. 141, 144
Scully, P. 168, 182
Segovia, F. 107, 114
Seibert, E. 111, 114, 129, 144
Seow, C.-L. 44, 51
Serio, T. 68, 79
Setume, S. D. 172, 182
Sharp, C. J. 4, 57, 59, 66, 69, 79, 108, 114, 130, 133, 144
Shields, M. E. 57–9, 66, 71, 79
Sibeko, M. 186, 202
Sjoberg, L. 36, 48, 50
Smith, C. 117, 127
Smith, J. Z. 109, 110, 114
Snaith, N. H. 89, 96
Stone, K. 104, 109, 110, 114
Strobel, M. 163, 164, 168, 182
Symonds, M. 26, 35

Thiessen, M. 89, 96
Torpey, J. 142, 144
Trevaskis, L. M. 86, 96
Trible, P. 44, 51, 186, 191, 192, 196, 202

Tsoffar, R. 103–6, 111, 112, 114
Turquet, L. 148, 159

Van Wolde, E. 80, 94, 95
Van der Woude, A. 86, 96
Van der Kolk, B. 22, 28, 29, 35
Van der Walt, C. 152, 160
Vawter, B. 153, 160
Vriezen, T. C. 86, 96

Waetjen, H. C. 196, 202
Walker, C. 164–7, 182
Walther, D. 163, 182
Wanke, G. 55, 66
Warrior, R. A. 131, 144
Watts, J. W. 90, 91, 96
Weems, R. J. 50, 51
Weiler, K. 190, 202

Weisaeth, L. 22, 35
Welch, S. D. 195, 202
Wellhausen, J. 86, 96
Wenham, G. J. 87, 90, 96
West, G. 44, 51, 149, 160, 185–93, 195, 196, 202, 203
Westermann, C. 25, 35, 124, 127
Whitfield, C. 22, 35
Wickware, M. E., Jr. 75, 78
Wilkes, K. V. 46, 47, 51
Wilson, S. 116, 117, 127
Wright, C. 25, 35

Yep, G. A. 148, 160

Žižek, S. 147, 151, 154, 155, 158, 160
Zondi-Mabizela, P. 186, 187, 203

Milton Keynes UK
Ingram Content Group UK Ltd.
UKHW050124270424
441800UK00004B/90